SCIENCE DICTIONARY
of the
Plant World

A
SCIENCE
DICTIONARY
of the
Plant World

AN ILLUSTRATED DEMONSTRATION OF TERMS
USED IN PLANT BIOLOGY

Michael Chinery, B.A.

1933

WITH OVER 400 COLOUR PICTURES

PUBLISHED BY
Franklin Watts, Inc.
575 Lexington Avenue
New York, N.Y. 10022

Published in 1966 by Sampson Low, Marston & Co. Ltd., London

First American publication by Franklin Watts, Inc., 1969
Made and printed by Purnell & Sons Ltd.
Library of Congress Catalog Card Number: 68–17110
© 1966 Sampson Low, Marston & Co. Ltd.

MADE AND PRINTED IN GREAT BRITAIN BY PURNELL & SONS LTD.
Filmset by Cox & Sharland Ltd.

THE DICTIONARY

Abaxial. Concerning the surface of a leaf directed away from the stem on which it arises.

Abcission Layer. A layer at the base of the petiole of a woody plant that breaks down and causes leaf fall. The layer is formed from the cells at the base of the leaf stalk. These cells are slightly smaller than the surrounding ones. They break down completely so that, just before leaf fall, only the vascular strand and the epidermis connect the leaf to the stem. Even light winds are enough to break these connections and the leaf falls. A protective, corky layer – the leaf scar – forms under the leaf before it falls. (See *Leaf*).

Achene. A type of fruit (q.v.) which normally contains only one seed and which is indehiscent – i.e. it does not split open and release the seed. The typical achene is leathery but there are several modifications, including the woody nut and the winged samara. (See Page 101).

Achlamydeous. (Of flowers) Lacking petals and sepals – e.g. ash flower. The term naked is also used for this.

Actinomorphic flowers are regularly arranged and can be cut into two similar halves in two or more directions. (See *Zygomorphic*), and (Plate 1).

Adaxial. Concerning the leaf surface facing the stem on which it arises.

Adventitious roots are those developing from the stem or leaf, not as branches from the main root. Adventitious buds develop from parts other than the leaf axil. (See *Root*), and (Plate 56).

Aerenchyma. A special aerating tissue found in the roots and stems of some marsh and aquatic plants (e.g. purple loosestrife). Large air-filled spaces occur between the cells. The tissue's function is to supply air to submerged parts.

Aerobic. Requiring free oxygen for respiration (q.v.).

After-ripening. For reasons imperfectly understood, many seeds (e.g. hawthorn) will develop only after certain chemical and physical changes have taken place in the embryo, even though it appears to be fully formed. When the seed falls from the plant it will not develop straight away, even if placed in the most favourable conditions. The period during which the changes take place and during which the seed will not germinate is the after-ripening period.

Agar (agar-agar). A polysaccharide obtained from the mucilages of certain red seaweeds. It is valuable as a culture medium on which to grow micro-organisms.

Agglutination. The clumping together of bacteria under the action of anti-bodies.

Aleurone Grains. Protein granules commonly found as storage materials in oil-containing seeds, such as those of castor oil and Brazil nut. They are probably formed from the entire contents of vacuoles rich in protein as the seeds lose water during ripening. The outer layers of potato tubers also contain protein grains – for which reason peeled potatoes are less nutritive than unpeeled ones.

Algae. Large division of flowerless plants, most of which live in water. They include many single-celled planktonic organisms of fresh and salt water, the filamentous pond scums, and the various-coloured seaweeds. Reproductive methods include simple division, the production of free-swimming or non-motile zoospores which can each develop into a new plant, and sexual methods involving the fusion of male and female gametes. There are many parallels in structure and life history with fungi but the algae are differentiated from fungi by the possession of chlorophyll. (See *Chlorophyceae; Chlamydomonas; Phaeophyceae; Rhodophyceae; Spirogyra; Desmid; Diatom*), and (Plates 1; 10; 13; 91–94; 98; and 120).

Plate 1

ACTINOMORPHIC

A regular or actinomorphic flower—one that can be cut in two or more directions to produce two similar halves.

ALGAE

Pleurococcus—a single-celled alga commonly found as a green 'crust' on tree trunks. (Below) *Pandorina*—a colonial alga composed of 16 similar cells each of which acts as an individual plant.

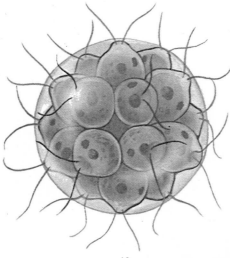

Plate 2

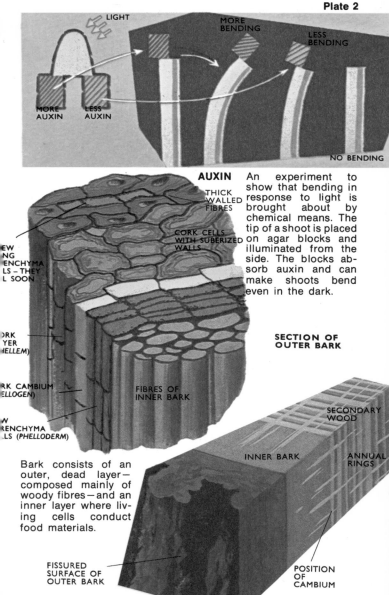

AUXIN An experiment to show that bending in response to light is brought about by chemical means. The tip of a shoot is placed on agar blocks and illuminated from the side. The blocks absorb auxin and can make shoots bend even in the dark.

LIGHT

MORE BENDING

LESS BENDING

MORE AUXIN   LESS AUXIN

NO BENDING

THICK WALLED FIBRES

CORK CELLS WITH SUBERIZED WALLS

EW NG ENCHYMA LS – THEY L SOON

ORK YER HELLEM)

RK CAMBIUM ELLOGEN)

W RENCHYMA LS (PHELLODERM)

FIBRES OF INNER BARK

SECTION OF OUTER BARK

SECONDARY WOOD

INNER BARK

ANNUAL RINGS

Bark consists of an outer, dead layer—composed mainly of woody fibres—and an inner layer where living cells conduct food materials.

FISSURED SURFACE OF OUTER BARK

POSITION OF CAMBIUM

BARK

Alismataceae. A family of herbaceous monocotyledons all of which live in water or wet places. The perianth is in two distinct whorls of three and the free carpels usually develop into achenes. Some members have erect and floating leaves. Examples include arrowhead and water plantain.

Alkaloids. Complex organic bases containing nitrogen occurring as by-products, particularly in some families of flowering plants, e.g. Solanaceae, Ranunculaceae, Umbelliferae, Papaveraceae. They may be present in the cell sap, in solution, or as solids, and are particularly important because of their poisonous and medicinal properties. Examples are atropine (occurring in all parts of deadly nightshade and especially the seeds of thornapple), cocaine (in a South American plant), morphine (in young fruits of the opium poppy), nicotine (leaves of tobacco), quinine (bark of *Cinchona*) and strychnine (from the seeds of *Strychnos*).

Allogamy. Cross-fertilisation.

Alternate. (Of leaves). (See *Phyllotaxis*).

Alternation of Generations. The alternation of two distinct stages in a life cycle. One form reproduces sexually and gives rise to the other which in turn reproduces asexually to give the first stage again. This phenomenon exists in all plants from the bryophytes upward and also in many algae, although it is often obscure. It is most obvious in ferns and other pteridophytes. The leafy fern plant is the asexual generation which reproduces by spores and is thus called the sporophyte generation. The sporophyte is diploid (q.v.) and the spores are formed after a meiotic division in which their chromosome number is halved. The spores are thus haploid (q.v.) and each gives rise to a haploid *prothallus* which is the gametophyte generation of the fern life cycle. The gametophyte produces gametes or sex-cells which join in pairs and give rise to a new sporophyte generation. In most ferns the gametophyte produces both male and female gametes but in seed plants there are separate male and female gametophytes. The spore giving rise to the female gametophyte is not shed from the parent and the tiny female gametophyte develops within the parent sporophyte generation. This is why the alternation of generations is not obvious in seed plants. The male spore is the pollen grain. (See *Filicales; Hepaticae; Musci; Seed; and Spore*).

Amaryllidaceae. A family of monocotyledonous flowering plants belonging to the order or cohort Liliiflorae (q.v.). Includes daffodil, snowdrop, and snowflake — perennial herbs with bulbs and long, narrow leaves. The flower is regular and has a *perianth* consisting of 6 petal-like segments. The ovary is inferior and develops into a capsular fruit. The unopened flower is protected by a spathe which remains as a scaly flap when the flower opens. (See Plate 126).

Amitosis. Nuclear division by simple fission without the appearance of chromosomes and spindle. It is of infrequent occurrence and normally confined to ageing cells or to certain tissues such as endosperm. (See *Mitosis*).

Amplexicaul leaves are those whose bases clasp the stem.

Anaerobic. Able to survive in the absence of free oxygen. (See *Respiration*).

Anandrous. (Of flowers). Lacking stamens — i.e. female flowers.

Anatropous Ovule. (See *Ovule*).

Androecium. The male parts of a flower — i.e. all the stamens (q.v.).

Anemophily. Pollination (q.v.) by wind.

AMARYLLIDACEAE

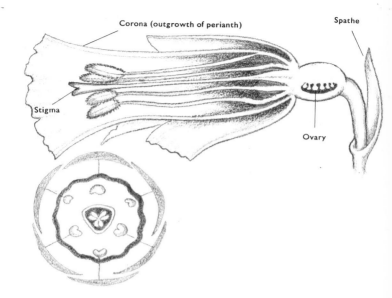

Corona (outgrowth of perianth)

Spathe

Stigma

Ovary

Half flower and floral diagram of daffodil.

Angiospermae. Flowering plants. As seed-bearing plants, they are placed, with the gymnosperms, in the division Spermatophyta, but they are distinguished from the gymnosperms by the fact that the seeds are enclosed in fruits, and by the possession of vessels in the xylem (q.v.). The classification of the many thousands of flowering plants into families and orders is based on floral characteristics but apart from the division into mono- and dicotyledons there is no general agreement on the higher groupings. The division of the dicotyledons into Archichlamydeae (flowers with free petals) and Metachlamydeae (joined petals) is useful but does not necessarily indicate close relationship (See Page 260) and (Plates 126-128).

Annual. A plant that completes its entire life cycle, from seed to seed, and dies in a single season.

Annual ring. The amount of growth shown each year in a woody stem. Because, in temperate climates, there is a distinct difference between xylem formed in spring and in autumn, the rings give the approximate age of the tree. In tropical climates, however, growth is constant throughout the year and no rings are seen. In temperate climates it is possible for more than one growth ring to form in one year. This may happen when a very cold spell occurs during the summer. (See Plate 116).

Annular Thickening. (See *Xylem*).

13

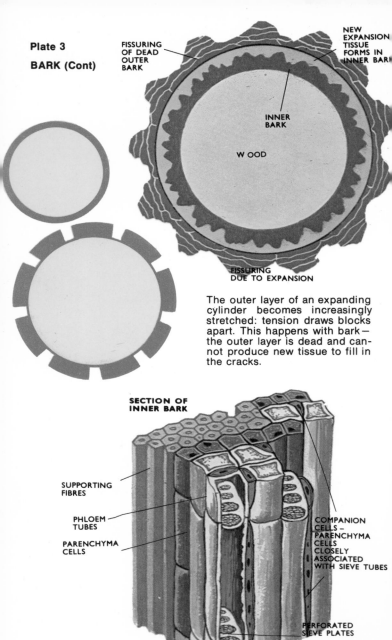

Plate 3
BARK (Cont)

FISSURING OF DEAD OUTER BARK

NEW EXPANSION TISSUE FORMS IN INNER BARK

INNER BARK

WOOD

FISSURING DUE TO EXPANSION

The outer layer of an expanding cylinder becomes increasingly stretched: tension draws blocks apart. This happens with bark — the outer layer is dead and cannot produce new tissue to fill in the cracks.

SECTION OF INNER BARK

SUPPORTING FIBRES

PHLOEM TUBES

PARENCHYMA CELLS

COMPANION CELLS — PARENCHYMA CELLS CLOSELY ASSOCIATED WITH SIEVE TUBES

PERFORATED SIEVE PLATES

Plate 4

BARK (Cont)

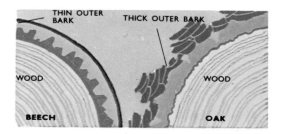

Beech bark forms very slowly and no great thickness builds up to become fissured as in oak.

SILVER BIRCH	CHERRY
TRANSITION FROM SMOOTH BARK SHOWING LENTICELS, TO RUGGED BARK, OBSCURING THEM	LIKE THE SILVER BIRCH, LENTICELS ARE HORIZONTAL, BUT THEY ARE MUCH MORE ELONGATED

15

ANGIOSPERMAE

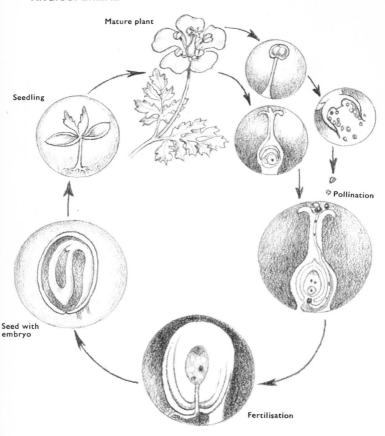

The life cycle of a typical angiosperm or flowering plant.

ANGIOSPERMAE (Cont)

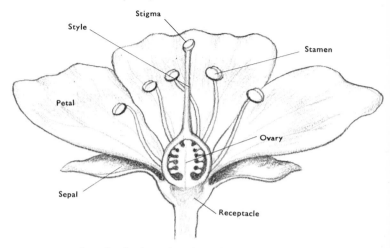

Longitudinal section through a typical flower.

Annulus. (1) A single row of specially differentiated cells in moss sporogonia and fern sporangia concerned with the liberation of the spores. (2) A ring of membranous tissue surrounding the stalk beneath the fruiting cap of basidiomycete fungi, such as the common mushroom. Before the cap of the latter expands to expose the gills, the annulus is an unbroken ring of tissue joining the edge of the cap to the stalk. (See Plates 31 and 66).

Anther. The part of a stamen containing the pollen. (See *Flower*) and (Plate 34).

Antheridium. The body containing the male sex cells in lower plants such as algae, fungi, mosses, liverworts, and ferns. (See Plates 20 and 33).

Antherozoid. Flagellated male gamete of mosses and liverworts and other lower plants.

Anthocyanins. Pigments that occur in solution in the cell sap of flowering plants. They are glycosides-long chain molecules composed of glucose units – and are responsible for the tints of many petals, the colours red, blue and violet depending on the pH of the cell sap: red when acid, blue when alkaline and violet when neutral. Some autumn colourings are also due to anthocyanins.

Anthoxanthins. Soluble pigments occurring in the cell sap of leaves, stems, and flowers. They may modify the colours of anthocyanins (q.v.).

Antibiotic. A substance produced strictly by a living organism which is

17

Plate 5

BARK (Cont)

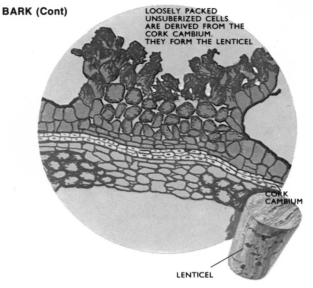

LOOSELY PACKED UNSUBERIZED CELLS ARE DERIVED FROM THE CORK CAMBIUM. THEY FORM THE LENTICEL

CORK CAMBIUM

LENTICEL

A section through a lenticel. Corks are cut so that the lenticels run across them: they are then air-tight.

BIOLUMINESCENCE

The toadstool *Mycena*—one of several luminous fungi.

Plate 6

BRACT

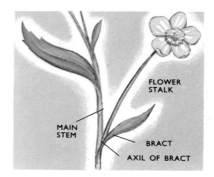

A Brussels sprout cut through the middle showing that a bud is actually an unelongated stem whose leaves are bunched tightly together.

BUD

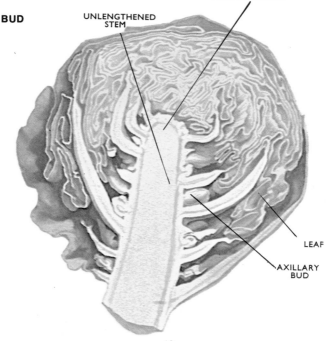

harmful to another species. Penicillin, produced by the mould *Penicillium notatum,* is antagonistic to many bacteria and was the first antibiotic to be used commercially. Other important ones are streptomycin, aureomycin, and terramycin. The term may also be extended to include such drugs as sulphonamides which are man-made. The first of these was Prontosil.

Apetalous. Without petals.

Aphyllous. Without leaves.

Apical Meristem. A growing point at the tip of a root or stem in a vascular plant. To begin with the actively dividing cells of a growing point are uniform in size and shape. But behind the tip they gradually differentiate, becoming mature cells some way behind the tip. (See *Meristem*).

Apocarpous. Having separate carpels. (See *Flower*).

Apomixis. Reproduction without sex, which is superficially similar to sexual reproduction but in which fertilisation does not take place.

Apothecium. A cup-shaped fruiting body characteristic of many ascomycete fungi, e.g. *Peziza,* a typical cup-fungus. (See Plate 122).

Archegonitae. Bryophytes and pteridophytes. Plants having female sex organs called archegonia. (See *Archegonium*).

Archegonium. The flask-shaped female sex organ of liverworts, mosses, and ferns, and also of most gymnosperms. (See *Filicales, Hepaticae*) and (Plates 20 and 33).

Archesporium. A single cell or mass of cells from which spores are derived. (See *Spore*).

Archichlamydeae. A subclass of the Angiospermae in which the petals, when present, are usually free.

Areole. (See *Cacti*).

Aril. Brightly-coloured structure enveloping or partly enveloping the seeds of some plants — e.g. yew and spindle (*Euonymus*). It forms from the base of the ovule or its stalk and is not, therefore, a fruit (q.v.). (See Plate 125).

Aristate. Having an awn (q.v.).

Ascocarp. The fruiting body of an ascomycete fungus. (See *Fungi*).

Ascomycetes. Sac fungi. (See *Fungi*).

Ascospore. A spore produced by an ascomycete fungus.

Ascus. A spore-sac of an ascomycete fungus.

Asexual Reproduction. The increase in numbers by simple division or budding without the fusion of two sex-cells. It may be by spore-formation or by *vegetative reproduction* (q.v.).

Association. A major plant community in which more than one plant is dominant, as in mixed deciduous woodland. It may also be applied in modern usage to any small unit of natural vegetation. (See *Community*).

Autogamy. A sexual process usually thought of as occurring in some protozoa but also occurring in some diatoms. A nucleus divides into two parts and these reunite.

Autonomic movements are produced as a result of some internal stimulus e.g. nutation (q.v.).

Autotrophic organisms are able to manufacture their own organic food from inorganic materials using energy from an outside source. Most green plants are completely autotrophic making organic foods from carbon dioxide, water, and mineral salts, using the energy of sunlight which is in some way fixed by the chlorophyll. Some bacteria are also autotrophic, using energy obtained by the oxidation of inorganic substances. The nitrifying bacteria of the soil, and the iron bacteria are examples. (See *Chlorophyll; Photosynthesis*).

Auxin. A plant growth substance or hormone. (See *Tropism*).

Awn. (=*Arista*). A slender, bristle-like appendage on the glumes of many grasses. (See *Gramineae*).

Axil. The angle between a leaf or bract and the stem on which it grows. (See Plate 53).

Bacillariophyceae. (See *Diatom*).

Bacillus. A genus of rod-shaped bacteria.

Bacteria. Minute, single-celled organisms, so small that they cannot be seen with the naked eye. The largest ones are only about $1/1800$ inch long. Many are essential to the processes of decay, helping to break down the dead remains of plants and animals and releasing materials that plants can absorb through their roots. Others have the ability to use atmospheric nitrogen in the building up of nitrates — mineral salts that are vital for healthy plant growth. Many of the bacteria present in the gut of animals break down food materials and thus provide substances that the animal would

otherwise be unable to obtain. Some bacteria are employed in important industrial processes — in the manufacture of acetic acid and cheese, for example. The most obvious effect of bacterial activity, however, is disease. Many bacteria live on or in the body without ever causing disease, but some may invade the tissues when conditions are suitable. It is fortunate that only a small proportion of the species of bacteria are pathogenic, but even so the list of diseases that they cause is a lengthy one. The variety of materials that different bacteria use as food is remarkable. Some obtain their energy by oxidising ammonium compounds, others (the sulphur bacteria) use sunlight to form carbohydrates from carbon dioxide and hydrogen sulphide, and the iron bacteria oxidise iron compounds. Yet others can grow and reproduce only inside other living things.

Many bacteria have lost the ability to utilise inorganic substances and have become parasitic, relying on their hosts to provide them with ready-made food. Most of these can reproduce only inside their hosts, though they may be able to survive outside the host by forming a protective coat or *spore*.

Bacteria may be arranged into three groups according to their shape: rod-shaped forms (*bacilli*), spherical forms (*cocci*), and curved or spiral forms (*spirilli*).

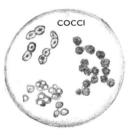

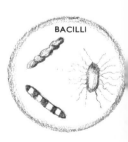

A variety of bacteria.

21

Plate 7

CACTI

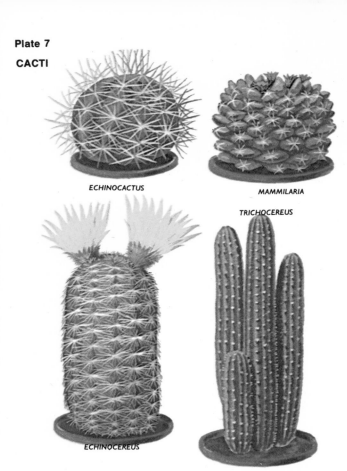

ECHINOCACTUS

MAMMILARIA

TRICHOCEREUS

ECHINOCEREUS

Various cacti: the spines or glochids (tiny barbed hairs) are all borne on small cushions called areoles.

REOLE WITH
PINES

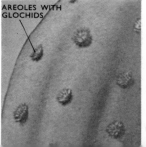

AREOLES WITH
GLOCHIDS

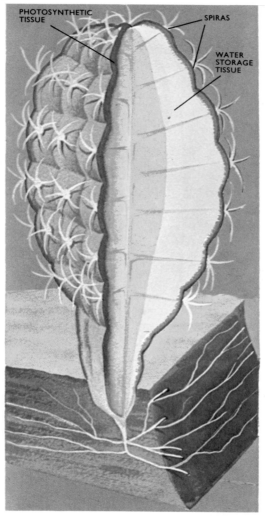

Diagram of a cactus showing the water storage tissue and the spreading root system which gathers all the available water after rain.

Most bacteria have a rigid cell wall. Although they have no nucleus like that of typical plant and animal cells, nuclear material is scattered through the cell. Bacteria reproduce only by division. Usually the cell elongates prior to splitting across the middle. Sometimes the separation is incomplete and a 'double bacterium' is formed such as the *diplococcus* that causes pneumonia. Repeated division without complete separation may produce long chains (e.g. *streptococci* and *streptobacilli*).

Some bacteria are able to move of their own accord, either by means of wriggling movements or by lashing whip-like hairs or *flagella*—this is possible only in moist situations—but the majority are distributed by means of wind and animals.

Some bacteria are *aerobic;* that is, they can live only in the presence of free oxygen. Others are *anaerobic,* and can live only in the absence of free oxygen. Thus aerobic forms (*aerobes*) are active in such situations as open wounds and the membranes lining the nose, throat and lung passages. Examples are those bacteria that cause colds, and sepsis in wounds. The organisms that cause tetanus and gas gangrene are *anaerobes* and normally infect deep wounds.

The effects of bacteria on the body vary considerably. By invading the tissues they may destroy vital cells so that a part is weakened or unable to work. But the main effect of a bacterial attack is produced in most cases by the chemical substances that they release during their growth or on their breakdown after they die. These substances are called *toxins* and are generally characteristic for particular bacteria producing a characteristic disease. Thus the anthrax bacillus always produces anthrax and the tetanus bacillus always produces tetanus. However, some diseases—pneumonia, for example—may be caused by a number of different organisms.

Pathogenic bacteria, like other parasites, must contact new hosts in order that the species shall survive. The method of spreading varies considerably between different bacteria. Those that infect the throat and respiratory passages will pass to the air during breathing, sneezing, or coughing. Hence the importance of using a handkerchief to prevent their spread. Other organisms (e.g. typhoid bacillus) may infect the faeces. During treatment of a person who has typhoid it is most important that his faeces are disinfected so that all the typhoid-causing organisms are killed.

Bacteria that are able to survive for long periods outside their host stand a better chance of infecting a new host than those that survive for only short periods. Thus the tuberculosis bacillus can survive in dark dusty places for many months and a person can become infected in a room in which a tuberculosis patient has lived.

Another problem is that some people (*carriers*) are resistant to bacteria and, though they carry them in their body, they are not affected by their presence. If such an individual comes into contact with a person who is susceptible, however, that person can become infected and may contract the disease. This has particular importance in the food industry where food may be handled by carriers. (See Plate 119).

Bactericide. Substance capable of killing bacteria.

Bacteriology. The study of bacteria.

Bacteriophage. A virus that can kill bacteria.

Bark. A protective tissue of dead cells that covers the stems and branches of woody plants. In some species, oak and elm for instance, it appears rough and fissured. In others, such as beech, it is smooth and shiny, while in yet others it is scaly (larch and sycamore). So distinctive is the bark of different plants, that in winter, when leaves have fallen, it is one of the most useful features for identifying trees.

But the bark seen on the outside of a tree is not the whole of the structure. In fact it is the least important section, consisting almost entirely of dead tissues. There is an inner region of bark which is much paler and which contains living cells. The cells of this inner bark make up the *phloem* (q.v.) — the tissue that conducts organic food through the plant. Removal of this layer will kill a tree.

Most of the food-conduction is carried out by cells in the innermost portion of the inside layer. As the phloem tissues are pushed further outwards by further growth, they become crushed and the living cells are destroyed. The dead tissues eventually go to make up the outer bark.

At the junction of the innermost surface of the bark and the wood inside, there is a thin layer of dividing cells (*the cambium*). Each year the cambium cells grow and divide. Of the two cells formed, one continues the multiplication while the other becomes adapted to another function. New cells on the inside of the cambium form more wood. On the outside of the cambial layer, the new cells form more phloem.

The phloem for ever pushes outwards. Original phloem of the inner bark is turned into the dead tissues of the outer bark. The thickness of the inner bark is always about the same, so old inner bark is turned into new outer bark at about the same rate as new inner bark forms at the cambium surface.

The new outer bark tissue becomes completely cut off from the inner bark by special thin layers of cork (*periderms*). Periderms form from the parenchyma cells which, though subjected to crushing, remain alive considerably longer than the sieve tubes of the phloem.

The cells which make up cork are tightly packed together. The cells walls are also reinforced (*suberised*) with fatty substances. Cork is consequently impermeable and forms a watertight protective coat about the inside of the bark.

The pattern of the cork layers varies with species of tree. Sometimes they are few and very extensive. Other times they are numerous and separate only a few square inches of outer bark. e.g. the plane tree. In comparison with the thickness of the outer bark, cork layers are usually insignificant. One exception, however, is the cork oak from which commercial cork is obtained. The cork here may be several inches thick while outer bark is very thin indeed.

The addition of new (*secondary*) wood to the stem of the tree, together with the formation of new inner bark, slowly increases the girth of a tree trunk. The new inner bark tissues are, of course, not subjected to strain. At the time of formation they completely cover the surface area of the tree at its particular stage of development.

Old inner bark is, however, put under strain. Its tissues are called upon to spread over a greater circumference than they originally covered. The problem is partially solved by a stretching of the cells. But this is not enough. New expansion tissue forms by division of the parenchyma cells but no expansion can go on in the dead, outer bark. Under the strain the dead tissues split apart, giving the gnarled, fissured surface familiar in so many trees.

Yet the bark of beech and some other trees is quite smooth. The outer bark of these trees is very thin as its growth rate is very slow. The outer bark surface breaks down into powder and disappears unnoticed.

The bark of the oak grows at least four times as fast as that of beech. Numerous cork layers form, each cutting off sections of outer bark. The amount of dead tissue is considerable. Some flaking off at the surface of outermost bark does occur, but the rate is not fast enough to remove all the accumulated dead tissues. The thick outer bark is particularly subject to strain and fissuring occurs, giving a rough surface.

Cork is not the only commercial product obtained from bark. The

25

Plate 9

CACTI (Cont)

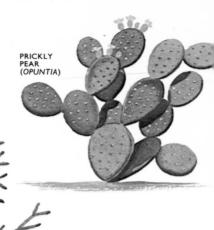

Two further examples of cacti.

CARBON CYCLE

A simplified carbon cycle.

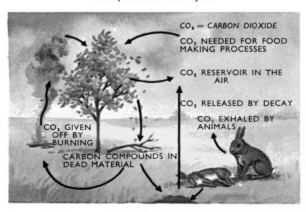

CO_2 = CARBON DIOXIDE

CO_2 NEEDED FOR FOOD MAKING PROCESSES

CO_2 RESERVOIR IN THE AIR

CO_2 RELEASED BY DECAY

CO_2 EXHALED BY ANIMALS

CO_2 GIVEN OFF BY BURNING

CARBON COMPOUNDS IN DEAD MATERIAL

Plate 10

CHLAMYDOMONAS

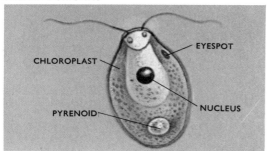

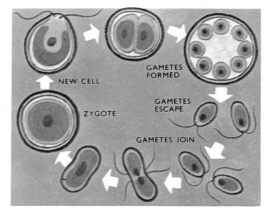

This very simple single-celled alga is found in ponds and ditches everywhere. It reproduces by simply dividing into two (bottom) or by producing gametes which join up to give new individuals (centre).

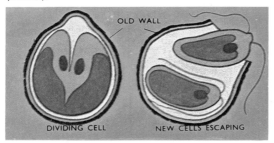

27

tannins used in leather tanning are obtained from bark — notably that of oak, hemlock, birch, and willow. Tannins are by-products of plant metabolism and they are deposited in several places, not just bark. The drug quinine — important in the treatment of malaria — is obtained from the bark of the *Chinchona* tree. Cinnamon is also a bark product. (See *Cork, Stem*) and (Plates 2, 3, 4, 5 and 12).

Basidiomycetes. Large division of fungi (q.v.) containing the mushrooms and toadstools and the parasitic rust fungi. (See Plates 14, 65 and 66).

Basidiospore. Characteristic spore of basidiomycete fungi. (See Plate 65).

Basidium. The cell on which basidiospores are formed. (See Plate 65).

Bennettitales. An extinct group of gymnosperms that was abundant in Mesozoic times. (See *Gymnospermae*).

Berry. A fleshy fruit (q.v.) usually containing many seeds. Examples include tomato, gooseberry, and orange. (See Plate 37).

Biennial. A plant that completes its life cycle in two seasons. Examples include the carrot, and beetroot. The first season is involved in the production and storage of food, in the carrot in an underground tap root, and in the second year this food store is used up in the production of flowers and seeds. The plant then dies.

Binomial System of Nomenclature. The system of naming plants and animals whereby each type receives two Latin names. The first is the generic name and is spelt with a capital letter. The second is the specific name and is spelt with a small letter. The great Swedish naturalist Linnaeus was the first to use this system on a wide scale. (See *Classification*).

Biological Control. The use of one organism to control another — usually

a pest. For example the use of a small moth to control prickly pear cacti in Australia.

Bioluminescence. The production of light by a living organism. Many animals produce their own light but among plants only the lower ones — toadstools such as *Mycena* and 'jack-o-lantern' (*Clitocybe*), and many moulds and bacteria. It is not known how, or even if the organisms benefit by their activity. 'Jack-o-lantern' is poisonous, as are many brightly coloured, non-luminous fungi. Possibly the luminescence has protective value therefore, but many luminous plants are non poisonous. The light produced is often referred to as 'cold light', for very little heat is evolved in its production. Measurements indicate that nearly one hundred per cent is released as light (contrast this with an ordinary electric light bulb which is only ten per cent efficient). The chemical reaction involved is a modification or side branch of the reactions that proceed in every living cell. It is promoted by an enzyme, *luciferase*. In the presence of oxygen and an organic compound rich in phosphate (adenosine triphosphate or A.T.P.) luciferase promotes the oxidation of *luciferin*. This causes the production of light. The chemical structure of luciferin has been established and it has been synthesised. The luciferase molecule is thought to be a protein chain made up of about one thousand amino acid molecules. (See Plate 5).

Biotic factors. The influences of living things in the environment as distinct from the influences of soil and climate.

Bipinnate. Compound pinnate leaves in which the leaflets themselves are pinnate as well. (See Page 136).

Bog. Community dominated by *Sphagnum* mosses and growing on wet peat. Bogs develop in regions of poor drainage and where the rainfall is very high. Blanket bogs cover large tracts of Ireland and northern Britain. Here the high rainfall exceeds evaporation and the soil has become leached and acidic. Such conditions favoured the growth of *Sphagnum* mosses. Bacterial decay is hindered by the acidic conditions and so the remains of mosses built up large accumulations of peat. This peat acts as a sponge and absorbs the rainfall, thus making a bog rather squelchy to walk on. The activity of man has, in many regions, caused erosion of the blanket bogs and they have tended to dry out and become heather-dominated moors. Valley bogs develop in low lying areas on acid soils – over podsols, for example. Bogs can sometimes form in region of alkaline rocks. If a pool becomes filled in with reeds and other fen vegetation, the accumulating remains may rise above the general water level. Rain water will then make it slightly acidic – suitable conditions for the growth of *Sphagnum*. This bog moss is able to carry its own water supply up with it and makes it more and more acidic. At the edge of the original depression, the influence of the alkaline soil water is felt to some extent but in the centre it has no effect and the growth of *Sphagnum* is greater there. The bog, therefore, becomes domed and is called a raised bog. The detailed surface of a bog is rarely even, but consists of numerous mounds and hollows. The hollows are wetter and moss growth is more rapid there. As the moss can carry its water supply up with it in large cells, the moss of a hollow grows up until it is above the original surrounding mounds. As it gets higher, it gets drier and drier and peat formation slows down. Heather and other woody plants may start to grow on the top of the new mound, while the original mounds are now hollows and the process starts again. In this way, a bog builds up considerable thicknesses of peat. In a living or growing bog, the *Sphagnum* mosses are the dominant plants but there are numerous others such as sundews, heathers, heaths, and sedges such as the cotton grass. As soon as the

Sphagnum cover is broken peat formation stops and, if the removal of the *Sphagnum* is accompanied by drainage, the mosses may not be able to re-establish themselves. The bog will then become a drier community called a moor, dominated by heather or sedges instead of *Sphagnum*. (See *Peat; Moor; Fen*) and (Plates 72–75).

Boraginaceae. (See *Tubiflorae*).

Bract. A small leaf in the axil of which a flower stalk develops. (See Plate 6).

Bracteole. A small leaf on a flower stalk.

Bryophyta. The group of plants containing mosses and liverworts. (See *Hepaticae; Musci*).

Bud. An unlengthened shoot all of whose leaves are clustered around it. (See *Stem*) and (Plates 6 and 101).

Budding. A form of propagation (q.v.). (See Plates 83 and 84). Also a form of asexual reproduction in which detachable parts are formed and released. The division of yeast cells into two is called budding. (See Plate 122).

Bulb. An underground storage and reproductive structure. Food is stored in thick, fleshy leaves that surround a short stem. The flowering shoots develop from buds in the axils of these leaves. After flowering, a new bud (or buds) swells up as food accumulates in its leaves and this forms the new bulb. (See *Stem; Corm*) and (Plate 100).

Bulbil. A tiny bulb – especially one that forms from a bud on an aerial stem and then falls to the ground.(See *Vegetative Reproduction*).

Cacti. Flowering plants of the family Cactaceae. The chief problem facing a plant in desert conditions is to obtain sufficient water, and, having obtained it, to conserve it. All deserts have

Plate 11

COMMUNITY

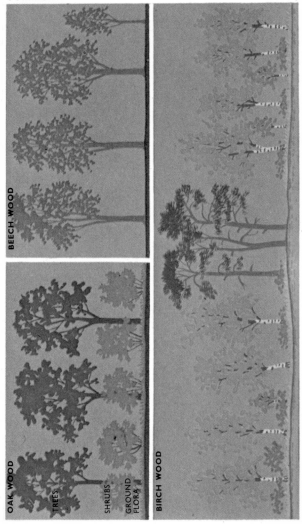

OAK WOOD

TREES

SHRUBS

GROUND FLORA

BEECH WOOD

BIRCH WOOD

Three types of woodland. The extent of the shrub and ground layers depends on the amount of shade cast by the dominant trees.

Plate 12

CORK

Virgin (left) and cultivated cork. Bottle corks are cut so that the pores (lenticels) run across them. The tough-walled air-filled cells (below) give cork its resilience.

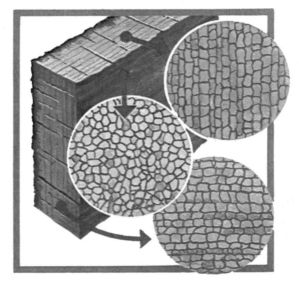

some rainfall, but it is meagre, and a year or more may elapse between each shower. Moreover, when it does rain, it is often as a torrential cloudburst lasting only a short while. Thus a plant has to take in water rapidly and to store it in large quantities. It has to use water sparingly and avoid losing too much through the drying effects of the air and the hot sun.

Cacti have the necessary qualities that enable them to do these things. Many have vast spreading root systems covering large areas close to the surface of the ground, and able to absorb great volumes of water quickly: the stems are distended and fleshy, sometimes forming enormous water stores. Often they are pleated, which allows them to expand, just as a concertina does, thus increasing their water-carrying capacity. Some (e.g. barrel cactus) are like giant water butts, others (e.g. Saguaro cactus) form long tubular columns stretching fifty feet in the air, while others are no bigger than a shirt button. The cells of the water storage tissues are rich in glue-like mucilage. This holds water very efficiently, and as cacti have no normal leaves – they are nearly always in the form of sharp protective spines – there are no large stomata-covered leaf surfaces through which water is lost in transpiration. A few stomata are present in the epidermis of the fleshy stems and it is thought that they open only at night (in the majority of plants the stomata open in the day and close at night). Also, since cacti are so compact, their surface area is relatively small, another important factor in keeping water loss to a minimum. As much as ninety per cent of a cactus' bulk is water. Such is their ability to conserve water, however, that in a laboratory experiment no more than a third of this amount was lost after some had been kept for several years without watering.

The stem, besides being a water-store, is the food-manufacturing centre of a cactus. It is green in colour, the photosynthetic tissue forming a thin outer layer surrounding the inner mass of colourless water storage tissue. Besides the barrel-shaped and column-like forms, many stems are flat and jointed, somewhat like green, spiky biscuits joined edge-to-edge. The opuntias have this form. Cacti are distinguished from all other succulents by the possession of *areoles*. These are the tiny 'pincushions' from which spines and *glochids* (barbed hairs) project.

There are about 1,300 species, most of which inhabit the desert and semi-desert areas of North America. The original home of the cactus family was in America but many species are now found in other parts of the world. The common prickly pear (*Opuntia*), for example, has grown for many years in South Africa and the Mediterranean region. After its introduction into Australia in the 19th century, it spread so rapidly that it became a pest. It was eventually controlled by the introduction of a moth whose caterpillar feeds on the cactus – an outstanding example of biological control.

The flowers of cacti are often large and showy and exquisitely coloured. The ovary is *inferior* and the fruit is a berry. In one species it is juicy and gooseberry-like and can be eaten. Cacti are of little practical use, however. In such countries as Mexico, prickly pear are grown as fences and hedges to enclose and protect houses. The thorns of certain cacti (e.g. barrel cacti) are hooked and are used by primitive tribes for fishing. In times of food shortage, prickly pear and similar cacti have been chopped up for animal foodstuffs, whilst many species are grown as decorative plants in greenhouses and homes. (See Plates 7, 8 and 9).

Caducous. Referring to parts such as sepals when they are not persistent, as in the poppy.

Calcicole. Lime-loving. Plants of this type are found almost exclusively on calcareous soils. Examples include salad burnet and old man's beard (*Clematis*).

Calcifuge. Lime-hating. Plants of this type are rarely found where there is free calcium carbonate in the soil. They are typical of sandy soils. Examples include heather and *Rhododendron*.

Callose. A carbohydrate material that may cover one or both surfaces of the sieve plates of sieve tubes. Deposits of callose are often permanent when the activity of the cells are brought to an end. In some plants, however, such as the vine, callose is laid down in the autumn, being redissolved in the spring. (See *Phloem*).

Callus. An outer mass of tissue formed by plant tissues especially those of the cambium in response to an injury.

Calyptra. The protective covering of the capsule of mosses. It is formed from the neck of the archegonium. (See *Musci*) and (Plate 64).

Calyptrogen. A row of cells from which the root cap is often formed. (See *Root*).

Calyx. The outer part of a flower, i.e. the sepals. These are usually green but sometimes are brightly coloured as in marsh marigold. They protect the inner parts of the flower. (See *Flower*).

Cambium. A tissue consisting of actively dividing cells. It is found in vascular bundles between the xylem and phloem and also between vascular bundles. Division of its cells produces additional xylem and phloem cells in *secondary thickening* (q.v.). (See *Stem; Root*).

Cambrian Period. Geological period beginning 5–600 million years ago. (See *Geological Time Scale*).

Campanulaceae. Family of dicotyledons containing the bell-flowers such

as the harebell and the cultivated Canterbury bells. Most of the members are herbs and the petals are joined into a bell-shaped tube in most species. (See Page 28).

Campanulate. Bell-shaped — as in the gamopetalous flowers of the family Campanulaceae.

Campylotropous. Referring to an ovule (q.v.) which is bent in such a way that the micropyle is close to the chalaza where the funicle joins the ovule. There is no fusion of the ovule and funicle over any distance as in the anatropous ovule.

Capitulum. An inflorescence (q.v.) typical of flowers of the family Compositae (q.v.).

Capsule. A type of dry, dehiscent fruit (q.v.) formed from two or more carpels and opening in a variety of ways. (See Plate 35).

Carbohydrate. An organic compound whose molecule contains carbon, hydrogen and oxygen atoms. The latter two are usually present in the same ratio as in water, namely two hydrogen atoms to each oxygen atom. Examples are glucose (grape sugar), fructose (fruit sugar), sucrose (cane sugar), starch — an important storage material — and cellulose — the principal structural material in plants. Carbohydrates are the main fuels that are burned to supply the energy needed to power living processes. But they are not merely energy providers, cellulose being produced in large quantities, for example, to form cell walls. Sugar molecules are often combined to form glycosides such as anthocyanins, pigments that give blue, red, and purple colours to flowers. There are three main groups of carbohydrates, mono-saccharides, disaccharides, and polysaccharides. Monosaccharides are simple sugars such as glucose and their molecules cannot be split into other simpler sugars. Two monosaccharide

Plate 13

COMPOSITAE

SCAPE
(LEAFLESS
FLOWERING
STEM)

DANDELION

The flower heads of members of the family Compositae are actually made up of numerous tiny florets: each of them contains sex organs and is a complete flower (see Plate 34).

DESMID

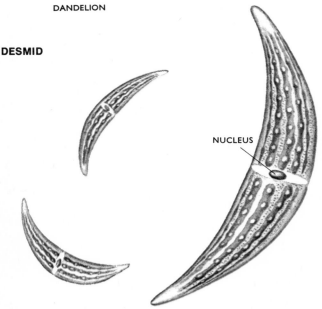

NUCLEUS

A single-celled alga called *Closterium*. It has a shell in two symmetrical halves.

Plate 14

DISEASES in PLANTS

CLUSTERS OF
SPORES ON BARBERRY

Black rust of wheat, caused by the fungus *Puccinia graminis*. The black streaks on the wheat are formed by masses of black spores breaking through the surface. There are several stages in the life cycle, including two on the barberry plant.

CAMPANULACEAE

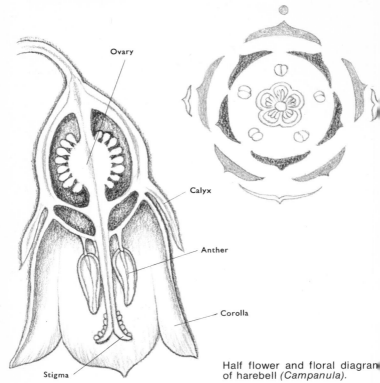

Ovary

Calyx

Anther

Corolla

Stigma

Half flower and floral diagram of harebell *(Campanula)*.

molecules can join up and form a disaccharide molecule, with the elimination of a molecule of water. Plants form sucrose from glucose and fructose in this way. Polysaccharides are formed when many monosaccharide molecules join up. Starch consists of about 200 glucose molecules. Cellulose consists of even more monosaccharide molecules, linked together in a slightly different way.

Carbon Cycle. The circulation of carbon atoms in nature, largely due to the activities of living organisms. Carbon from atmospheric carbon dioxide is incorporated in plant tissues as a result of photosynthesis: such compounds are consumed in respiration with the liberation of carbon dioxide: plants die, after which their remains are broken down by microorganisms with the further liberation of carbon dioxide: plants may also be eaten by herbivores which produce carbon dioxide waste in respiration and which die and whose remains are broken down with the release of carbon dioxide. Natural phenomena such as volcanoes and bush fires also contribute valuable quantities of carbon dioxide to the atmosphere. (See Plate 9).

Carboniferous Period. Geological period beginning about 260 m'llion years ago and famous for the vast swamp forests in which the coal-forming plants grew. (See *Geological Time Scale*).

Carotene. An orange pigment occurring particularly in chloroplasts with chlorophyll and xanthophyll and concerned with photosynthesis. Carotene is a long chain hydro-carbon. It also occurs in parts of plants which lack chlorophyll and gives the colour to carrot storage organs. It is important to man as a precursor of vitamin A. (See *Photosynthesis*).

Carpel. The female structure of a flower. There are often more than one and they may be joined (e.g. the plum has one carpel, the orange has several joined ones, while the buttercup has many separate ones). Each carpel contains one or more ovules that later become seeds. The carpel(s) develop into the *fruit* (q.v.). (See *Flower*).

Carr. (See *Fen*).

Caruncle. A warty outgrowth on the seeds of some flowering plants (e.g. castor oil). In this plant the caruncle obscures the hilum and the micropyle. It absorbs water before germination and passes this on to the adjacent radicle. (See *Germination; Seed*).

Caryophyllaceae. (See *Centrospermae*).

Caryopsis. The fruit (q.v.) of grasses. The ovary wall is joined to the seed coat. (See *Gramineae*).

Catkin. A spike, often hanging, of simple flowers – e.g. hazel. (See *Inflorescence*).

Cauline. Of the stem. Cauline leaves are carried on the upper part of a stem but do not bear flower shoots in their axils.

Cell. A mass of protoplasm surrounded by a thin membrane and (in plants) a cellulose cell wall. (The term is also used to refer to a structure that has lost its protoplasm – e.g. a xylem cell.) The larger plants are composed of many such units of which there may be many kinds, each designed for a specific job or jobs. A mature plant cell is typically small – between a

CELL

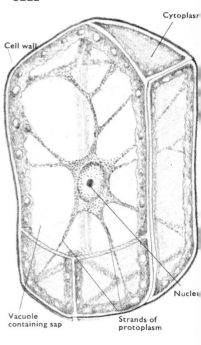

Block diagram of a plant cell.

Plate 15

DISEASES in PLANTS (Cont)

SPORE-BEARING
BRANCHES
(CONIDIOPHORES)
BREAKING THROUGH
LEAF SURFACE

CONIDIA

Potato blight on leaves and tuber. The disease starts in an infected tuber and spreads from there to the leaves. Spores produced in the mildewy regions of the leaves then spread to other plants. (Right) Wart disease of potato, caused by the fungus *Synchytrium endobioticum.*

Plate 16

SPORES DEVELOPING IN WART TISSUE. THEY ARE RELEASED WHEN THE TISSUES DECAY

tenth and a hundredth of a millimetre in diameter – and its protoplasm consists of a denser part, the nucleus containing the chromosomes (q.v.), and a clearer cytoplasm. The latter does not fill the cell in an animal cell, but acts as a lining to the cell wall. It surrounds a vacuole filled with watery cell sap, containing minerals and other substances in solution. The cytoplasm contains various bodies such as plastids, which include the chloroplasts (q.v.), and the mitochondria (q.v.). (See *Phloem; Xylem*).

Cell Division. (See *Mitosis* and *Meiosis*).

Cell sap. A watery solution in the vacuole of a plant cell which contains many substances, such as salts and sugars, in solution. (See *Cell*).

Cell theory. A theory put forward in the 19th century, in the first place by Schwann and Schleiden, that all plants and animals are made up of cells. Growth and reproduction are basically due to cell division. (See *Mitosis* and *Meiosis*).

Cellulose. A carbohydrate (q.v.) that forms the principal structural elements in plants, composing the cell walls. Its molecules are formed by the condensation of many glucose molecules, forming fibres. The latter are of great use to man as the basis of textiles.

Cell Wall. The limiting layer of a plant cell surrounding the cell contents. It is formed by the lining layer of protoplasm and consists largely of cellulose (q.v.). (See *Cell*).

Cenozoic Era. Geological Era embracing the last 70 million years of the Earth's history. (See *Geological Time Scale*).

Centrospermae. An order of dicotyledons containing the families Chenopodiaceae and Caryophyllaceae. The former includes the beetroot, *Chenopodium,* and the sea blite. The family Caryophyllaceae contains the stitchwort, campions, pinks, and chickweeds. The majority of these plants are herbaceous. (See Plate 127).

Cereal. A member of the grass family (Gramineae) whose seeds are used for food. Examples include rye, oats, wheat, maize, and barley. (See Plate 44).

Chalaza. The region of a flowering plant ovule (q.v.) where the funicle or ovule stalk is primarily attached and where the vascular trace from the funicle enters the ovule itself. (See Plate 29).

Chemosynthetic. (=*Chemotrophic*). Obtaining energy from some inorganic reaction, such as the oxidation of hydrogen sulphide to sulphur. Several species of bacteria use this method of nutrition. (See *Autotrophic*).

Chemotropism. A directional response to a chemical stimulus, such as the growth of the pollen tube towards the ovule through the stigma of a flower. (See *Tropism*).

Chenopodiaceae. (See *Centrospermae*).

Chimaera. A plant structure which is a mixture of two genetically different tissues. It may be produced as a result of a mutation or by natural or artificial grafting. For example, a shoot may exhibit a mixture of characters of the scion and the stock. (See *Mutation; Propagation*).

Chlamydomonas. A genus of tiny, single-celled green algae that swim freely near the surface of water. It is one of the commonest plants in the freshwater plankton. Its single oval cell, which has a rigid cellulose wall, is so tiny that fifty of them would only just stretch across a pin's head. From one end two fine flagella emerge and drive the organism forwards as they lash about. There is a large cup-shaped *chloroplast* containing the chlorophyll. A lighter area in the chloroplast is the *pyrenoid* and is concerned with starch production. All the processes in the cell are controlled by the nucleus. There is no problem in getting oxygen for respiration—it just diffuses through the cell wall. The same goes for the carbon dioxide used in photosynthesis. Towards the front of the organism is a red *eye-spot* concerned with the detection of light. *Chlamydomonas* is able to respond to light and moves to where the light is best for photosynthesis. When the light and temperature are just right for it, *Chlamydomonas* grows rapidly and each one may split into two or more new individuals every day. Huge numbers result and, together with other algae, may make the water green. When the cell is about to divide, the flagella are withdrawn and the organism stops swimming. The nucleus, protoplasm, and chloroplast all divide once or more and a new cell wall develops around each new group giving two, four, or eight new cells. They produce flagella and swim away as new *Chlamydomonas* plants when the cell wall of the parent breaks up. If the conditions are not favourable (i.e. lack of sunlight and low temperature) *Chlamydomonas* may reproduce in another way. Each one splits up (within its wall) into perhaps sixty-four tiny bodies called *gametes*. When the cell wall bursts, the gametes are released and they join up in pairs (not necessarily from the same parent) to form *zygotes*. The flagella are lost and a thick wall develops. In this state the organism is very resistant to drought and cold. When better conditions return the thick wall breaks down and two or more young individuals are released: the zygote has divided within the thick wall. (See *Chlorophyceae; Algae*) and (Plate 10).

Chlorophyceae. The green algae—the largest group of algae. The green chlorophyll is not masked by other

pigments as it is in the red and brown algae. Members live in salt and fresh water as well as on land. *Pleurococcus* (Plate 1) lives on tree trunks and other similar surfaces. *Chlamydomonas* (q.v.) lives in fresh water. *Volvox* and *Pandorina* (Plate 1) are colonial forms made up of lots of cells like *Chlamydomonas*. *Spirogyra* (q.v.) is a common filamentous green alga with many cells in each strand. *Vaucheria* is composed of strands but they are not divided into cells. *Ulva lactuca*—the sea lettuce is a common sea-shore member of this group. (See *Algae*) and (Plates 10, 94, 98, and 120)

Chlorophyll. The green colouring matter found in almost all plants other than fungi and usually contained in the chloroplasts. Its molecules contain carbon, hydrogen, oxygen, nitrogen and magnesium atoms. An essential part of the photosynthetic system in plants, chlorophyll, in some way, is able to pass on the energy of sunlight to the enzyme systems so that these can facilitate the manufacture of foods such as sugar from atmospheric carbon dioxide, and water. It is significant that the absorption spectrum shows strong absorption of wave-lengths at the red and blue ends and that starch manufacture is much greater in red and blue light than in light of other wave-lengths. (See *Photosynthesis*).

Chloroplast. A chlorophyll-containing body in plant cells. (See *Chlorophyll*).

Chlorosis. An unhealthy condition in green plants in which parts that are normally green become yellow (chlorotic), due to failure of chlorophyll formation. One cause is magnesium deficiency.

Chromoplast. A plastid (q.v.) containing a pigment in plant cells. The pigment may be green (in which case the chromoplast is called a chloroplast), red, orange or yellow. Some flower colours are due to pigments in

41

Plate 17

DISEASES in PLANTS (Cont)

A LEAF FROM A SWEDE PLANT LACKING
MAGNESIUM, AND A NORMAL LEAF (RIGHT)

Deficiency diseases are very common, although they can normally be cured quite easily by the addition of the missing element(s) to the soil.

Plate 18

EMERGENCES

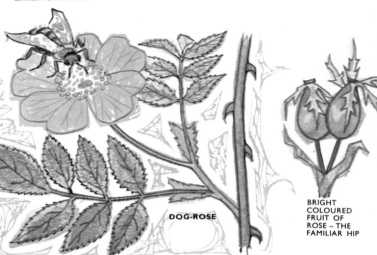

DOG-ROSE

BRIGHT
COLOURED
FRUIT OF
ROSE – THE
FAMILIAR HIP

The prickles of the dog rose are outgrowths of the stem and help the plant to climb and display its flowers and fruits.

EPIGYNOUS

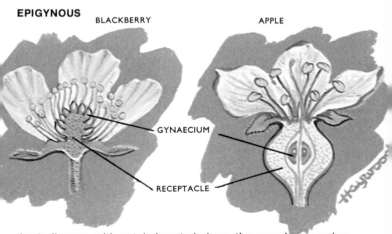

BLACKBERRY   APPLE

GYNAECIUM

RECEPTACLE

Apple flowers, with petals inserted above the carpels, are epigynous. Blackberry flowers are perigynous.

43

chromoplasts in the petals, as is the red colour of a ripe tomato fruit.

Chromosome. Double thread-like structure made of nucleoprotein which can be seen in cell nuclei when the cells are dividing. In normal body cells the chromosomes occur in pairs, the number of pairs depending on the species. The members of each pair look alike and are said to be homologous. Chromosomes carry the genes that control the features of the cell — and of the whole body. When a cell divides the two daughter cells must — at first anyway — be exactly like the parent. During the division of the nucleus the chromosomes all divide along their length, each producing two identical daughter-chromosomes. One daughter from each new pair goes to each new cell, carrying identical instructions, so the new cells will be exactly alike. This process of division is called *mitosis* (q.v.).

Although the body cells contain pairs of chromosomes (*diploid* condition), the sex-cells or gametes contain only half the normal number — i.e. one of each pair. This is the *haploid* condition and a special form of nuclear division called meiosis is involved in the formation of gametes: the homologous chromosomes come together and then separate, one of each pair going to each new cell. At fertilisation, two gametes join and so the diploid number of chromosomes is obtained again. (see Gene; Heredity).

Circinate Vernation. The way in which young fern fronds unroll. The apex is at the centre of the coil and is the last part to be exposed. The individual parts of a frond are also coiled in this way.

Cladode. A stem that is leaf-like in appearance and function, as found in the butcher's broom and asparagus and some cacti.

Classification. The division of the plant kingdom into groups of related plants. There are nearly 350,000 known different kinds of species. No two plants are exactly alike. One fir tree will always differ slightly in shape and height from another, yet two fir trees are more alike than a fir tree and an oak tree. Amongst the many different kinds of plants some are more alike than others. The differences and likenesses are used to place them into groups which may be subdivided many times, the members of a sub-group having more features in common than the members of a group. A classification is necessary so that the relationships of the many kinds of plants are understood. Besides taking into account the plants living today, any system of classification must include plants which are now extinct. From the many fossils which have been found the ancestry and the relationships of the various groups have become much clearer. The plant kingdom may be divided into four main groups, the Thallophyta (algae and fungi), the Bryophyta (mosses and liverworts), the Pteridophyta (ferns and fern-like plants) and the Spermatophyta or seed-bearing plants (i.e. angiosperms or flowering plants and gymnosperms). Another classification recognises only three main groups placing the Pteridophyta and Spermatophyta into the one group — Tracheophyta or vascular plants (i.e. plants with a system of veins carrying food and water from one part of the plant to another). Each person has a christian name and a surname and plants are named in a similar way except that the plant 'surname' comes first. Each kind of plant (and animal too) has two Latin names, the first is its *genus* ranking, the second its *species* ranking. Closely related species all belong to the same genus. Thus the different kinds of buttercup all belong to the genus *Ranunculus*. One species is called *Ranunculus repens*, another *Ranunculus acris* and a third *Ranunculus bulbosus*. The Latin names may appear cumbersome and hard to pronounce but they are standard throughout the world. Common names not only vary locally, but from country to country and 'buttercup' may mean something completely different to a person from another area – if it means anything at all. All the species of the genus *Ranunculus* have certain features in common. The flowers have a calyx and a corolla, many stamens, the fruit is made up of many achenes and each petal has a pocket-like nectary at its base. The species differ in such respects as the shape of the leaves, stems, and roots but it is the flowers that indicate relationship. Closely related genera are grouped into families. For example *Ranunculus*, *Clematis* (e.g. old man's beard), *Caltha* (e.g. marsh marigold) and anemone are grouped in the family Ranunculaceae. Related families are arranged into orders or cohorts. Thus the Ranunculaceae are in the order Ranales and this order, with many others, forms the class Dicotyledonae of the subdivision Angiospermae. The Angiosperms or flowering plants are divided into two classes, the Monocotyledonae and the Dicotyledonae. The Angiosperms are a subdivision of the division Spermatophyta, the seed-bearing plants. The classification of *Ranunculus repens* may be written: –

Division:	Spermatophyta
Subdivision:	Angiospermae
Class:	Dicotyledonae
Order:	Ranales
Family:	Ranunculaceae
Genus:	*Ranunculus*
Species:	*repens*

(See Pages 48—49 and 245—264) and (Plates 119—128).

Cleistogamy. Fertilisation occurring within a flower that is not open.

Climax Vegetation. A plant community the composition of which is more or less stable, and whose character is mainly determined by the prevailing climatic conditions. In British lowland conditions, for example, open country is gradually invaded by trees of various kinds until oak becomes the dominant plant species. (See *Community; Consociation; Succession*).

Club Moss. (See *Lycopodiales*).

Cohort. Term sometimes used in plant classification (q.v.). Equivalent to order.

Coleoptile. The sheath surrounding the young shoot of grass seedlings. (See *Germination*) and (Plate 42).

Coleorhiza. The sheath surrounding the young root of grass seedlings. (See *Germination*).

Collenchyma. The supporting tissues of young stems. The cell walls of the living cells are strengthened with cellulose.

Columella. A dome-shaped partition separating internally the sporangium from the sporangiophore stalk of pin mould fungi. (See *Mucor*) and (Plate 39).

Community (of plants) is applied to any collection of plants which make up a distinct type of vegetation – from woodlands to the scant plant growth on the flanks of a sand-dune. An oak-wood in springtime: close to the ground clumps of moss, white anemones, lesser celandines, winter aconites, and thick green spreads of dog's mercury; above, an undergrowth of stouter woody shrubs such as hazel, hawthorn, and sloe; higher still, branches of the oak trees themselves, supported on tough rigid trunks. All these plants are growing on a similar sort of soil; all are subjected to the same sort of climate. Together they make up a recognisable community of plants. For greater precision of meaning, according to the scale of the plant community, a number of other terms can be used. A plant formation refers to a community in very broad terms. The great belts of vegetation found throughout the world – the rain forests, desert vegetation, deciduous forests, coniferous forests – are examples. Studied in greater detail each plant formation breaks down into a number of subsidiary categories. An oakwood,

Plate 19

EPIPHYTE

An orchid growing epi-phytically on a branch and showing the aerial roots through which it absorbs water.

EQUISETALES

The field horsetail, *Equisetum arvense.*

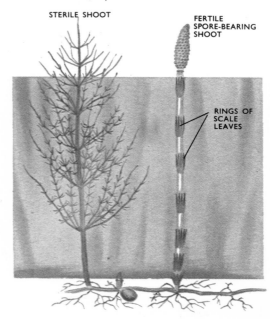

STERILE SHOOT

FERTILE SPORE-BEARING SHOOT

RINGS OF SCALE LEAVES

Plate 20

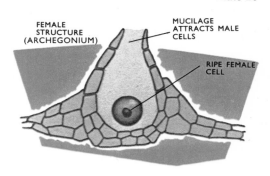

FEMALE
STRUCTURE
(ARCHEGONIUM)

MUCILAGE
ATTRACTS MALE
CELLS

RIPE FEMALE
CELL

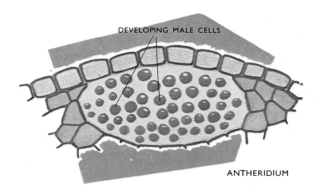

DEVELOPING MALE CELLS

ANTHERIDIUM

The tiny horsetail prothallus (centre) bears female archegonia
near the middle and male antheridia around the outside.

47

CLASSIFICATION

A chart showing the evolution and classification of plants. An asterisk by a name indicates that the plant is extinct.

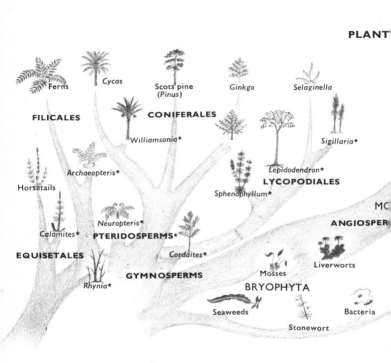

PLANT

FILICALES

CONIFERALES

Ferns

Cycas

Scots pine
(Pinus)

Ginkgo

Selaginella

Williamsonia*

Sigillaria*

Archaeopteris*

Lepidodendron*

LYCOPODIALES

Horsetails

Sphenophyllum*

Neuropteris*

MO

ANGIOSPER

Calamites*

PTERIDOSPERMS*

Cordaites*

EQUISETALES

Liverworts

GYMNOSPERMS

Mosses

Rhynia*

BRYOPHYTA

Seaweeds

Bacteria

Stonewort

PRIMITIVE ALGAE

THALLOPHYTA

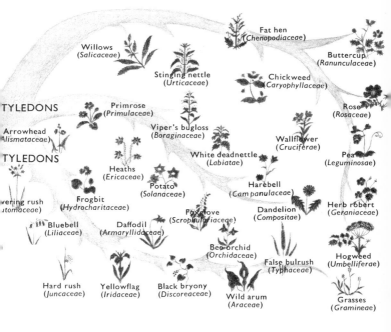

Fat hen
(*Chenopodiaceae*)

Willows
(*Salicaceae*)

Buttercup
(*Ranunculaceae*)

Stinging nettle
(*Urticaceae*)

Chickweed
(*Caryophyllaceae*)

TYLEDONS

Primrose
(*Primulaceae*)

Rose
(*Rosaceae*)

Arrowhead
(*Alismataceae*)

Viper's bugloss
(*Boraginaceae*)

Wallflower
(*Cruciferae*)

TYLEDONS

White deadnettle
(*Labiatae*)

Pea
(*Leguminosae*)

Heaths
(*Ericaceae*)

Harebell
(*Campanulaceae*)

Potato
(*Solanaceae*)

vering rush
utomaceae)

Frogbit
(*Hydrocharitaceae*)

Dandelion
(*Compositae*)

Herb robert
(*Geraniaceae*)

Foxglove
(*Scrophulariaceae*)

Bluebell
(*Liliaceae*)

Daffodil
(*Armaryllidaceae*)

Bee orchid
(*Orchidaceae*)

False bulrush
(*Typhaceae*)

Hogweed
(*Umbelliferae*)

Hard rush
(*Juncaceae*)

Yellowflag
(*Iridaceae*)

Black bryony
(*Discoreaceae*)

Wild arum
(*Araceae*)

Grasses
(*Gramineae*)

49

Plate 21

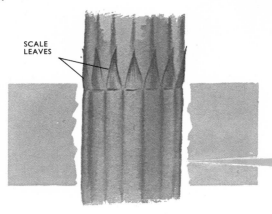

SCALE
LEAVES

EQUISETALES (Cont)

(Above) The ridges of the horsetail stem correspond with the scale leaves of each segment. Branches (if any) grow from the nodes. The section (right) shows the arrangement of the tissues. (Below) 'Cone' of the field horsetail with (right) an enlarged sporophyll scattering spores, and an enlarged spore.

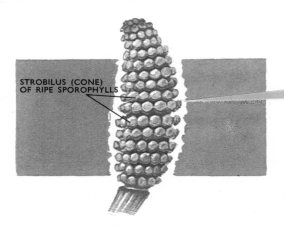

STROBILUS (CONE)
OF RIPE SPOROPHYLLS

Plate 22

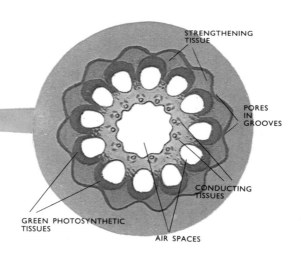

STRENGTHENING
TISSUE

PORES
IN
GROOVES

CONDUCTING
TISSUES

GREEN PHOTOSYNTHETIC
TISSUES

AIR SPACES

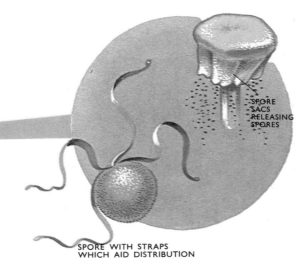

SPORE
SACS
RELEASING
SPORES

SPORE WITH STRAPS
WHICH AID DISTRIBUTION

for example, is a smaller community falling within the larger community of the deciduous forest plant formation. For such a community, dominated by a single species (i.e. the oak tree) the term *consociation* is used. If there are two or more species of equal importance, then the community is called an association (e.g. mixed oak-ash woods). Finally, very small but distinct communities may occur inside associations or consociations. Within an oakwood for instance, there may be a local predominance of ash trees. This lowest category is referred to as a plant society. Why are rain forests found only in tropical regions? What causes the beech wood consociation to dominate the chalk and limestone hills of Southern England while oak woods cover the low-lying valleys? The occurrence and distribution of any plant community rests with three sets of factors. There is the *climatic* factor – including the influence of sunlight, temperature, wind, rainfall and humidity; there is the soil or *edaphic* factor – the composition and properties of the soil supporting the plant community. And there is the *biotic* factor – primarily the influence of the animal population on the plant community.

The climatic factor is without any doubt the most important of the three. It is the world-wide variation in climate that produces the characteristic vegetation belts or plant formations. No matter what the soil is, a rain forest would never grow in Western Europe. Rain forests need moisture, warmth and strong sunlight throughout the year and only in the tropical regions are those needs satisfied. Western Europe, however, with its warm, moist summers and coldish winters, is ideal for deciduous forest. The soil or edaphic factor has a strong secondary influence on plant communities. The types of associations and consociations within a plant formation are largely determined by soils. Within the deciduous forest category for example, oakwoods usually monopolise the low-lying regions. The reason is that oaks are suited to the moist, heavy

clays generally forming low areas. Beech woods favour light, shallow, calcareous soils and hence grow scattered over chalk downs and limestone hills. Shallow, sandy, well-drained soils favour the growth of birch trees and pines. Oakwoods may be found here as well, but this oak tree – the durmast oak or *Quercus petraea* – is a different species from the pedunculate oak (*Quercus robur*) of the low-lying clay soils. The biotic factor theoretically means the action of all organisms on the plant community, including the influence of the plants upon one another. But usually the phrase is taken to mean the effect of the animal population alone. It includes soil-dwellers such as earthworms, bacteria and viruses, the pollinating insects, destructive grubs, the browsing and grazing animals such as deer and rabbits, the seed-dispersing birds and of greatest importance of all – Man himself. Man's impact on plant communities with his axe, plough, and herds of grazing animals is immense. For instance, three thousand years ago lowland Britain was completely wooded – that is all but the bogs and swamps. Centuries of agriculture have pushed the forests back to today's scanty woodlands. In their place are highly artificial plant communities – fields of crops and pastures carefully tended by Man to prevent unwanted, useless plants (weeds) from encroaching. For sheer size, the tree dominates the plant kingdom. Its tough, woody stem enables leaves and flowers to open scores of feet above the ground. But trees dominate in one other way. Their leaves, supported high in the air, receive the maximum amount of sunlight available. Considerably less light penetrates the trees' foliage to reach the smaller shrubs, and less still reaches the herbaceous plants growing near to the ground and the mosses actually in contact with the earth. This layering effect or stratification is a characteristic of all plant communities. In woodlands it reaches its greatest development with four 'stories' – trees, shrubs, herbs, and mosses. Out-

COMPOSITAE

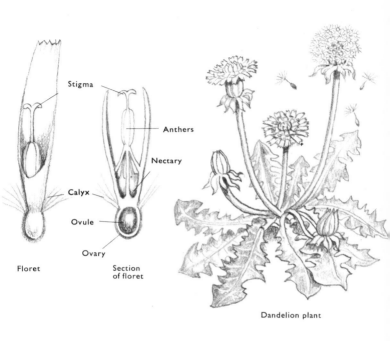

Stigma

Anthers

Nectary

Calyx

Ovule

Ovary

Floret

Section
of floret

Dandelion plant

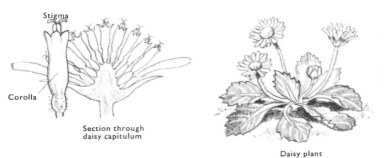

Stigma

Corolla

Section through
daisy capitulum

Daisy plant

Some features of composite flowers.

Plate 23
EQUISETALES (Cont)

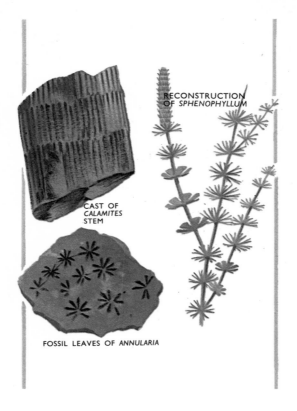

RECONSTRUCTION
OF *SPHENOPHYLLUM*

CAST OF
CALAMITES
STEM

FOSSIL LEAVES OF *ANNULARIA*

Some extinct horsetails and the related *Sphenophyllum.*

Plate 24

EQUISETALES (Cont)

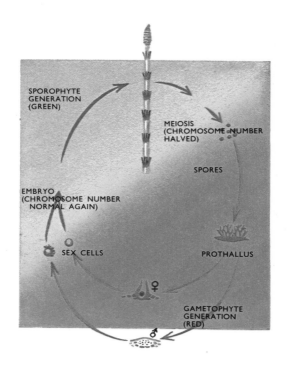

Diagrammatic life cycle of a horsetail.

side the woods, the layering may not be so complete yet nevertheless is still present. Grasslands, for instance, consist of an upper layer of tall grasses and herbs while beneath are rosette plants and short grasses. The tree as a dominant plant in a woodland community strongly influences the lower levels of growth. Beech trees cast a very deep shade. Consequently, in such a wood, the vegetation nearer the ground is scanty or absent altogether. Oaks and ashes, casting less shade, enable far more abundant and varied undergrowths and ground floras to flourish. Apart from the differences in light intensity, slight variations can also be detected in the air's carbon dioxide, oxygen and water content at each level of a plant community. Thus, superimposed on the broad climate of the community as a whole, each plant layer has its own peculiar micro-climate. (See Plates 11 and 45).

Companion Cell. (See *Phloem*).

Compositae. Family of flowering plants including the dandelion, daisy, thistle, and many others. It is the largest of all families of flowering plants with members in all sorts of habitats. What is normally called the flower is actually an inflorescence (capitulum) composed of large numbers of tiny flowers called florets. These florets may or may not have strap-shaped ligules developed from an irregularly-shaped corolla. Some composite flowers have ligulate florets only round the outside (e.g. daisy). Each floret has a calyx which frequently develops into the pappus of hairs which carries the fruit away. Florets may be of one sex or the other, or hermaphrodite. (See *Flower; Inflorescence*, Page 53 and Plates 13, 34, and 128).

Composite. Member of the family Compositae.

Compound Leaf. One that is divided into separate leaflets.

Conceptacle. A small chamber con-

taining the sex organs, on the swollen tips of certain branches of the thallus of some brown algae. They occur in groups. Both sex organs may be carried in the same chamber or there may be separate chambers for male and female. (See Plate 92).

Cone. A spore- or seed-bearing structure made up of tightly packed special leaves (*sporophylls*). (See *Coniferales*) and (Plates 21 and 77).

Conidiophore. Specialised hypha bearing asexual spores (*conidia*) as in *Phytophthora*, the fungus causing potato blight. (See Plate 15).

Conidium. An asexual spore carried on the conidiophores of some fungi. (See *Conidiophore*) and (Plate 15).

Coniferales. The conifers – a group of gymnosperms containing the typical cone-bearing trees such as pine, spruce, larch, and juniper. True conifers are all trees and they make up an important part of the vegetation of the cooler parts of the world. There is some variation in structure and habits but the main features of the group can be illustrated by studying the pine (*Pinus*).

The young pines, and many other conifers, are somewhat conical in shape but the lower branches are lost as the trees age and the shape is destroyed. There are two types of leaf: small brown scale leaves, and the green 'needles'. The latter are formed only on dwarf sideshoots (spurs), never on the main shoots or branches. The dwarf shoots arise in the axils of scale-leaves on the main shoots. The needles contain a great deal of strengthening tissue and are able to withstand very cold and dry conditions. The spurs and their needles last only a few years but in most conifers they are not shed all at once as are the leaves of deciduous trees. The larch does drop all of its leaves in autumn.

The root system is normally a tap-root with branches. Root hairs are not

CONIFERALES

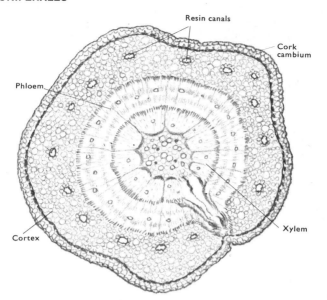

Transverse section of a young pine stem and (below) transverse seotion of a pine leaf or needle.

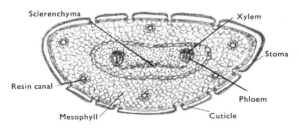

well developed but there is a close relationship with a fungus which helps in the absorption of water.

Male and female cones are formed on one tree. Clusters of male cones develop in spring at the base of young shoots. Above the cones, the shoots bear spurs. Each male cone consists of a central stem and numerous spirally arranged scales. Each scale carries two pollen sacs on its lower surface. Attached to the pollen grains are tiny airsacs which aid in wind dispersal. The female cones first appear at the ends of some of the young shoots, as small, red, erect structures. A number of tiny bract

57

Plate 25

EVOLUTION

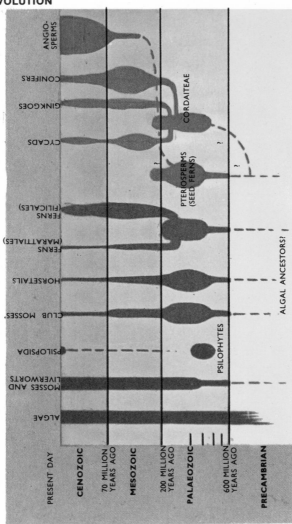

A chart showing the sequence of the main plant groups in geologic time. Because of an incomplete fossil record the evolution from one group to another is uncertain. The origin of the angiosperms is particularly

58

Plate 26

A Carboniferous swamp forest: flowering plants did not exist but the other main lines of plants had appeared. The counterparts of modern horsetails were woody trees (eg *Calamites*) up to 100 feet high. *Cordaites* was probably related to the monkey puzzle tree. Ferns and tree-ferns were common although structurally different from modern ones. Seed-ferns—possible ancestors of flowering plants—were very numerous.

scales are arranged spirally round the axis, and on each bract scale there is a large ovuliferous scale which carries two ovules. Each ovule consists of a mass of tissue (the nucellus) surrounded by an integument. One of the cells of the nucellus divides a number of times and then, by a reduction division (meiosis), forms four haploid spores. Only one survives and is called the embryo-sac. At about this stage (May or June in the Northern Hemisphere) the female cones are pollinated. The scales separate and pollen from the male cones can enter and reach the ovule. After pollination the scales close up and the cone stalk bends over so that the cone hangs among the needles. The pollen grain reaches the nucellus via the micropyle and a pollen tube grows into the nucellus. Development of the pollen grain then stops for about

a year in the pine, although this is not so in most conifers. During this interval many changes occur in the female cone and ovule. The cone as a whole enlarges and turns green. The embryo-sac grows and forms inside it a mass of tissue that corresponds to the pro-thallus of the fern. Female cells develop in this prothallus. In the spring of the second year (i.e. nearly a year after pollination) the pollen-tube again begins to grow and reaches the female cells. Within the pollen tube the pollen cells have been dividing and eventually produce a male cell that joins with one of the female cells to produce an embryo. This is the act of fertilisation. Repeated division of the embryo cells produces a tiny pine plant consisting of root, stem and some seed-leaves (cotyledons). The prothallus becomes swollen with food tissues and

CONIFERALES (Cont)

The life cycle of the pine *(Pinus)* (See also Plate 77).

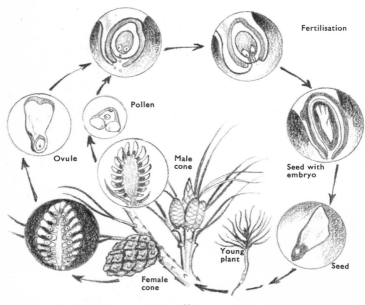

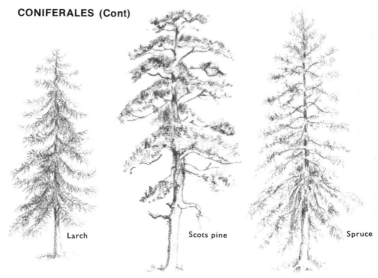

Larch   Scots pine   Spruce

Various conifers.

the nucellus almost completely disappears. The covering of the ovule hardens and becomes the seed coat. The changes associated with fertilisation and seed development take about a year. The female cones, when ripe, are brown and woody. The scales open in dry weather and release the seeds which are provided with a thin membrane from the upper surface of the scale. Thus, in the pine, the seeds are shed in the third year of the life of the cones, a little over two years after their first appearance. The majority of the conifers, however, require only one year for the process. (See *Gymnospermae; Ovule; Seed*) and (Plates 77 and 125).

Conjugation. The process in which the contents of two structurally similar cells behave like gametes, as in *Spirogyra* (q.v.) (See Plate 98).

Connate Leaves. Opposite leaves which grow together around the stem. (See Page 136).

Consociation. A plant community (q.v.) dominated by a single species.

Convergent Evolution. The phenomenon whereby organisms living under similar conditions tend to show similar characteristics. The phenomenon is powerful support for the theory of Natural Selection (q.v.). Similar features that have arisen *independently* in two or more groups will all be selected if they are of value in that particular habitat. Thus several different groups of swamp-living plants possess aeration tissue in their roots and stems. This feature has evolved independently in each group because it is of use under the conditions in which the plants live. Care must be taken in classifying organisms to see that similar features are really the result of a common ancestry and not the result of convergent evolution.

Convolvulaceae. (See *Tubiflorae*).

Cordaitales. An order of extinct gym-

Plate 27

EVOLUTION (Cont)

The first plants probably resembled our present-day algae. They lived in the sea and had no vascular tissue or cuticle. Perhaps most of today's group of land plants descended independently from algae. They would have passed through a simple stage resembling the primitive fossilized *Psilophytes*.

SPORANGIA

VASCULAR TISSUE

PSILOPHYTES FROM DEVONIAN ROCKS

SOME PRESENT-DAY ALGAE

Seed ferns looked like ferns but bore true seeds like gymnosperms and angiosperms. They were abundant in Carboniferous times but died out in the Cretaceous period. Their seeds were enclosed like the angiosperms – not borne naked on cones like the gymnosperms. Perhaps they were the ancestors of the angiosperms.

FLOWERING PLANTS ALSO HAVE ENCLOSED SEEDS

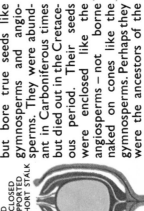

THE SEED WAS ENCLOSED AND SUPPORTED ON A SHORT STALK

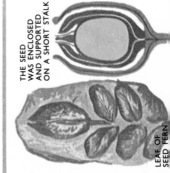

LEAF OF SEED FERN

62

Plate 28

PRESENT-DAY MOSS

Mosses and liverworts have very delicate tissues which are rarely preserved in the fossil record. They are however very ancient groups, and probably date from Cambrian times.

DELICATE TISSUES OF PAST MOSS PRESERVED IN CARBONIFEROUS ROCK

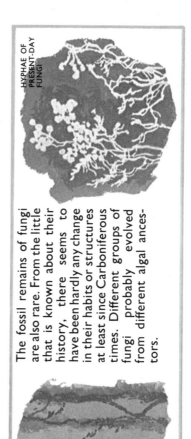

HYPHAE OF PRESENT-DAY FUNGI

The fossil remains of fungi are also rare. From the little that is known about their history, there seems to have been hardly any change in their habits or structures at least since Carboniferous times. Different groups of fungi probably evolved from different algal ancestors.

FUNGI PRESERVED IN THE WOOD OF A CARBONIFEROUS TREE

63

CRUCIFERAE

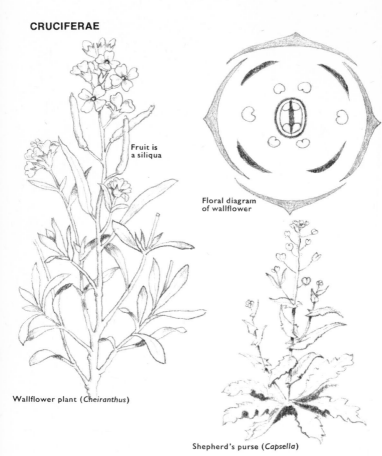

Fruit is
a siliqua

Floral diagram
of wallflower

Wallflower plant (*Cheiranthus*)

Shepherd's purse (*Capsella*)

nosperms. They flourished especially in the great forests of Carboniferous times. Some were trees reaching a height of a hundred feet, with large simple leaves having parallel venation. (See Gymnospermae).

Cordate. A particular leaf shape. (See Page 136).

Cork. A protective tissue formed around the outside of woody plants,

and where the plant has been injured. It is also formed under leaf scars. The main source of commercial cork is the cork oak (*Quercus suber*). Its cork-producing tissues continue to grow year after year and can buid up a considerable thickness of cork. After the cells are formed, the corky substances are deposited in the walls and the cells then die. The cell liquids are withdrawn as the walls thicken. The cork cells then contain nothing but air. (See *Bark;*

Abcission Layer) and (Plate 12).

Corm. A short, swollen, underground stem that carries buds. It acts as a storage organ and also as an agent of vegetative reproduction (q.v.). The food is stored in the swollen stem and not in leaves as in the case of bulbs. (See Plate 100).

Corolla. The petals of a flower.

Cortex. The region of a stem or root between the epidermis and the vascular tissues. (See *Root; Stem*).

Corymb. A type of *inflorescence* (q.v.). (See Plate 48).

CYCADALES

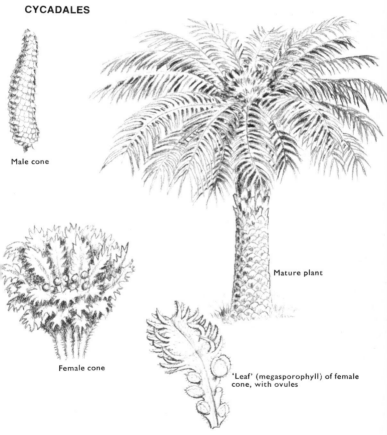

Male cone

Female cone

Mature plant

'Leaf' (megasporophyll) of female cone, with ovules

Some features of *Cycas*. The female cones of other cycads are compact and more typically cone-like.

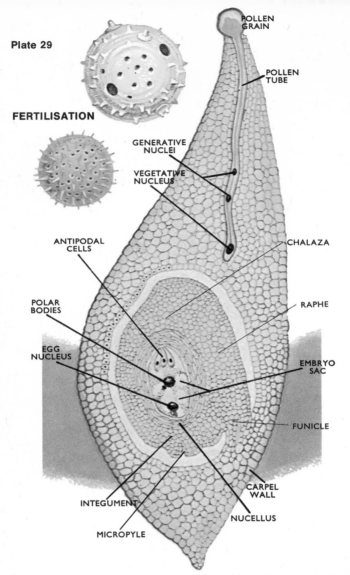

Plate 29

FERTILISATION

POLLEN GRAIN

POLLEN TUBE

GENERATIVE NUCLEI

VEGETATIVE NUCLEUS

ANTIPODAL CELLS

CHALAZA

POLAR BODIES

RAPHE

EGG NUCLEUS

EMBRYO SAC

FUNICLE

INTEGUMENT

CARPEL WALL

MICROPYLE

NUCELLUS

Greatly enlarged section of buttercup carpel showing ovule structure, germinating pollen grain, and two different types of pollen grain (top left).

Plate 30

FERTILISATION (Cont)

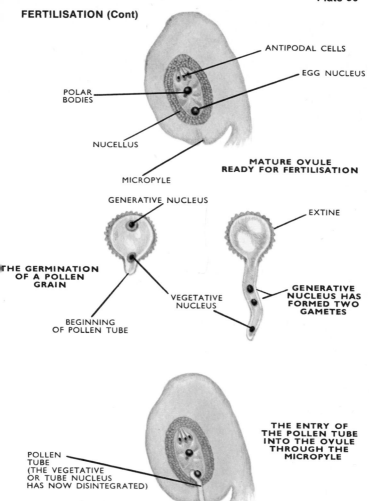

ANTIPODAL CELLS

EGG NUCLEUS

POLAR BODIES

NUCELLUS

MICROPYLE

MATURE OVULE READY FOR FERTILISATION

GENERATIVE NUCLEUS

EXTINE

THE GERMINATION OF A POLLEN GRAIN

VEGETATIVE NUCLEUS

GENERATIVE NUCLEUS HAS FORMED TWO GAMETES

BEGINNING OF POLLEN TUBE

THE ENTRY OF THE POLLEN TUBE INTO THE OVULE THROUGH THE MICROPYLE

POLLEN TUBE (THE VEGETATIVE OR TUBE NUCLEUS HAS NOW DISINTEGRATED)

The stages of fertilisation.

Cotyledon. A seed leaf. Cotyledons may or may not emerge from the seed as it germinates. (See *Seed; Germination*) and (Plates 41 and 47).

Crassulaceae. Family of herbaceous, usually succulent plants, including the stonecrops and the houseleeks. (See *Rosales*).

Cretaceous Period. Division of the *Geological Time Scale* (q.v.).

Cross-fertilisation. The joining of male and female gametes from different flowers of the same species. (See *Fertilisation*).

Cross-pollination. The transfer of pollen from the stamens of one flower to the stigma of another of the same species. (See *Pollination*).

Cruciferae. Large family of dicotyledons commonly called crucifers. There are always four petals and the fruit is a siliqua or silicula (See page 101). The family contains all the varieties of cabbage plant, wallflowers, shepherd's purse, and many other common plants. (See *Rhoedales*) and (Plate 127).

Cryophytes. Plants that live on ice and snow; mainly small plants such as algae, fungi, and mosses.

Cryptogam. (See *Phanerogam*).

Cucurbitaceae. Family of dicotyledons — frequently climbing plants — including the melon, marrow, cucumber, and the white bryony. The flowers are unisexual and the fruit is a berry or a pepo, which is a special kind of berry.

Cuticle. An outer layer of a plant (or animal) produced by the epidermis and not made up of cells. Aerial parts such as leaves have a cuticular covering which is broken only by the stomata. Its main role is that of restricting water loss.

Cyanophyceae. The blue-green algae. Their colour is due to the pigment phycocyanin which masks the colour of the chlorophyll with which it is distributed throughout the cytoplasm. Not common in the sea, they are common in freshwater as planktonic creatures that are either colonial, single-celled forms, or filamentous. Some species are also found on land in such situations as soil and moist stonework. Reproduction is entirely asexual. Examples include *Gloecopsa, Nostoc, Chroococcus*. (See *Algae*) and (Plate 120).

Cycadales. The most primitive living plants that reproduce by means of seeds. Mostly extinct, living forms are restricted to the tropics and subtropics. The unbranched stem may be short and partly underground or columnar, reaching a height of some sixty feet. The leaves borne at the top are large and fern-like. Male and female organs are borne on different plants, in cones, the male cone being terminal and the female ones on either side of the stem. The male pollen is wind-dispersed and the male cells are flagellated. Cycads exhibit secondary thickening as do woody dicotyledons. The pith is considerable. The sago palm, a typical cycad, has pith rich in starch and for this reason is commercially important. (See *Gymnospermae*) and (Plate 125).

Cycadofilicales. An order of extinct gymnosperms that flourished particularly in Carboniferous times. They reproduced by means of seeds, but showed many fern-like characters. The reproductive organs were not arranged in cones.

Cyme. A type of inflorescence (q.v.) in which each axis ends in a flower. (See Plate 48).

Cyperaceae. Family of monocotyledons sometimes included with the grasses in the order Glumiflorae. These plants are the sedges — rhizomatous herbs usually growing in damp places. The stem is often triangular in cross-section. As in the grasses, the flowers are arranged in spikelets surrounded by glumes. There may be one or more flowers in each spikelet and the spikelets are arranged in various types of inflorescence. The genus *Carex* is large and widespread. In this genus the male and female flowers are separate — usually on separate parts of the inflorescence. (See *Gramineae*) and (Plate 126).

Cystolith. A local deposit of calcium carbonate on an ingrowth of the wall of an epidermal cell, in plants such as the stinging nettle.

Cytogenetics. The science that brings together cytology and genetics (q.v.). (See *Cytology*).

Cytology. The study of cells.

Cytoplasm. The protoplasm of a cell other than the nucleus. (See *Cell*).

Deciduous. (Of plants) Shedding all their leaves at a certain season of the year and passing a period without leaves. Oak, elm, beech and most other British flowering trees are examples. (See *Abcission Layer*).

Decumbent. Stems that creep along the ground and turn up at the ends are said to be decumbent.

Decurrent. (Of a leaf). With the base extended and running down the petiole or stem as a 'wing'.

Decussate. Arrangement of leaves on a stem in which the leaves are in opposite pairs and in which each pair is at right angles to the pairs above and below. This arrangement is typical of the family Labiatae.

Dehiscent. Fruits that split open and release their seeds are said to be dehi-

scent. The mode of splitting varies. (See *Fruit*) and (Page 101).

Denitrifying Bacteria. Bacteria living in the soil which break down nitrates to nitrites in the absence of free oxygen, and yield nitrogen gas to the atmosphere. (See *Nitrifying Bacteria* and *Nitrogen Cycle*).

Dentate. (Of leaves). Having a toothed margin, the teeth being larger than in the serrate or saw-edged leaf, and pointing outwards rather than towards the tip.

Dermatogen. (See *Histogen*).

A leaf with a decurrent base and (bottom) part of a stem with opposite decussate leaves.

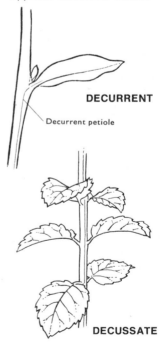

DECURRENT

Decurrent petiole

DECUSSATE

Plate 31

FILICALES

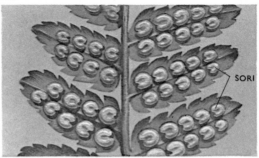

SORI

The male fern *(Dryopteris felix-mas)* carries numerous groups (sori) of sporangia on the underside of its fronds. The sporangia are protected by a flap called the indusium.

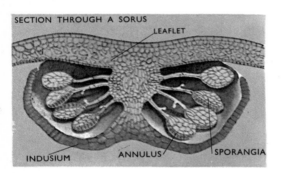

SECTION THROUGH A SORUS

LEAFLET

INDUSIUM   ANNULUS   SPORANGIA

(Below) The prothallus of the male fern, carrying the sexual structures.

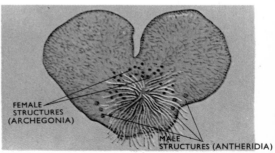

FEMALE STRUCTURES (ARCHEGONIA)

MALE STRUCTURES (ANTHERIDIA)

Plate 32

FILICALES (Cont)

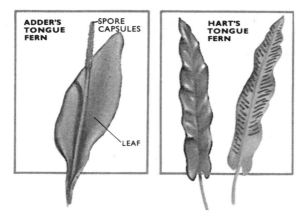

Four types of fern showing the different arrangements of the sporangia.

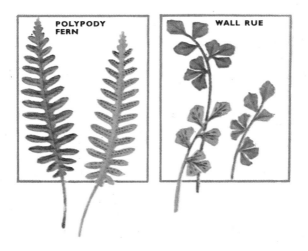

Desmids. Members of the algae group Conjugales that are unicellular and usually have elaborate chloroplasts. The cell is usually of two symmetrical halves, each half having one or two chloroplasts. The two halves may be separated by a median constriction where the nucleus is sited. The cellulose cell wall is either covered with spines or is elaborately sculptured. The desmids occur in fresh water. (See *Algae*) and (Plate 13).

Devonian Period. Division of the *Geological Time Scale* (q.v.).

Dextrose. An alternative name for glucose (q.v.).

Diadelphous. Referring to stamens united by their stalks to form two bundles or, as in many papilionaceous flowers, one united group and one free stamen.

Diageotropism. A growth response at right angles to gravity. It is exhibited by the rhizomes of many plants, which grow horizontally. (See *Tropism*).

Diatoms. A group of algae (q.v.) consisting of unicellular or colonial forms abundant in freshwater and in the sea. The chloroplasts contain a brown pigment in addition to chlorophyll. The cell wall consists of two halves, one of which fits inside the other much as the base and lid of a polish tin fit together. The cell wall is impregnated with silica and the vast deposits of these cell walls on the sea bed are known as siliceous or diatomaceous oozes. *Coscinodiscus* is a typical diatom. (See Plate 120).

Dichasium. A type of inflorescence (q.v.).

Dichlamydeous. (Of flowers). With the perianth arranged in two separate whorls.

Dichotomous. Dividing regularly into two equal branches.

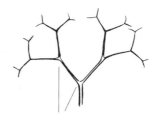

Regular division into two

Dicotyledon. Widely used term used to denote a member of the class Dicotyledoneae.

Various diatoms and desmids.

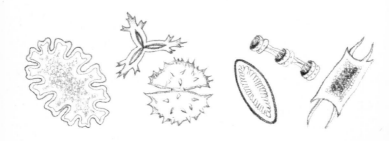

Dicotyledoneae. The class of flowering plants whose members have two seed leaves (cotyledons) in each seed. Their leaves are net-veined. (See Pages 261-264).

Didynamous. (Of a flower) With two pairs of stamens of unequal length.

Digitate. (= *Palmate*).

Dikaryon. A fungal hypha or mycelium made up of binucleate cells. The nuclei divide at the same time when new cells are formed.

Dimorphism. The occurrence of an organ or organism in two forms – e.g. the pin-eyed and thrum-eyed forms of the primrose (Plate 81), and the floating and submerged leaves of water crowfoot.

Dioecious. Having male and female flowers on separate plants – (e.g. willow).

Diploid. Having two sets of chromosomes per cell. (See *Chromosome*).

Diseases of Plants. The study of plant disease is called plant pathology and is an important branch of science because so much damage is caused by disease. Plant diseases are almost as old as plants themselves, for clear signs of disease are shown in many ancient fossils. Cultivated plants, however, suffer far more than wild ones – largely because many plants of the same kind are grown closely together. In the wild, a plant is not always surrounded by others of the same kind and germs have less chance of spreading. In the 17th century it was noticed that the weather seemed to affect the health of the crops. Mildews and other fungi were known to be associated with many diseased plants but it was believed that the fungi sprang up in the dying tissues. Not until the 19th century, when Pasteur showed that living things could not arise from nothing, was it realised that the fungi actually caused the disease in many cases.

Fungi of one sort or another are the causes of the majority of plant diseases. Some diseases, such as the black-spotting of sycamore leaves, do not appear to do much harm although every leaf may be affected. Others are more serious. *Potato blight* – the disease that caused widespread famine in Europe (especially Ireland) in the 1840's – is a very serious disease and can rapidly destroy the whole plant. *Rusts* and *smuts* are important fungal diseases of cereals. 'Damping off' of seedlings is also caused by fungi, and results in collapse of the seedlings just above ground level. The fungus body consists of a mass of fine hyphae which get into the plant through injuries, through the leaf pores or even through undamaged cuticles. The threads then divide and branch through the tissues of the host, absorbing food materials. Blemishes and discolourations appear on the plant and these are often the sites of spore production. Many fungus diseases, notably potato blight, thrive best in damp conditions.

A large number of rots of fruit and vegetables are caused by bacteria (q.v.). The organisms invade the tissues and break them down by enzyme action into a watery, smelly mess.

Viruses (q.v.) also cause many plant diseases. They frequently produce a mottling (mosaic) of the leaves or flowers. The food-making ability of the leaves is reduced and the plant often becomes spindly. There is a serious loss of yield. Potatoes suffer from a number of serious virus diseases such as leaf-mosaic and leaf-roll. A few diseases are caused by protozoans and by nematode worms that get into the tissues. Symptoms include galls and stunted growth. Some insects cause disease-like symptoms by injecting poisonous substances into the plant. The symptoms often resemble those of virus diseases but are not so persistent, and recovery is common.

Physiological diseases are serious but easily remedied. They result from the lack of some food material – it may be a trace-element such as boron that is required in minute quantities, or it

Plate 33

FILICALES (Cont)

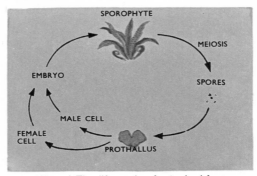

(Above) The life cycle of a typical fern.

Female archegonia (A) develop on the prothallus together with the male antheridia (C) which release flagellated male cells (antherozoids) (B). These are attracted to the female cells by the mucus exuding from the necks of the archegonia.

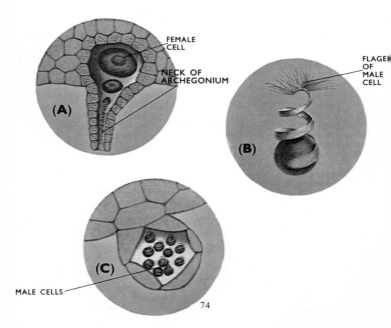

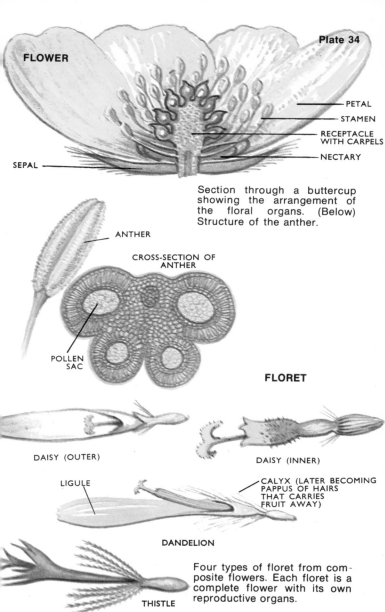

FLOWER

Plate 34

PETAL

STAMEN

RECEPTACLE WITH CARPELS

NECTARY

SEPAL

Section through a buttercup showing the arrangement of the floral organs. (Below) Structure of the anther.

ANTHER

CROSS-SECTION OF ANTHER

POLLEN SAC

FLORET

DAISY (OUTER)

DAISY (INNER)

LIGULE

CALYX (LATER BECOMING PAPPUS OF HAIRS THAT CARRIES FRUIT AWAY)

DANDELION

Four types of floret from composite flowers. Each floret is a complete flower with its own reproductive organs.

THISTLE

75

may be something like phosphate that is needed in larger amounts. Soil analysis soon gives the answer and addition of the missing element or elements cures the trouble.

It is rarely practical (or even possible) to cure a diseased plant. Control is based on *prevention*. The golden rule for gardeners dealing with a diseased plant is 'dig it up and burn it'. Only in this way can the germs be completely destroyed. However, before the diseases can be controlled, it is necessary to know how they are transmitted from plant to plant. It is useless to treat the seed if infection is transmitted by insects. Nor is there any use in controlling insects if the disease germs lurk in the soil from year to year. Many diseases, however, pass to other plants in more than one way. Soil-borne diseases — such as *club-root* of cabbages and *wart disease* of potatoes — pass from plant to plant by means of spores resting in the soil. The spores are released into the soil and remain there, waiting for another crop to attack. Many of the soil-borne diseases — mainly caused by nematodes, fungi and bacteria — can be avoided by rotating crops. The spores perish before a susceptible crop is returned to the land. Some fungi, however, including those causing club-root and wart disease, have very long-lived spores and crop-rotation will not necessarily avoid these diseases. A number of diseases are transmitted from one crop to the next by means of seed or other reproductive bodies (e.g. tubers). Fungus diseases are commonly transmitted in and on seeds. They can be avoided to some extent by treating the seed with fungicide. Virus diseases rarely pass on in the seed but commonly do so in tubers and other vegetative organs.

Even when clean, disease-free seed is planted in clean land, diseases can still be contracted. Airborne spores from neighbouring crops can cause heavy infection. Potato blight and wheat rust are two major air-borne diseases, caused by fungi. The growing of resistant vegetables helps to overcome disease. Keeping down weeds that might harbour the germs is important and the use of 'clean' seed is essential. If only a few seeds are infected, a disease can later spread from these plants to the whole field. When effective fungus-killing compounds are known, they should be sprayed or dusted onto the plants to kill fungus spores *before they are able to get into the plant*. Of the insect-borne diseases, viruses are the most important. They are frequently carried by aphids that suck up sap. The viruses get into the saliva and are then injected into the next plant at the next meal. Usually only one or a few species of insect can transmit a particular virus and if the insect can be controlled, the virus disease will also be controlled. (See Plates 14, 15, 16 and 17).

D.N.A. Desoxyribose nucleic acid. (See *Nucleic Acid*).

Dominant. (1) The major plant in a community. (2) A gene that over-rules the action of another affecting the same feature(s). (See *Gene*).

Dormancy. A state of very low metabolic activity — almost inactivity — found in seeds and spores when the conditions are not suitable for their development. Deciduous trees that drop their leaves in autumn pass the winter in a state of dormancy. (See *After-ripening*).

Dorsiventral. Referring to leaves which grow more or less horizontally and whose upper and lower surfaces are very different in structure. The leaves of most dicotyledons are of this type, in contrast with the leaves of monocotyledons which are frequently upright and whose two surfaces are more of less similar. (See *Leaf*).

Double fertilisation. The process of fertilisation in angiosperms is a double one involving fusion of one male nucleus with that of the egg and the other with the primary endosperm nucleus to produce the zygote and endosperm respectively. (See *Fertilisation*).

Drupe. A fleshy fruit (q.v.), the inner layer of which is hard and normally encloses a single seed (e.g. plum).

Ecad. A plant the form of which is a result of environmental conditions rather than inherited ones.

Ecology. The study of living things in relation to their environment.

Ecotype. Plants of a species which, though genetically adapted to a certain habitat, are still able to cross naturally with other members of that species.

Ectoplasm. The thin membrane covering the protoplast or living matter of a plant cell.

Ectotrophic. Referring to a mycorrhiza forming an external cover to a root. (See *Mycorrhiza*).

Edaphic factors. Influences of the soil and its contents, living and non-living.

Elaters. Long cells found in the spore capsules of liverworts. They twist in response to humidity changes and help to scatter the spores. (See *Hepaticae*).

Embryo. The young plant that develops from an egg usually as a result of sexual reproduction, but sometimes through parthenogenesis. An embryo is entirely dependent upon food reserves provided by the parent.

Embryology. The study of embryos and their development.

Embryo Sac. A large, oval cell occupying most of the nucellus of an ovule in flowering plants and otherwise known as the megaspore for it corresponds to the female spore of ferns. (See *Spore*). Initially the embryo sac contains a single nucleus but through divisions eight are formed. Three are sited at the end away from the micropyle, two

central polar bodies fuse to form the primary endosperm nucleus and at the micropylar end are the egg nucleus and two synergidae. This is the position prior to fertilisation (q.v.). (See *Ovule*) and (Plate 29).

Emergences. The prickles of such plants as the bramble and rose which aid climbing. They are stem outgrowths including epidermis and cortex but not normally vascular tissues. (See Plate 18).

Endemic. Native to a given area. Especially used of pests and disease-causing parasites which consistently occur in a given area. Isolated islands, such as New Zealand, are characterised by the large number of endemic species.

Endodermis. The innermost layer of the cortex surrounding the cylinder of vascular tissue in all roots and the stems of fern-like plants and some dicotyledons. (See *Root; Stem*) and (Plate 88).

Endoplasm. The cytoplasm within the ectoplasm or plasma membrane.

Endosperm. In seed-bearing plants a special food-tissue outside the embryo. It is formed from the endosperm nucleus by its division after fertilisation. (See *Seed; Fertilisation*) and (Page 204).

Endotrophic. Referring to a mycorrhiza (q.v.) within the root cortex cells, as in bird's nest orchid.

Entire. (Of a leaf). Having a margin quite smooth and not toothed in any way — e.g. privet. (See Plate 53).

Entomogenous. Referring to a fungus that is parasitic on an insect.

Entomophily. Pollination (q.v.) by insects.

Environment. All the factors in an organism's surroundings, including

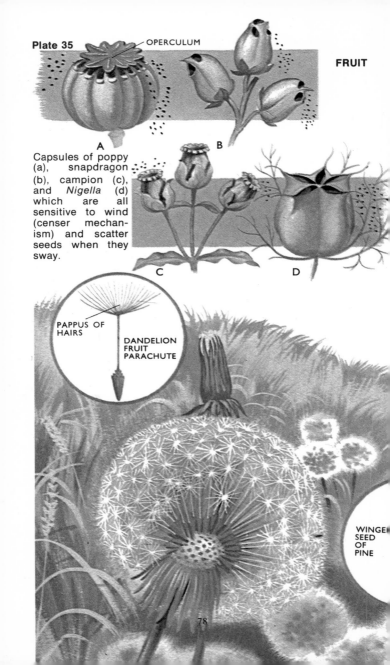

Plate 35

OPERCULUM

FRUIT

A

B

Capsules of poppy (a), snapdragon (b), campion (c), and *Nigella* (d) which are all sensitive to wind (censer mechanism) and scatter seeds when they sway.

C

D

PAPPUS OF HAIRS

DANDELION FRUIT PARACHUTE

WINGED SEED OF PINE

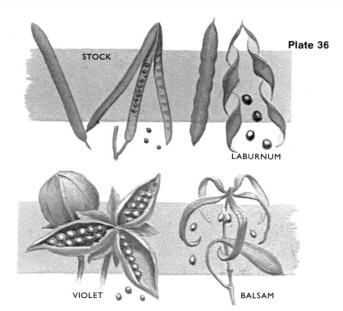

STOCK

Plate 36

LABURNUM

VIOLET

BALSAM

(Above) Examples of mechanical dispersal of seeds by explosive or twisting movements of fruits.

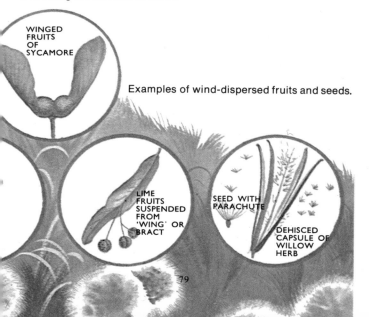

WINGED FRUITS OF SYCAMORE

Examples of wind-dispersed fruits and seeds.

LIME FRUITS SUSPENDED FROM 'WING' OR BRACT

SEED WITH PARACHUTE

DEHISCED CAPSULE OF WILLOW HERB

other living things, climate, temperature, wind, etc.

Enzyme. An organic catalyst produced by living things. Enzymes promote chemical reactions in living things. Their action is usually specific, i.e. an enzyme controls only one reaction or one kind of reaction. All enzymes isolated and investigated so far are proteins. The activity of an enzyme is very sensitive to changes in such conditions as pH, temperature etc.

Eocene Period. A geological period of the earth's history which lasted for 15 million years from around 60 million years ago. (See *Geological Time Scale*).

Epicalyx. A whorl of bracts (leafy processes) adjacent to and outside the true sepals, as in strawberry.

Epicotyl. The part of a young stem above the cotyledons.

Epidermis. The outermost layer of cells in a plant (or animal).

Epigeal. Referring to germination in which the seed leaves come above ground (e.g. cabbage).

Epigynous. Condition in which the petals etc. arise from above the enclosed carpels: the carpels are inferior (e.g. apple). (See *Flower*) and (Plate 18).

Epinasty. The much faster growth of the upper side of an organ such as a leaf resulting, in this instance, in a downward curving.

Epipetalous. Referring to stamens which are attached to the petals, and which come away with them.

Epiphyte. A plant growing on another but using it only for support and not drawing food from it. Examples are mosses and orchids that grow on trees. (See Plate 19).

Equisetales. Horsetails. These are non-flowering plants related to the ferns. Only about 25 living species are known in the world today and most of them are small plants about 2 or 3 feet high. Horsetails were very common in Carboniferous times and the remains of many large, woody forms are often found in coal. Living horsetails — all belonging to the genus *Equisetum* — are but relics of this once large group.

The horsetail plant consists of a branching, underground rhizome and a number of upright aerial shoots. The rhizome lasts from year to year but

EPIGEAL

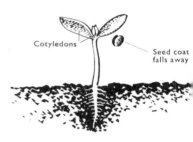

Cotyledons

Seed coat falls away

Epigeal germination (above) and hypogeal germination.

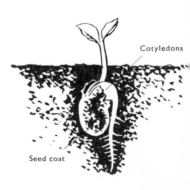

Cotyledons

Seed coat

its roots and the aerial stems are usually renewed each year. The branching underground rhizomes, and the ability of some species to form reproductive tubers, make horsetails very difficult plants to get rid of when once they are established. In some species, the stems are branched while in others there are no branches at all. The stems are all ridged to some extent and the outer cells contain a lot of silica crystals. This makes them rough to the touch and led to the old name of 'scouring rushes'. Leaves are present only as tiny scales at each node. The stem itself is green and photosynthetic. In this connection the stem is provided with stomata just as the leaves of other plants are. Branches — if any — arise in whorls at the nodes and break through the sheath of scale leaves. The stems are hollow except at the nodes but the branches are solid. Horsetail stems readily snap at the joints because there is a layer of tender growing cells (meristems) at each joint. The new cells produced by the meristems increase the length of the stem between each joint and so the plant grows in height. Internally, there is a small amount of conducting tissue and a number of large air-filled spaces. This is to be expected in plants that are essentially marsh-living. When water is abundant, there is no need for elaborate conducting tissue but air spaces are necessary to prevent waterlogging of the tissues. The majority of strengthening tissue is concentrated in the ridges round the outside of the stem. Horsetails, in common with other fern-like plants, show a well marked alternation of generations.

The plant so far described is the sporophyte generation. The spores are formed on special leaves called sporophylls that are grouped into 'cones'. In most species the 'cones' develop at the tips of ordinary shoots but, in the field horsetail and some others, special reproductive shoots develop. These shoots contain little or no chlorophyll and do not branch. At first the 'cones' are tightly closed

but, as they mature, the 'leaves' open to expose the spore sacs. These then split and release the spores. Strap-like projections from the spores are sensitive to humidity and their twisting movement helps to scatter the spores. The spores contain chlorophyll and germinate fairly rapidly to form a flat plate of green cells — the prothallus. This is the other stage of the life cycle — the gametophyte — whose cells are haploid.

The prothallus itself grows into a tiny green cushion with a number of upright leaf-like lobes. It grows at the edge and may reach one centimetre across. Flask-like female archegonia arise at the base of the upright lobes. Each contains a female cell. Male antheridia develop a little later, around the edge of the prothallus. When the prothalli are crowded together or poorly nourished, they are small, and they often produce only antheridia. The antheridia liberate tiny male cells. These are ciliated and, in damp conditions, they can swim around and reach a female cell. The two cells fuse together and form an embryo — the beginning of a new sporophyte generation. The embryo is at first nourished by the prothallus but soon puts out its own roots and stems and the prothallus dies. Horsetails and related plants first appeared in the Lower Devonian times, about 325 million years ago. They were very common in Carboniferous times but only one family survived until the Jurassic. This family flourished with the dinosaurs but only very few species remain alive today. *Sphenophyllum* was not a true horsetail but resembled them and flourished with them in coal-forming times. It was a woody plant known mainly from its leaves. *Calamites* was a true horsetail of huge size — reaching perhaps to 100 feet. It had a rhizome and small, green leaves. The conducting tissue was elaborate and there was a lot of woody tissue. The branches themselves branched and when lower branches fell, the plant looked very tree-like. In spite of its size the stem was

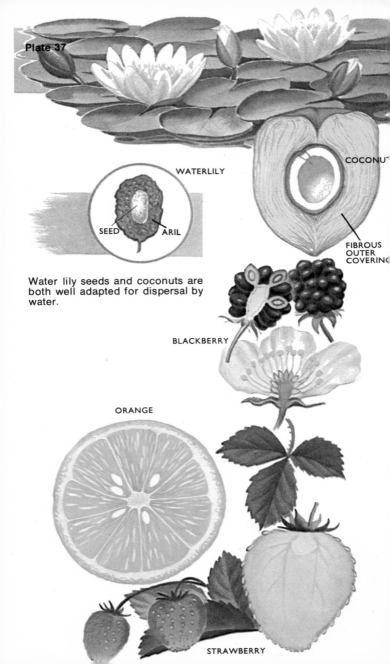

Plate 37

WATERLILY

SEED   ARIL

COCONUT

FIBROUS OUTER COVERING

Water lily seeds and coconuts are both well adapted for dispersal by water.

BLACKBERRY

ORANGE

STRAWBERRY

Plate 38

FRUIT (Cont)

The pineapple is a composite fruit formed by the fusion of many flowers. Blackberries (opposite) are compound fruits made up of several small drupes—each derived from a single carpel. The orange is a berry derived from several carpels whose outer walls form the peel. The carpels are fleshy and each may contain one or more seeds. Strawberries are false fruits formed from the swollen receptacles. The true strawberry fruits are the tiny pips on the surface.

83

hollow and fossil casts of the inside are common in the rocks. (See *Filicales; Alternation of Generations*) and (Plates 19–26).

Ergot. Common name for the ascomycete fungus *Claviceps* which infests the ovaries of rye, oats, and many other grasses. The fungus overwinters as hard black, banana-shaped bodies called *sclerotia,* each about half an inch long, which lie dormant in the soil. In spring stalked swellings grow out and produce spores. The thread-like spores are carried in the wind and may infect a grass-flower if they land on the stigma. The spores germinate, eventually infecting the whole of the ovary. Tiny spores called *conidia* are budded off from the ends of some of the hyphae and insects, attracted by a sugary secretion, carry them from one flower to another so causing a rapid spread of the fungus. Towards the end of the summer the production of conidia stops and the hard, dark sclerotia are produced, giving the grass plants their characteristic diseased appearance.

Ericales. An order of flowering plants including the family Ericaceae containing the lings and heathers. All are small shrubs or trees. Members of the Ericaceae are characterised by having pollen tetrads, the pollen grains failing to separate. The fruit is usually capsule or a berry. Besides the lings and heathers the family includes *Rhododendron* and *Azalea* and cranberry, bilberry, and whortleberry.

Escape. A cultivated plant that is found growing in the wild.

Etiolation. The pale and spindly growth of plants kept in the dark.

Euphotic zone. The upper sunlit zone of the sea where the light intensity is great enough to permit photosynthesis. Usually regarded as being to a depth of a hundred metres though there are obvious differences between different parts of the sea depending on such factors as the amount of solid carried in suspension. Water in a river estuary is obviously less transparent than that in mid-ocean.

ERGOT

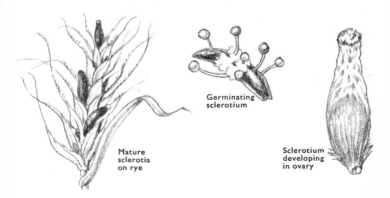

Mature
sclerotia
on rye

Germinating
sclerotium

Sclerotium
developing
in ovary

ERICALES

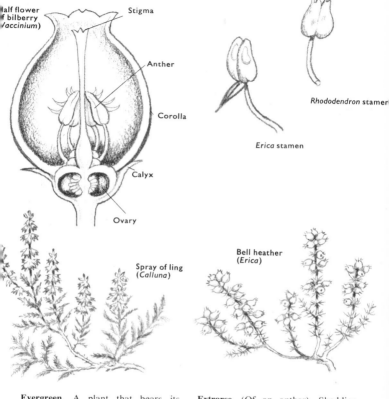

Half flower of bilberry (Vaccinium)

Stigma

Anther

Corolla

Calyx

Ovary

Rhododendron stamen

Erica stamen

Spray of ling (Calluna)

Bell heather (Erica)

Evergreen. A plant that bears its leaves all the year round e.g. holly. Leaf fall is not a seasonal process but a continuous one.

Evolution. The theory that complex organisms have originated from simpler ones by a process of gradual cumulative change. (See *Natural Selection*) and (Plate 25).

Exodermis. Outer layer of mature root, consisting of corky cells. (See Plate 88).

Extrorse. (Of an anther). Shedding pollen away from the centre of the flower.

F₁. The first filial generation (the first generation of offspring of a certain pair) is referred to as the F_1 generation. (See Plate 61).

F₂. The second generation offspring of a particular pair of individuals – the second filial generation. (See Plate 61).

Fagales. Order containing woody

Plate 39

FUNGI

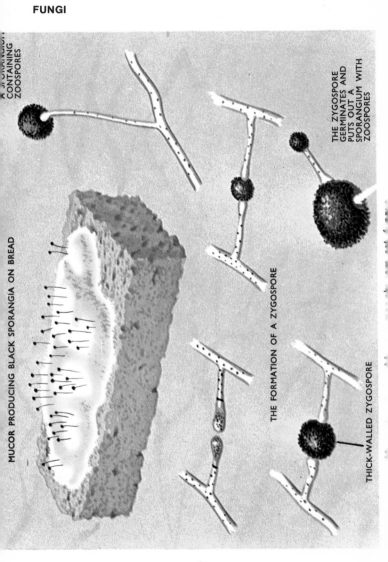

A SPORANGIUM CONTAINING ZOOSPORES

MUCOR PRODUCING BLACK SPORANGIA ON BREAD

THE FORMATION OF A ZYGOSPORE

THICK-WALLED ZYGOSPORE

THE ZYGOSPORE GERMINATES AND PUTS OUT A SPORANGIUM WITH ZOOSPORES

86

Plate 40

FUNGI (Cont)

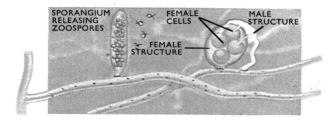

Saprolegnia, a water-living saprophyte which reproduces by motile zoospores (left) and by sexual fusion of male and female cells (right).

GALL

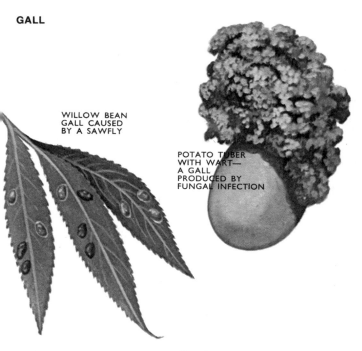

WILLOW BEAN GALL CAUSED BY A SAWFLY

POTATO TUBER WITH WART— A GALL PRODUCED BY FUNGAL INFECTION

trees or shrubs of the familes Betulaceae (birch), Corylaceae (hazel), and Fagaceae (beech, oak and the Spanish or sweet chestnut). The male flowers are usually in catkins and the female flowers are often surrounded by bracts which persist and protect the fruit which is a nut. (See Plate 127).

False Fruit. Fruit (q.v.) not developed entirely from a carpel or carpels but including other organs.

Family. A group of related genera. An important classificatory grouping. The family names of plant normally end in -aceae. (See *Classification*).

Fasciation. The coalescence of organs or their expansion to form abnormally wide or thick structures.

Fascicular. Cambium (q.v.) that occurs within the vascular bundles is called fascicular or intrafascicular cambium.

FAGALES

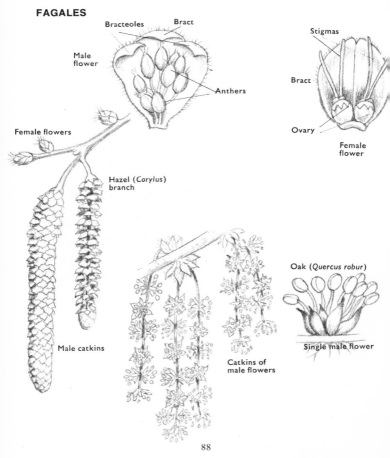

Bracteoles

Bract

Male flower

Anthers

Female flowers

Hazel (*Corylus*) branch

Male catkins

Catkins of male flowers

Stigmas

Bract

Ovary

Female flower

Oak (*Quercus robur*)

Single male flower

That which occurs between the bundles (as in secondary thickening) is called inter-fascicular cambium.

Fen. A community developing in water overlying alkaline rocks. The typical plants are reeds and sedges. Mineral particles are trapped by the plants and, together with the remains of dead plants, they build up on the bottom. Waterlogging prevents bacterial decay and fen peat is formed. This differs from bog peat in being alkaline and in containing a certain amount of mineral matter. As the surface of the peat rises it may be colonised by willow and alder scrub forming a *carr* or, if it rises sufficiently, it may be transformed into a bog by colonisation with *Sphagnum*. (See *Bog; Peat*).

Fermentation. The decomposition of organic materials, especially carbohydrates, by micro-organisms. A good example is the breakdown of sugars into alcohol in the process of winemaking. Yeasts are the organisms concerned here.

Fern. (See *Filicales*).

Fertilisation. The fusion of two gametes to produce a new generation. It is quite a simple process in many lower plants but in the flowering plants there are a number of associated features all of which are conveniently considered under this topic.

By the time the pollen grain reaches the stigma its nucleus has usually divided into *vegetative* and *generative nuclei*. A fine *pollen tube* grows out from the grain and grows down into the ovary. It appears to be chemically attracted to an ovule which it enters through the micropyle. Within the pollen tube the generative nucleus divides to give two gametes.

Within the ovule is the embryo sac corresponding to the spore of a fern. The embryo sac contains the actual female gamete with which one of the male gametes fuses. This is the actual act of fertilisation. The other male gamete fuses with other nuclei in the embryo-sac. The fused gametes develop into the embryo consisting of plumule, radicle, and cotyledons, while the other fused nuclei divide and grow into the endosperm tissue which nourishes the embryo. By this time the ovule has become a seed (q.v.). (See Plates 29 and 30).

Fibre. Elongated sclerenchyma cell. (See *Sclerenchyma*).

Fibrous Root. (See *Root*).

Filament. The stalk of a stamen (q.v.).

Filicales. Ferns — a subdivision of the *Pteridophyta* (q.v.). There is a well marked *Alternation of Generations* (q.v.), the sporophyte generation being the typical fern plant with large leaves. Most ferns have distinct root, stem, and leaf and a vascular system. The stem is usually small and underground, except in the tropical tree-ferns which may reach a height of 60 feet. It is rarely branched although in the bracken it is in the form of a branching rhizome which throws up new fronds over a wide area. It is this feature that makes bracken such an invasive plant. The leaves or fronds are usually large and normally, but not always divided (Plate 32). Roots are all adventitious, developing from the leaf bases or from the stem. There are no flowers.

The life-cycle of a fern is best studied by taking a typical example such as the male fern, *Dryopteris*, which has a wide distribution in the Northern Hemisphere. The stem is a stocky underground structure that puts up a crown of fronds each year. The fronds, which may be 4 feet high, take two years or more to develop and the next year's fronds can be seen tightly coiled at the top of the stem. They uncoil from the base and are covered in brown 'fur' at first. When the fronds wither and die their bases remain attached to the stem which thus appears to increase in thickness each year.

On the underside of a mature frond there appear numerous brown patches

89

Plate 41

GERMINATION

A sweet corn cob and the germination of one of its seeds. The radicle appears before the plumule which is surrounded by a protective sheath *(coleoptile)*. The cotyledon remains below ground.

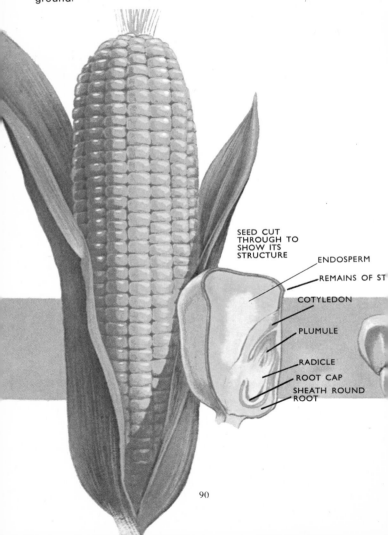

SEED CUT THROUGH TO SHOW ITS STRUCTURE

ENDOSPERM

REMAINS OF ST

COTYLEDON

PLUMULE

RADICLE

ROOT CAP

SHEATH ROUND ROOT

GEMMA

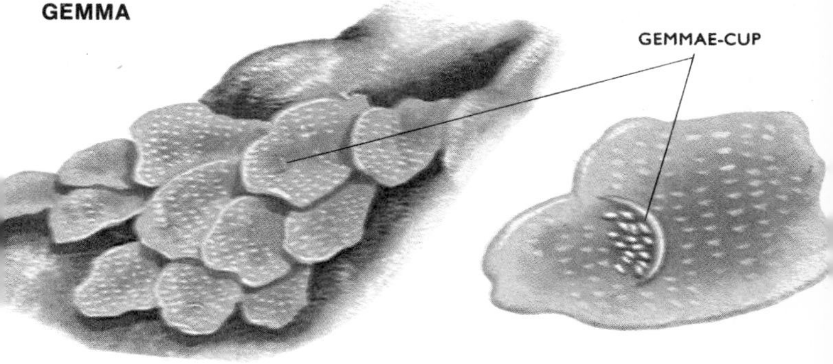

Plate 42

GEMMAE-CUP

Many liverworts reproduce vegetatively by small detachable buds called gemmae which are formed in cup-shaped pits.

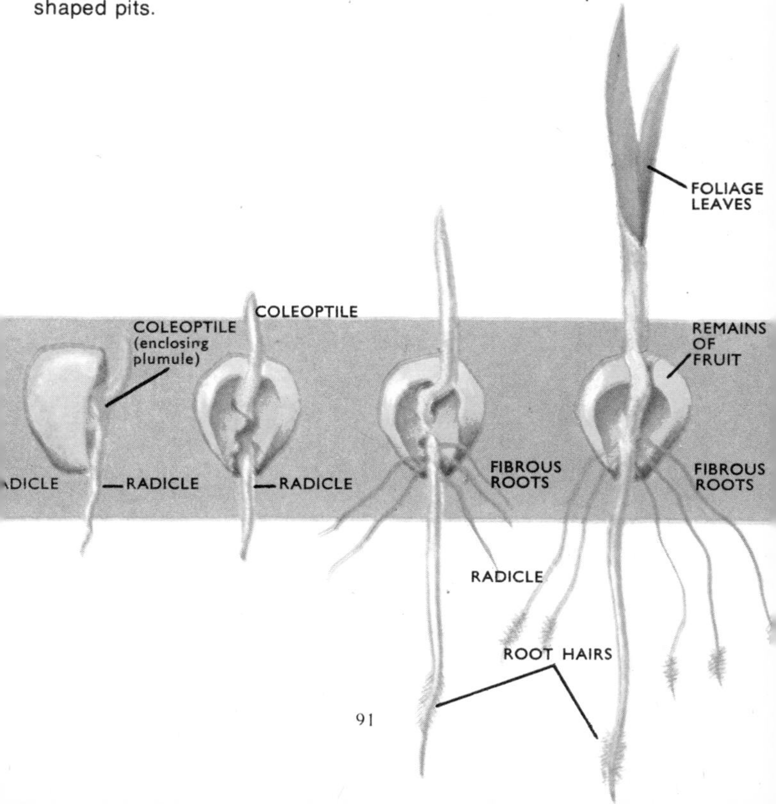

FOLIAGE LEAVES

COLEOPTILE
(enclosing plumule)

COLEOPTILE

REMAINS OF FRUIT

ADICLE — RADICLE — RADICLE

FIBROUS ROOTS

FIBROUS ROOTS

RADICLE

ROOT HAIRS

91

FILICALES

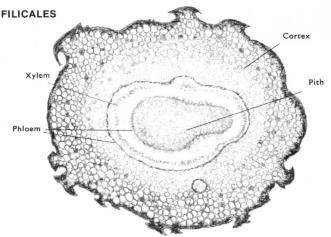

Cortex

Xylem

Pith

Phloem

Transverse section through a fern stem.

which, if examined in detail, will be seen to consist of a number of stalked swellings covered by an umbrella-shaped flap of tissue called the *indusium*. Each stalked swelling is a sporangium and each group of sporangia is called a *sorus*. The arrangement of these sori on the frond varies (Plate 32) and in some species — e.g. hard fern and adder's tongue — they may not be borne on ordinary leaves at all.

The cells inside the sporangia undergo meiosis and haploid spores are formed. When these spores are ripe the indusium withers and the sporangia split, releasing clouds of the tiny spores. These are very resistant to drought and can survive for a very long time. If they fall on moist soil each will develop into a tiny plate of green cells which is the gametophyte generation of the fern life cycle and is called the *prothallus*. Because of their small size, prothalli are rarely seen in nature but they can be grown at home by shaking spores on to damp peat.

The prothallus is similar in most ferns in that it is heart-shaped and it bears a number of rhizoids on the underside. The prothallus bears the sex organs — male antheridia and female archegonia — on the underside. Most species have male and female organs on one prothallus but a few have separate male and female prothalli. The antheridia are spherical structures and the archegonia are flask-shaped. When the female cell in the base of the archegonium is ripe, cells in the neck of the archegonium break down into mucus which attracts the flagellated male cells (*antherozoids*). These are released only in wet conditions and they swim towards the archegonia, each eventually fusing with a female cell and forming a zygote which is the first cell of the new sporophyte generation.

The zygote begins to divide and forms an embryo fern which grows at the expense of the prothallus. After a short while leaves develop in the embryo; roots develop from its tiny stem, and the young fern becomes self-supporting. The prothallus then withers away. The first fronds of the new sporophyte fern are relatively simple. Later ones become progressively more divided until the mature, spore-bearing fronds are formed. (See Plates 31, 32 and 33).

Flagellum. Whip-like hair found singly or in numbers on various single-celled algae such as *Chlamydomonas* (q.v.).

Flora. The plant population of an area is collectively called the flora. The term is also applied to any list or description of the plants of a given region.

Floral Diagram. Diagrammatic representation of a flower showing the number and arrangement of the parts. It is basically a series of concentric circles on which the parts are arranged. The outer circle represents the calyx, the next, the corolla, and the inner ones the androecium and gynaecium. Any joining or overlapping of parts can be shown on the diagram. The position of the main stem is indicated by a small circle and bracts and bracteoles are also indicated when they are present. Together with a floral formula (q.v.) and a longitudinal section through a flower, the floral diagram can tell a flower's story far better than a lengthy description in words. (See Page 96).

Floral Formula. A way of expressing the number and arrangement of parts in a flower. The floral formula for a primrose is:

$$K(5) \, \overbrace{C(5) \, A5 \, G(\underline{5})}.$$

K stands for calyx, C for corolla, A for androecium, and G for gynaecium. The formula above tells us that there are five parts in the calyx and the brackets round the 5 indicate that the sepals are joined to each other. There are similarly 5 joined petals in the corolla. There are 5 stamens in the androecium but, as there are no brackets round the figure, it is known that they are not joined to each other. The long bracket joining the C and the A indicates that the stamens are joined to the petals. G(5) indicates that there are 5 joined carpels and the line under the figure indicates that the carpels are superior (above the insertion of the petals). The formula for the buttercup is K5 C5 A ∞ G $\overset{\infty}{}$. indicating that the parts are free. The sign ∞ means numerous. In many flowers (e.g. tulip) there is no division into sepals and petals and here the letter P is used in the formula to denote perianth. A small line above the figure for the carpels indicates that they are below the insertion of petals (i.e. the flower is epigynous). A floral formula does not give a complete description of a flower—for example it does not show whether any of the parts overlap or not—but when it is combined with a floral diagram (q.v.) and a longitudinal section of a flower all the information is given.

Floret. One of the elements of a composite flower such as a dandelion. Each floret is actually a complete flower in that it has its own sex organs, calyx and corolla. The strap-shaped part of the dandelion floret and of the outer florets of daisies is called the ligule. (See *Compositae* and Plate 34).

Flower. That part of the flowering plant (Angiospermae) that is concerned with reproduction. A flower is thought to be an unlengthened shoot whose leaves are modified as the *floral organs*—petals, stamens, etc.

The buttercup is a convenient, simple flower to study. The stalk of each flower is called the *pedicel* and is swollen at the tip, forming the *receptacle*. The floral organs develop in more or less concentric circles on the receptacle but in some of the more primitive flowers (water lily) they are arranged spirally on the receptacle. The first-formed organs are the *sepals,* of which there are five in the buttercup. They are green and leaf-like and together form the *calyx* whose chief function is the protection of the developing flower. Above the sepals are the five yellow *petals,* each with a small *nectary* at the base. The group of petals is called the *corolla* and, with the calyx, forms the *perianth*. The petals and nectaries attract pollinators to the flowers and also help to protect the *essential* organs within. These essential organs are the *stamens* and *carpels*. The stamens are the male, pollen-producing organs and form the *androecium*. Each stamen

Plate 43

GRAMINEAE

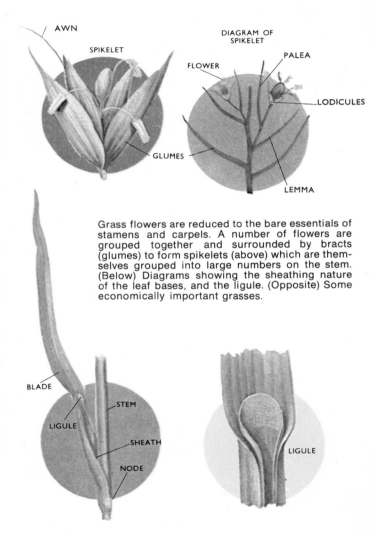

AWN
SPIKELET
DIAGRAM OF SPIKELET
PALEA
FLOWER
LODICULES
GLUMES
LEMMA

Grass flowers are reduced to the bare essentials of stamens and carpels. A number of flowers are grouped together and surrounded by bracts (glumes) to form spikelets (above) which are themselves grouped into large numbers on the stem. (Below) Diagrams showing the sheathing nature of the leaf bases, and the ligule. (Opposite) Some economically important grasses.

BLADE
STEM
LIGULE
SHEATH
NODE
LIGULE

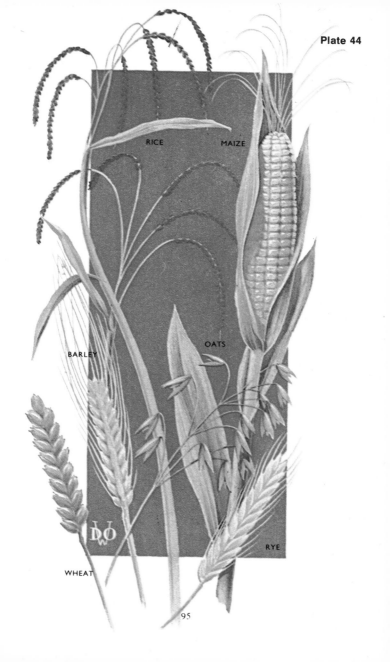

Plate 44

RICE

MAIZE

BARLEY

OATS

WHEAT

RYE

FLORAL DIAGRAM

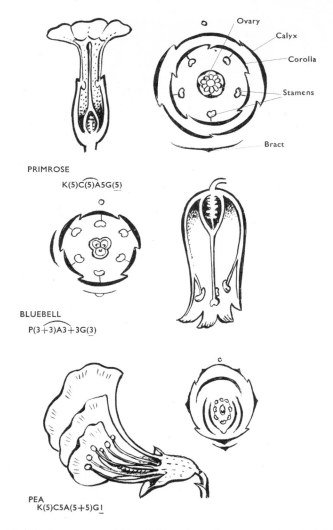

Ovary
Calyx
Corolla
Stamens
Bract

PRIMROSE
K(5)C(5)A5G(5)

BLUEBELL
P(3+3)A3+3G(3)

PEA
K(5)C5A(5+5)G1

Floral diagrams and floral formulae of some common plants, together with longitudinal sections of the flowers.

consists of a filament and anthers. The carpels, each containing an ovule, form the *gynaecium* in the centre of the flower. The *stigma* is the tip of the carpel through which the male cell from the pollen grain gains access to the ovule. The buttercup has many stamens and carpels but this is not so in all flowers. Below the flower there may be one or two tiny leaves called *bracteoles*. These are the very earliest floral leaves and the pedicel continues to grow after they are formed, but when once the sepals are formed the pedicel more or less ceases growth so that the floral organs are all closely grouped on the receptacle. A leaf at the base of a flower stalk is called a *bract* — the pedicel grows in its axil.

The buttercup has all four types of floral organ (the so-called 'perfect' flower) and the parts are arranged in a regular manner. There are, however, many variations of this pattern. The buttercup is a *hypogynous* flower — one in which the petals are inserted below the gynaecium. This is the most common condition but *perigynous* flowers are also common. Here the receptacle spreads at the top so that the petals are inserted around the carpels. In *epigynous* flowers the carpels are surrounded by the receptacle and the petals are inserted above the carpels.

Not all plants have bisexual flowers — the hazel for example has separate male and female flowers with only stamens *or* carpels. The flowers of peas and many orchids are highly irregular and have oddly-shaped petals. Petals (and sepals) often join and form a tube (e.g. primrose, bluebell) or may even be absent — grass flowers have neither petals nor sepals. The marsh marigold has no petals but the sepals are bright yellow and act as petals. Nectaries are not always present and if they are their positions vary a great deal. Stamens are of a fairly constant structure but may be joined together or to the petals. Carpels may contain one or more ovules each of which gives rise to a seed. The pea pod is derived from a carpel with several ovules. The carpels may be free (separate) or they may be joined to each other. These are just a few of the variations found among flowers.

The flowering plants are classified according to the structure of the flower — similarity in number and arrangement of petals etc. is a much better guide to relationships than similarity in leaf form or other vegetative characteristics.

Inflorescences (q.v.) are heads composed of numbers of individual flowers. (See *Fertilisation; Pollination; Seed; Ovule*) and (Plates 34, 48, 49, 78, 79, 80 and 126–128).

Follicle. A type of dry, dehiscent fruit (q.v.) which splits on only one side.

FLOWER

Perigynous (cherry) and epigynous flowers.

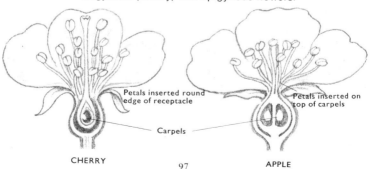

Petals inserted round edge of receptacle

Petals inserted on top of carpels

Carpels

CHERRY

APPLE

Plate 45
HALOPHYTE

A high salt content in the soil is lethal to many plants but a number—called halophytes—are specially adapted and can stand the high salt concentrations found around the coasts. Here, marram grass, sea spurge, and sea holly begin colonising shifting sand dunes. Fixed dunes, where succession is more advanced, are in the background.

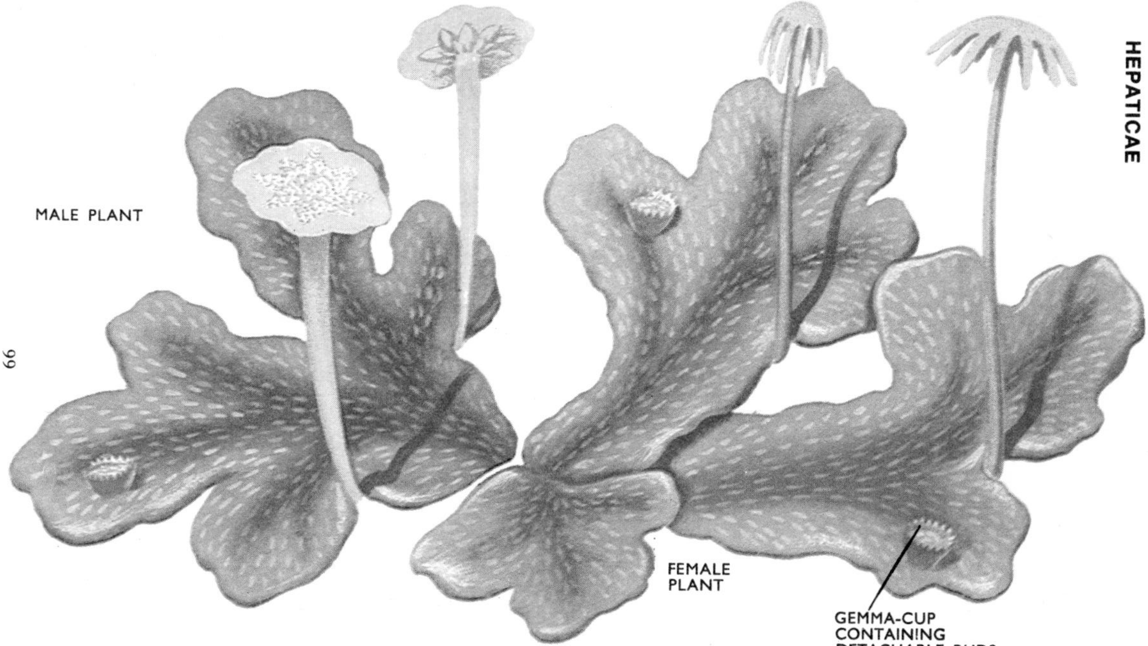

Plate 46

HEPATICAE

GEMMA-CUP CONTAINING DETACHABLE BUDS

FEMALE PLANT

MALE PLANT

The liverwort *Marchantia* showing the special male and female structures on which the sex organs are borne.

Food Chain. Aphid feeds on plant, spider eats aphid, bird eats spider, cat eats bird. This is an example of a simple food chain — a series of organisms, each of which feeds on the one before it in the chain. As one proceeds along the chain the animals get larger and also fewer in number. There are many simple food chains in a given population and they are nearly all linked to each other by cross links, for example, the above chain would be connected to others because spiders also eat flies and birds also eat worms. All food chains start with plants because animals cannot make their own food — they must obtain organic food either directly or indirectly from plants. The food chains of a community all link together and form the food cycle.

Frond. Leaf, especially the large, compound leaf of ferns. (See *Filicales*).

Fructose. A very common simple sugar found especially in fruits (fruit sugar).

Fruit. Feature of flowering plants which is formed from the carpel(s) and which helps to protect and distribute the seeds. Fruit production is normally triggered off by fertilisation

of the ovules but pollination may provide the necessary stimulus in some cases. This is of a chemical nature and it is now possible to produce seedless fruit artificially by dusting the flowers with a hormone powder.

Fruits which are derived from the carpel(s) alone are called *true fruits:* those that contain parts of other organs as well are *false fruits.*

True fruits are classified in many ways. *Simple fruits* are those derived from a single carpel or from a number of joined carpels. *Compound fruits* are true fruits derived from a number of separate carpels in one flower — they are in fact collections of simple fruits.

In the formation of true fruits the carpel wall gives rise to the layers of the fruit (the *pericarp*). These layers may be fleshy or more or less dry. The two main types of fleshy fruits are the *drupe* and the *berry*. The drupe, typified by the plum and the cherry, differs from the berry in that the inner layer of the carpel wall (the *endocarp*) becomes hard and woody, forming the stone. The plum stone is not the seed — it is part of the fruit and the seed is inside it. Drupes normally contain only one seed but berries contain several and are normally derived from several

FRUIT

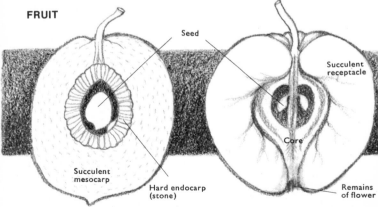

PLUM   APPLE

Sections through a drupe (left) and a pome.

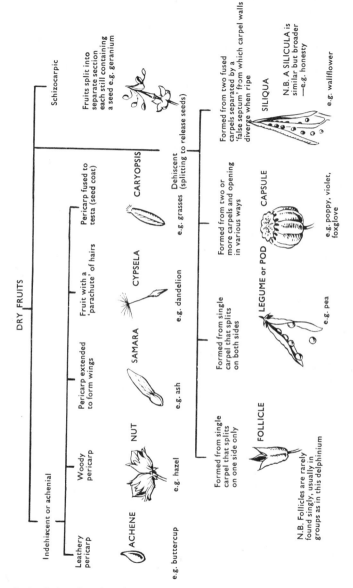

DRY FRUITS

Indehiscent or achenial

Leathery pericarp
ACHENE
e.g. buttercup

Woody pericarp
NUT
e.g. hazel

Pericarp extended to form wings
SAMARA
e.g. ash

Fruit with a 'parachute' of hairs
CYPSELA
e.g. dandelion

Pericarp fused to testa (seed coat)
CARYOPSIS
e.g. grasses

Dehiscent (splitting to release seeds)

Formed from single carpel that splits on one side only
FOLLICLE
N.B. Follicles are rarely found singly, usually in groups as in this delphinium

Formed from single carpel that splits on both sides
LEGUME or POD
e.g. pea

Formed from two or more carpels and opening in various ways
CAPSULE
e.g. poppy, violet, foxglove

Formed from two fused carpels separated by a 'false septum' from which carpel walls diverge when ripe
SILIQUA
N.B. A SILICULA is similar but broader —e.g. honesty
e.g. wallflower

Schizocarpic

Fruits split into separate section each still containing a seed e.g. geranium

A chart showing the classification of the main types of dry fruits.

Plate 47

HEPATICAE (Cont)

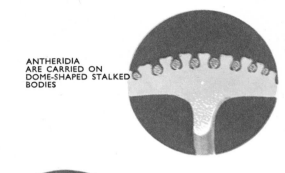

ANTHERIDIA
ARE CARRIED ON
DOME-SHAPED STALKED
BODIES

ARCHEGONIA
ARE CARRIED ON
THE UNDERSIDE
OF THESE
UMBRELLA-SHAPED
BODIES

FLASK-SHAPED
ARCHEGONIA

Detail of the structures which carry the sex organs in *Marchantia*.
(See Plate 46.)

HYPOGEAL

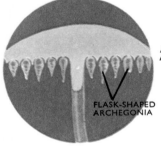

PLUMULE

SEED
LEAVES
(COTYLEDONS)

Hypogeal germination, in
which the cotyledons re-
main below ground.

102

Plate 48

HYPOGYNOUS

The buttercup, with its petals inserted below the carpels, is a hypogynous flower.

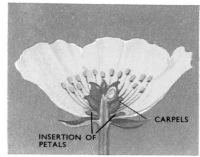

CARPELS

INSERTION OF PETALS

INFLORESCENCE

Various types of flower head.

CORYMB

YARROW

CYME

STITCHWORT

UMBEL

HOGWEED

103

fused carpels. Examples include oranges and tomatoes. The blackberry is a compound fruit consisting of a number of separate small drupes.

Dry fruits are of many types but they are primarily divided into *dehiscent, indehiscent,* and *schizocarpic* types. Dehiscent fruits split in some way or other and release the seeds. Examples include the *capsule* of the poppy (Plate 35) and the *pod* of the pea (Plate 57). Other types are illustrated in the accompanying diagram. Indehiscent fruits do not split open—the seed is not released until the fruit rots or is otherwise damaged. Fruits of this type are called achenial fruits. The true *achene* is leathery: the *nut* is hard and woody; while the *samara* is winged and easily distributed by wind. (See accompanying diagram). Schizocarpic fruits split but they split into sections which still contain seed. Each section behaves rather like an indehiscent fruit and is called a *mericarp*. The *lomentum* is a legume or pod which does not split open but which breaks into sections each containing a seed. The *regma* of geraniums splits into individual carpels, each still containing a seed.

False fruits include the apple and strawberry among many others: both of these fruits include the receptacle. The apple carpels are surrounded by the receptacle which swells and forms the fleshy part of the fruit. The carpels containing the seeds form the core. Fruits of this type are called pomes. Strawberries are actually swollen receptacles carrying a number of true fruits (the small pips) formed from the separate carpels.

Composite fruits are false fruits formed from whole inflorescences, not single flowers. Examples include figs, pineapples, and mulberries. Bracts, sepals, and flower stalks all take part in forming these fruits. (See *Flower; Seed*) and (Plates 35–38).

Fucoxanthin. Brown pigment masking the chlorophyll of the brown algae (*Phaeophyceae*, q.v.).

Fungi. A large group of plants including moulds, mushrooms and yeasts. The body of a fungus normally consists of fine threads called *hyphae*. Chlorophyll is completely absent and fungi cannot therefore manufacture their own food. They are not capable of photosynthesis and not dependent upon sunlight. Many of them live in complete darkness. They must rely for food on ready-made organic matter which is absorbed from the material on which they grow. In this respect fungi resemble animals which also need ready-made food. The hyphae often release digestive juices which liquefy the food material. Many fungi are *parasites,* absorbing food from living organisms. Those which exist on dead material are called *saprophytes.* They play an important part in the economy of nature for they break down dead organisms and release material for use by other plants.

As food and water are absorbed the hyphae increase in length and frequently branch. Growth is far less complicated than in the higher plants for there are no special tissues in the fungi. The hyphae are simple, tubular structures whose walls consist of various types of cellulose and nitrogen compounds. They contain protoplasm, nuclei, and droplets of oil which act as food reserves. The hyphae are sometimes divided into cells, each with one or two nuclei.

Fungi are classified according to their structure and the way in which they reproduce. There are three major groups.

PHYCOMYCETES. The threads of these fungi are not divided up into separate cells. Many of the species live in water, or are parasites of flowering plants.

Saprolegnia lives in water where its white threads are common on dead twigs, insects, and even on injured fishes. The hyphae branch over and through the tissues and frequently swell at the tips. The swollen tips, containing many nuclei, are partitioned off by a wall. Each nucleus becomes associated with a piece of protoplasm which rounds off and produces two whip-like flagella. The tip of the hypha opens and the tiny bodies swim away by means of their flagella. Actively swimming bodies like this are common among lower plants. They are called *zoospores*. Each zoospore, if it reaches a suitable place, grows into a new hypha. Because of the large number produced, it is rare for a single zoospore to develop alone — there are usually a number of others close at hand. The zoospores are thus agents of *asexual* or *vegetative* reproduction.

Saprolegnia has another method of reproducing itself, especially towards the end of its life. Tips of branch-threads swell up and become partitioned off. There are two types of swelling — usually close together. The larger one is the female oogonium whose nuclei and protoplasm form sex-cells. The male structure is club-shaped and grows into contact with the oogonium. The male cells then pass over and join with the female sex-cells forming a number of *oospores* or 'eggs'. The nuclei join together and a hard wall forms around the 'egg'. It can resist bad conditions such as drought and then, after division by meiosis, which reduces the chromosome number, it puts out a new thread with a single set of chromosomes in the nuclei.

Mucor — the common pin mould of bread, leather, etc. — is another member of this group of fungi but differs in two important ways. The asexual zoospores have no flagella for they would be no use in the drier conditions under which *Mucor* lives. The spores are distributed by wind or by insects. There are no distinct male and female structures but not all the threads act alike. There are two physiologically different strains (called *plus* and *minus*) and when the two meet they form reproductive structures. The occurrence of two physiologically different strains is called *heterothallism* and is found in most of the higher fungi.

In *Mucor*, the tips of side-threads

are partitioned off and those of opposite strains join together. These swollen tips are called gametangia. Their nuclei join in pairs and a hard wall forms around them. This is the *zygospore*, corresponding to the 'egg' of *Saprolegnia*. When the zygospore germinates, after meiosis, it puts out a single thread which bears zoospores at its tip. These are distributed and form new threads. Most of the life of these fungi is spent in the *haploid* state. Only the sexual zygospores have two sets of chromosomes. This is in contrast to the higher plants and animals whose body cells have two sets. This is because in the higher organisms the reduction of the chromosome number takes place just before sex-cells are formed.

ASCOMYCETES. The threads of these fungi are divided into 'cells' each with, normally, a single nucleus. Many are important parasites but the most obvious are the brightly coloured cup-fungi, such as *Peziza*, which live on dead logs and the like. The sexual spores are formed inside special cells called *asci* — which normally occur in 'fruiting bodies' made up of masses of tightly packed threads. The fruiting bodies are often brightly coloured.

There are usually two different strains of threads which will produce fruiting bodies only when they meet. The threads join but the nuclei remain separate. The threads continue to grow and produce more cells, each with *two* nuclei. These threads and branches of the original ones form the fruiting body. The asci develop at the tips of the threads which have two nuclei. In a cell, at or near the tip, the nuclei fuse and then divide into eight. Each new nucleus takes on some protoplasm and forms a spore. The spores are released when the spore-chamber opens. Spores of both strains are produced, and later grow into new fungus threads.

BASIDIOMYCETES. To this group belong the most familiar fungi — the mushrooms and toadstools. Their early life is much like that of the previous group — they exist as fine

Plate 49

INFLORESCENCE (Cont)

SOLITARY FLOWER
ANEMONE

ONE-SIDED RACEME
BLUEBELL

Various types of flower head.

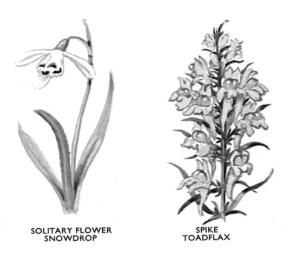

SOLITARY FLOWER
SNOWDROP

SPIKE
TOADFLAX

Plate 50

INSECTIVOROUS PLANT

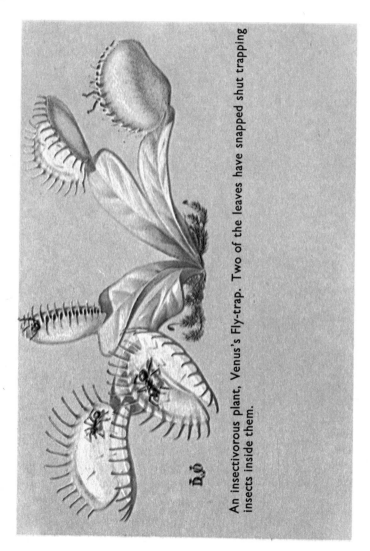

An insectivorous plant, Venus's Fly-trap. Two of the leaves have snapped shut trapping insects inside them.

FUNGI

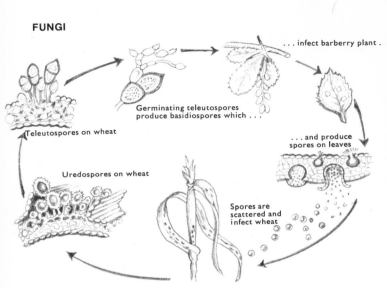

... infect barberry plant.

Germinating teleutospores
produce basidiospores which ...

Teleutospores on wheat

Uredospores on wheat

... and produce
spores on leaves

Spores are
scattered and
infect wheat

The life cycle of the rust fungus *Puccinia* (See also Plate 14).

branching threads on dead leaves, manure, etc. When threads of opposite type meet, they again produce fruiting bodies of closely matted threads, some of which have two nuclei in their cells. The fruiting body of the mushroom develops underground as a small knot of threads. Its structure is almost fully formed before it appears above ground, and then, by absorbing large amounts of water, it grows up into the air and opens out into the typical umbrella-shape. On the underside of the cap there are many radiating gills which bear the spores. The threads bear club-shaped cells at the tip and in these cells (the basidia) the two nuclei fuse. They then divide by meiosis and the four new nuclei pass into four tiny swellings on the outer end of the cell. These are the tiny spores (*basidiospores*). They fall when ripe and are distributed by wind.

In the cultivated mushroom, only two spores are formed at the tip of each cell so that each spore has two

nuclei. There is no need for two different threads to meet before producing fruiting bodies in this case, because the threads already have two nuclei.

Some other fungi of this group have numerous pores on the underside instead of gills. The spores are produced on the linings of the pores in these fungi. Many of the bracket fungi on trees are of this type. The rust fungus (See Plate 14) is an important parasitic member of this group. Its body is nothing like that of a toadstool but the important link is the formation of basidiospores. (See Plates 14, 15, 16, 39, 40, 65, 66, 90, 106, 121 and 122).

Fungicide. Fungus-killing substance.

Funicle. Stalk of an ovule (q.v.).

Gall. Abnormal plant growth produced in response to infection with a parasite. Examples include robins' pincushions and oak-apples caused by infection

108

with insect parasites; potato wart and other swellings caused by fungi; and even the swelling caused by mistletoe growing on an apple branch. (See Plate 40).

Gametangium. Organ, especially of lower fungi, in which gametes are formed. (See Plate 39).

Gamete. Sex-cell.

Gametocyte. Cell that produces gametes by meiotic division.

Gametophyte. Haploid stage of the life cycle that develops from a spore and bears sex organs. The moss plant and the fern prothallus are examples of gametophytes. (See *Alternation of Generations*).

Gamopetalous. Having joined petals.

Gamosepalous. Having joined sepals.

Gemma. Small detachable bud formed by certain mosses and liverworts as a means of vegetative reproduction (q.v.). (See Plate 42).

Gemmation. The formation of gemmae.

Gene. An hereditary factor passed on from cell to cell and from generation to generation, which has a particular effect on the cell or organism containing it. Genes are carried on the *chromosomes* (q.v.) in the cell nuclei and each gene has a particular place (*locus*) on a certain chromosome. Because each body cell has two sets of chromosomes, it also has two sets of genes concerned with each feature. But the two genes are not necessarily identical: every now and then the molecular structure of a gene may become altered so that, although it still affects the same feature, it has a different effect. The gene is said to have mutated. A pair of different genes that occur at the same place on the chromosomes but have different effects on the development of the organism are said to be alleles or

allelomorphic genes. As a rule, one allele over-rules the effect of the other and is said to be dominant. The other allele is the recessive and its presence is made apparent in the organism only if it is present on both chromosomes of a pair. If the two chromosomes of a pair carry identical genes the organism is *homozygous* for that character. If two different alleles are carried on the chromosomes the organism is *heterozygous*.

Genes are believed to be composed of nucleic acids which control the development of the cells by controlling the types of protein formed. The vast number of instructions carried by the genes of an organism is made possible by the enormous variation in the arrangement of the molecules making up the nucleic acids. When a cell divides (except when forming sex-cells) the chromosomes and genes duplicate themselves exactly so that the same instructions go to each new cell. But even then the new cells may not be exactly like the parent cell for their position in the organism also influences their development. When sex-cells are formed the chromosomes do not duplicate themselves but one member of each pair goes to each sex-cell. When sex-cells join again at fertilisation there are again two sets of chromosomes but the genes that they carry are not identical with those of either parent and, as the effect of a gene is modified by the action of those genes around it, the new generation will not be identical with either parent even if grown under identical conditions. (See *Heredity; Natural Selection*).

Generic. Of a genus.

Genetics. The study of genes (q.v.) and the way in which characteristics are passed on from one generation to the next. (See *Heredity*) and (Plate 61).

Genotype. The actual genetic constitution of an organism, which may not be apparent from the outward appearance. (See *Phenotype*).

Plate 51

INSECTIVOROUS PLANT (Cont)

A 'see-through' drawing of the pitcher of *Nepenthes* showing a fly trapped in the liquid at the bottom.

Plate 52

LEAF

RACHIS

The top three leaves are unicostate—each having a single main vein. The left-hand one is simple, with a serrated margin. The oak leaf (centre) is also a simple leaf but it is lobed fairly deeply *(pinnatifid* condition) and this tendency is carried further in the compound pinnate leaf on the right. The three bottom leaves are multicostate—several main veins each—and again stages can be recognised from simple to compound. The horse-chestnut leaf on the right is an example of a *palmate* leaf.

111

Gentianaceae. Family of dicotyledons including the common centaury and yellow-wort as well as the famous blue gentians. The fruit is a capsule containing many small seeds. The corolla does not fall when it withers but remains and protects the capsule.

Genus. An important grouping used in classification (q.v.) and containing a number (maybe only one) of closely related species all of which share the generic name.

Geological Time Scale. During the Earth's long history there have been many changes: land has been submerged and uplifted many times: animal and plant groups have appeared, flourished, and become extinct. Geological time has been divided into a number of periods separated by episodes of mountain building or abrupt faunal changes. The time scale is of great importance to biologists dealing with evolution and with fossil groups.

GERANIALES

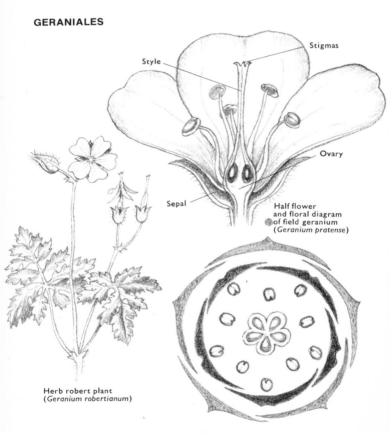

Half flower and floral diagram of field geranium (*Geranium pratense*)

Herb robert plant (*Geranium robertianum*)

Geological Time Scale

			Years since beginning	Plant life
QUATERNARY PERIOD	PRESENT DAY			
	HOLOCENE EPOCH	25000		
	PLEISTOCENE EPOCH	1 million		
TERTIARY PERIOD	PLIOCENE EPOCH	12 ,,		
	MIOCENE EPOCH	25 ,,		
	OLIGOCENE EPOCH	40 ,,		
	EOCENE EPOCH	60 ,,		
	PALAEOCENE EPOCH	70 ,,		
CRETACEOUS PERIOD		135 ,,	FLOWERING PLANTS	
JURASSIC PERIOD		170 ,,		
TRIASSIC PERIOD		200 ,,		
PERMIAN PERIOD		230 ,,		
CARBONIFEROUS PERIOD		280 ,,	FIRST SEED PLANTS	
DEVONIAN PERIOD		325 ,,	FERNS	
SILURIAN PERIOD		360 ,,	FIRST LAND PLANTS	
ORDOVICIAN PERIOD		425 ,,		
CAMBRIAN PERIOD		500 - 600 ,,		

QUATERNARY PERIOD / TERTIARY PERIOD: CENOZOIC ERA (RECENT LIFE)
CRETACEOUS / JURASSIC / TRIASSIC: MESOZOIC ERA (MIDDLE LIFE)
PERMIAN / CARBONIFEROUS / DEVONIAN / SILURIAN / ORDOVICIAN / CAMBRIAN: PALAEOZOIC ERA (ANCIENT LIFE)

PHANEROZOIC EON (EVIDENT LIFE)

CRYPTOZOIC EON (HIDDEN LIFE) — ALGAE

The Cryptozoic Eon occupies some 80% of all geological time. Although Cryptozoic means 'hidden life', signs of life at this very early stage have been discovered since the divisions were named.

A chart showing the main divisions of geological time and the times at which the main groups of plants are thought to have come into being.

Geotaxis. Movement of a whole organism under the influence of gravity. (See *Taxis*).

Geotropism. Bending movement of part of a plant brought about by the force of gravity. (See *Tropism*).

Geraniales. Order of flowering plants containing the geraniums (family Geraniaceae), flaxes, and balsams.

Gill Fungi. Fungi belonging to the family Agaricaceae (mushrooms, etc) in which the spores are borne on radiating gills on the underside of the cap. (See *Fungi*).

Ginkgoales. Order of Gymnospermae containing only one living member — the maidenhair tree *(Ginkgo biloba)*. (See Page 257) and (Plate 125).

Glabrous. Hairless.

Gland. Organ in which certain sub-

113

Plate 53

(*Left*) Netted venation of a dicotyledon and (*right*) the parallel veins of a mono-cotyledon such as the Lily of the Valley.

The rose leaf (note the separate leaflets) has green stipules at the base.

Haywood

LEAF (Cont)

A privet shoot showing the entire leaves with only a single main vein and the axillary bud at the base of each leaf.

Plate 54

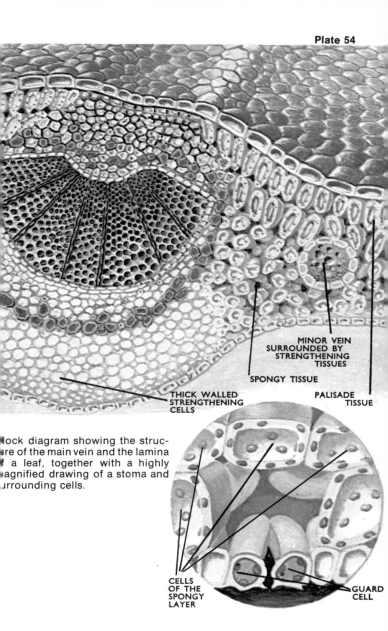

MINOR VEIN
SURROUNDED BY
STRENGTHENING
TISSUES

SPONGY TISSUE

PALISADE
TISSUE

THICK WALLED
STRENGTHENING
CELLS

Block diagram showing the structure of the main vein and the lamina
of a leaf, together with a highly
magnified drawing of a stoma and
surrounding cells.

CELLS
OF THE
SPONGY
LAYER

GUARD
CELL

115

stances are built up and from which they are discharged – usually to the outside in plants. Examples in the plant world include the stinging hairs of nettles, and the nectaries of flowers.

Glochid. (See *Cacti*).

Glucose. A simple sugar found as a food reserve in many plants.

Glume. Tiny bract that encloses a grass spikelet. (See *Gramineae*) and (Plate 43).

Glumiflorae. Order of flowering plants containing the grasses (family Gramineae) and sometimes taken to include the sedges (family Cyperaceae) as well. These plants have no perianth in the normal sense of the word – the sex organs are surrounded by tiny bracts called *glumes* and a number of other scales or bristles.

Gnetales. Strange group of plants containing only three genera which are very different from each other and which are grouped together merely for convenience. The Gnetales are classed as gymnosperms but they show many characteristics of flowering plants. (See Page 257) and (Plate 125).

Graft. (See *Propagation*).

Gramineae. Large family of flowering plants – grasses – many of which are of great economic importance. The woody bamboos are members of this family although most members are herbs. Some are annuals and biennials but the majority of grasses are perennial plants.

A characteristic of grasses is the production of numerous side-shoots from the bases of older shoots. Grazing or mowing stimulates greater production of these side-shoots and this is why grasses can stand up to continued cutting. Fibrous roots arise from the bases of these shoots and a thick sward is rapidly produced. Grasses are thus valuable aids in the stabilisation of exposed soil.

In its first year the grass shoot is normally short and vegetative but, sooner or later, it grows up and produces an inflorescence. The stems are normally hollow, except at the nodes. The linear leaves arise on alternate sides of the stem and sheathe the stem for a certain distance. At the junction of sheath and blade there is usually a collar called a *ligule* and the shape of this is frequently of use in identifying grasses.

The flowers are borne in *spikelets* – small branches almost completely enclosed by greenish scales called *glumes*. There may be one or more flowers in each spikelet, according to species and the spikelets are arranged in many ways in the inflorescence. Each individual flower stalk within the spikelet has a number of other small scales connected with it. Each flower stalk arises from the axil of a bract called the *lemma*. This often carries a projection called an *awn*. On the actual flower stalk there is another scale or bracteole called the *palea*, and two tiny *lodicules*. There is no perianth but some botanists believe that the lodicules represent the remains of it. The anthers are borne on long slender filaments and the stigmas are usually large and feathery. The flowers are usually hermaphrodite and are pollinated by wind. When the flower is fully formed the scales separate and expose the stamens and stigmas. The fruit is normally a caryopsis (see *Fruit*) and the seed is rich in carbohydrate and vitamins. Grain of one type or another is the staple diet in most parts of the world. (See Plates 43 and 44).

Gram's Stain. A special stain used in the study of bacteria. Some bacteria, because of a certain compound they contain, take up the stain and these are called gram-positive bacteria. Those bacteria without the compound do not take up the stain and are called gram negative.

Grass. (See *Gramineae*).

Growing Point. The tip of a stem or root where active cell division takes place. New cells are formed here but actual growth takes place further back where the new cells elongate. (See *Stem* and *Root*) and (Plate 62).

Growth. Increase in size.

Guard Cell. Cell surrounding stoma of a leaf (q.v.). (See Plate 54).

Guttation. Exudation of water droplets from plants in a humid atmosphere. (See *Hydathode*).

Gymnospermae. Division of seed-bearing plants differing from the flowering plants (Angiospermae) by the fact that the ovules are not enclosed in carpels — they are naked (Greek *gumnos* = naked). The seed is, therefore, not enclosed in a fruit. Another distinguishing feature is that the gymnosperms (apart from Gnetales) do not have vessels in their xylem tissue. The conducting cells are all tracheids. The sporophylls are normally arranged in cones — the two sexes sometimes on different plants. There are many extinct members which had large leaves. This type of gymnosperm is still represented by the palm-like cycads (See *Cycadales*). Most modern gymnosperms have small leaves and are typified by the members of the *Coniferales* (q.v.) — the spruce, larch, pine, and juniper. The yew *(Taxus)* is also a gymnosperm. Although its seed appears to be surrounded by a fruit, the red structure is actually an aril — an outgrowth of the seed itself. The *Gnetales* (q.v.) are a heterogeneous group consisting of three very dissimilar genera which show several angiosperm-like features. (See Page 257) and (Plates 77 and 125).

Gynaecium. The female region of a flower — the carpel or carpels. Often called the ovary or pistil. (See *Flower*).

Gynodioecious. With female and hermaphrodite flowers on separate plants.

Gynomonoecious. With female and hermaphrodite flowers both on the same plant.

Hairs. (See *Trichome*).

Halophyte. A plant able to tolerate high salt content in the soil. (See Plate 45).

Haploid. Having only a single set of chromosomes (q.v.) in the nucleus and not paired chromosomes as in the *diploid* condition.

Haustorium. Special branch of a parasite — fungus or higher plant such as dodder — that penetrates the host tissues and absorbs food. (See *Parasite*) and (Plate 71).

Heartwood. Central region of a tree-trunk, composed of xylem but with no living cells and not actually involved in conduction of water — the vessels have been compressed and impregnated with various resins, etc. that make the wood very hard and resistant to decay.

Heath. A region of acidic, sandy soil with low fertility. There is usually a thin layer of dry peat and the dominant plants are heather or ling.

Heliotropism. (=*Phototropism*).

Hemicellulose. Cellulose-like material found in the walls of many plant cells and often acting as a food reserve.

Hepaticae. Liverworts — a group of non-vascular plants which, with the mosses (*Musci*, q.v.), makes up the Bryophyta. There is no real distinction into root, stem, and leaf, although the majority — the so-called leafy liverworts — have leaf-like processes on an upright axis. *Pellia* and *Marchantia* are two common examples of the other type — the thalloid liverworts — which are like flat green seaweeds. All live in damp places and absorb water through single-celled rhizoids.

The green plant is the haploid or gametophyte generation (See *Alternation of Generations*) and it bears sex organs — male antheridia and female archegonia. The antheridia develop in pits on the upper surface of *Pellia*

Plate 55
LEAF (Cont)

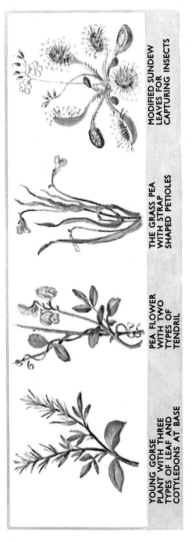

YOUNG GORSE PLANT WITH THREE TYPES OF LEAF AND COTYLEDONS AT BASE

PEA FLOWER WITH TWO TYPES OF TENDRIL

THE GRASS PEA WITH STRAP SHAPED PETIOLES

MODIFIED SUNDEW LEAVES FOR CAPTURING INSECTS

Various leaf modifications.

Plate 56

LEAF (Cont)

ADVENTITIOUS ROOTS
ON STEM

Many plants have more than one kind of leaf. On the climbing stems of ivy the leaves are deeply lobed and almost star-shaped, whereas higher up they are entire and rounded.

while the flask-shaped archegonia develop in groups near the tips of the branches, each group being covered by a flap of tissue. In *Marchantia* the sex organs are borne on stalked structures above the general plant surface (Plate 46) and there are separate male and female plants, but their sex organs are similar.

An egg-cell develops in the base of each archegonium and when it is ripe the cells in the neck of the archegonium break down into a mucus which appears to attract the flagellated male cells released by the antheridia. These male cells (*antherozoids*) swim in the film of water on the plant and one eventually joins with each egg-cell, forming a zygote which is the beginning of the sporophyte generation. The zygote cell divides and soon produces a large number of cells which form three regions—a foot embedded in the thallus, a capsule, and a short stalk joining the two. This embryo is surrounded by the enlarged base of the archegonium. The cells in the capsule multiply and some undergo meiotic division and form spores. The others become strap-shaped and are called *elaters*. All this goes on during the summer while the capsule is still under the flap that protected the archegonia. The following spring the stalk elongates and the capsule appears above the plant. This capsule and its stalk are the sporophyte generation of the liverwort and, as they do not contain chlorophyll they are dependent on the gametophyte for nourishment. The capsule splits and the spores are distributed by the elaters which twist about in response to changes in humidity. The spores give rise to new gametophyte plants.

A number of liverworts reproduce asexually by producing detachable buds called *gemmae* which are washed out of their cups by rain splashes and then grow into new plants.

Liverworts differ from mosses in several ways, notably in the simple spore capsule, single-celled rhizoids, and lack of a protonema. (See Plates 46, 47, and 123).

Herb. Any non-woody plant without persistent aerial parts.

Herbaceous. Non-woody.

Herbarium. A collection of dried or preserved plants.

Heredity. The study of the way in which characteristics are passed on from one generation to the next, or inherited. Gregor Mendel, a monk living in the middle part of the 19th century, was the first person to study this subject systematically and the term 'mendelism' is often used to refer to this subject.

Mendel experimented with garden peas which he grew in the monastery garden. He noticed that not all of the plants were alike: some were tall, others were short; some seeds were round, while others were wrinkled. These features were clear-cut and obvious and Mendel decided to study them individually. The fact that these flowers are normally self-pollinated was a great help, for Mendel's flowers were not contaminated by pollen from 'unknown' flowers. Mendel selected plants with opposed features—e.g. tall and short—and bred them individually until he was satisfied that he had true-breeding plants—i.e. all the tall ones would produce only tall ones. He then transferred pollen from tall plants to short ones and vice versa. In both cases the next generation (the F_1 generation) were all tall—the shortness characteristic of one parent had been suppressed and Mendel stated that tallness is produced by some factor in the cells which is *dominant* to a factor for shortness. This shortness factor is said to be *recessive*. When the new generation of plants was allowed to set seed naturally after self-fertilisation, Mendel found that from each parent he got about three times as many tall plants as short ones. Obviously the shortness factor was present in the F_1 generation and was passed on in the pollen or ovule to some of their offspring—the second filial or F_2 generation.

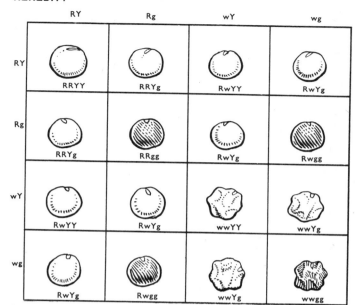

	RY	Rg	wY	wg
RY	RRYY	RRYg	RwYY	RwYg
Rg	RRYg	RRgg	RwYg	Rwgg
wY	RwYY	RwYg	wwYY	wwYg
wg	RwYg	Rwgg	wwYg	wwgg

The results of crossing round, yellow-seeded pea plants with wrinkled, green-seeded plants. (See text.) Four types of plant occur among the offspring: shaded seeds are green.

The constant appearance of the 3:1 ratio led Mendel to what is now called Mendel's First Law or the *Law of Segregation*. He suggested that the tallness and shortness factors in the F_1 plants separate when gametes are formed so that half of the gametes carry the tallness factor and half carry the shortness factor.

Mendel's First Law states that *only one of two opposed characters can be carried as a factor in a single sex-cell or gamete* (i.e. in a pollen grain or an ovule).

If we accept this we can show how the 3:1 ratio is produced. Let the tallness factor be called T and the shortness factor be called t. As Mendel started with pure lines, the original tall plants would have produced gametes with only T, and the short ones only t. When these combine in the F_1 generation we have Tt. Because T is dominant all the plants are tall. According to Mendel's First Law, when these plants produce pollen and ovules there will be equal numbers of T and t gametes. Any pollen cell may fuse with any ovule when the pollen is released, and there are therefore four possible combinations in the F_2 generation – TT, Tt, tT, and tt. Three of these combinations contain T and these plants are therefore tall while the remaining quarter are short. Two-thirds of the tall plants contain the shortness factor and, when self-pollinated, produce the monohybrid 3:1, tall : short ratio. The other tall F_2 plants, however, are pure-breeding as are all the short ones — they have only one type of factor and are called homozygotes. The impure plants (i.e. those with two different factors) are heterozygotes.

121

Plate 57

LEGUMINOSAE

Trifolium pratense, the red clover, showing the root nodules and, inset, one of the bacteria that live in the nodules and 'fix' atmospheric nitrogen.

LEGUME

The characteristic fruit of the leguminous plants is a pod or legume which splits along both edges and scatters the seeds by twisting movements brought about by humidity changes.

Plate 58

LEGUMINOSAE (Cont)

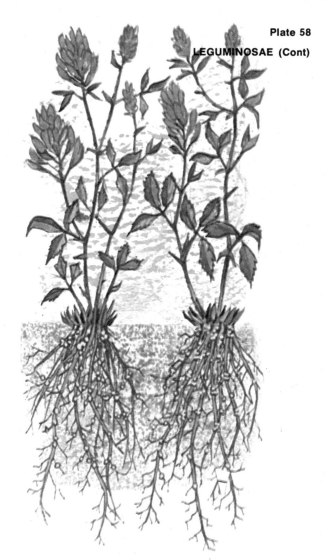

Lucerne *(Medicago sativa)*, an important leguminous plant which, because of its deep roots, can be grown as a fodder crop in quite dry regions.

Similar results are obtained with any pair of opposed characters. Mendel then went on experimenting with peas which differed in two characters. He chose two types of plant—one with round, yellow seeds (RY), the other with wrinkled, green seeds (wg), and cross-pollinated them. The resulting F_1 generation plants all had round, yellow seeds, so we can see that the factor for round seeds is dominant to that for wrinkled and that yellow dominates green. When the F_2 generation plants grew up and produced seed they showed all four characters in every possible combination. The proportions were very close to 9 round, yellow: 3 round, green: 3 wrinkled, yellow: 1 wrinkled, green. Mendel then stated his second law, known as the *Law of Independent Assortment: the factor for each one of a pair of opposed characters may combine with any one of another pair when the sex-cells are formed*. He reasoned that the impure F_1 plants would be RYwg and that they would produce the gametes RY, Rg, wY and wg. Rw and Yg cannot be produced because according to the first law a gamete can carry only one of a pair of opposed factors. Any pollen cell can again combine with any ovule and from the accompanying table we can see how Mendel explained the $9 : 3 : 3 : 1$ dihybrid ratio on this basis. Whenever R and Y occur together there will be round yellow seeds, for these two factors are dominant. When R is absent they will be wrinkled, and when Y is absent they will be green.

When Mendel published his results in 1865 scientists paid little attention to his work, and it was not until after 1900 that the truth of his statements was realised. By then the chromosomes had been discovered and it was realised that these were the 'vehicles' on which Mendel's 'factors' could be carried. We now call the 'factors' *genes* (q.v.).

The behaviour of the chromosomes during gamete formation (meiosis) is exactly what Mendel had suggested in his laws: the chromosome pairs separate and one of each pair goes to each gamete. Therefore, even if the parent cells contain two opposed factors, the gamete can have only one or the other —as Mendel stated in his first law. Again, when gametes are formed, any one of a pair of chromosomes can go to a sex cell with either of any other pair and so Mendel's second law is obeyed as far as the chromosomes are concerned. But it does not always hold true for the individual genes.

Because of the enormous number of genes necessary to control all the features of an organism, each chromosome has to carry many genes. Because they are *linked* in this way the genes on each chromosome do not normally separate during meiosis.

Mendel was very lucky in that the characteristics he selected were all controlled by genes on separate chromosomes. Had he selected any that were linked he may never have arrived at his second law.

Mendel's laws can be used to predict the features of the offspring of particular parents as long as the genetic make-up of the parents is known. This is of great importance in the breeding of improved strains of plant and animal. (See *Meiosis*) and (Plate 61).

Hermaphrodite. Having organs of both sexes in one individual flower.

Heterochlamydeous. Having two separate types of perianth segment—sepals and petals.

Heteroecious. (Of a parasite). Having one reproductive stage on one host and another different reproductive stage on another unrelated host. Rust fungi are good examples of heteroecious parasites. (Plate 14).

Heterosporous. Producing two kinds of spore—megaspores and microspores. (See *Spore*).

Heterostyly. Having more than one arrangement of the style and stigma. Flowers may be of any one type. The condition is an aid to cross-pollination. (See *Dimorphism*) and (Plate 81).

Heterothallism. A phenomenon found in algae and fungi where, although all the thalli may look exactly alike, there are two physiologically different types, usually referred to as + and − strains. Reproduction can take place sexually only between thalli of opposite strains.

Heterotrophic. Unable to synthesise organic food from inorganic material and therefore requiring complex organic food. Most plants can make their own food and are autotrophic but fungi, and other parasites and saprophytes are heterotrophic.

Heterozygous. (See *Gene*).

Hexose. A sugar with six carbon atoms in its molecule, e.g. glucose, fructose. Chains of hexoses make up many important plant materials such as starches and cellulose.

Higher Plants. Rather vague term embracing the seed-bearing plants and sometimes also used to include ferns.

Hilum. The scar on a seed marking the point where the funicle was attached.

Hirsute. Clothed with fairly long, soft hairs.

Hispid. Clothed with long, coarse hairs.

Histogen. Name given to any one of the three regions of tissue—*dermatogen, periblem,* and *plerome*—which some botanists believe exist in stem and root tips and which they believe later give rise to the epidermis, cortex, and stele. (See *Apical Meristem*).

Histology. The study of tissues.

Holocene. Division of the geological time scale (q.v.).

Holophytic. (=*Autotrophic*).

Homochlamydeous. With two groups of perianth segments all of which are of one type—not distinguished as petals and sepals. E.g. tulips.

Homologous Chromosome. Apart from gametes, each cell has two sets of chromosomes (q.v.), which can be arranged in pairs. The members of each pair are said to be homologous and each carries genes affecting the same characteristics.

Homosporous. Producing spores all of one type—not micro—and megaspores. (See *Spore*).

Homozygous. (See *Gene*).

Horsetail. (See *Equisetales*).

Host. Organism attacked by a parasite (q.v.).

Humus. Decayed and decaying organic material in the surface layers of the soil. It gives soil its dark colour. Humus is a very complex jelly-like material and *not a single substance*. A very important property of humus is its ability to link up with clay particles and form them into small groups. Thus addition of humus (or compost) to clay soils helps to break them up and make them workable. The water-holding ability of humus also makes it a valuable addition to sandy soils that tend to dry out rapidly. The ability of humus to adsorb mineral salts and ions makes it of great importance to plant nutrition.

Hybrid. Offspring resulting from the pairing of two different species. Hybrids are very often sterile.

Hybrid Vigour. The sturdiness often seen in a hybrid as the result of new genetic combinations.

Hydathode. Gland, found on the edges of many leaves, that secretes water especially when the atmosphere is too humid to allow much transpiration.

Hydrophyte. Plant normally growing in water or damp places.

Hydroponics. The science of growing plants in nutrient solutions without soil.

Plate 59

LEGUMINOSAE (Cont)

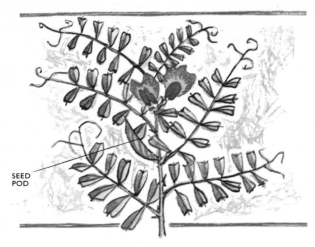

SEED
POD

The common vetch showing the typical pea-shaped flowers and the tendrils formed from the terminal leaflets.

LICHEN

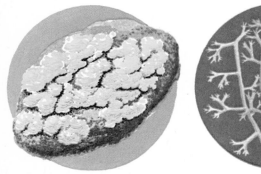

A SPECIES OF *CANDELARIELLA*
(A CRUSTOSE LICHEN)

CLADONIA IMPEXA
(A FRUTICOSE LICHEN)

Plate 60

LICHEN (Cont)

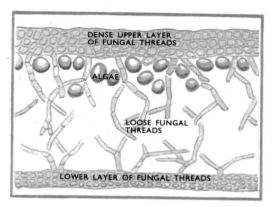

Section of a lichen showing the algae among the fungal threads. In some species the algae are more scattered.

CLADONIA COCCIFERA
WITH RED SPORE CUPS

A SPECIES OF *PELTIGERA*
(A FOLIOSE LICHEN)

Hydrosere. An example of plant succession (q.v.) starting in water. (See Plate 104).

Hydrotropism. Bending movement or tropism (q.v.) in which the stimulus for movement is water.

Hymenium. Layer of spore-bearing tissue in many of the higher fungi, e.g. toadstools. (See Plate 65).

Hyperplasia. Increase in size due to increase in the number of cells. Occurs in the formation of some galls in response to parasitic infection.

Hypertrophy. Increase in size due to increase in size of cells but not increase in number.

Hypha. The filament or thread of a fungus.

Hypocotyl. The region of a seedling shoot below the cotyledons. Also used to describe the part of a mature plant where the stem merges with the root. This part, of course, develops from the seedling hypocotyl.

Hypodermis. Layer of cells just under the epidermis of certain leaves (q.v.).

Hypogeal. Hypogeal germination is the condition in which the seed leaves or cotyledons do not come above ground as the seed germinates. (See *Epigeal*) and (Plate 47).

Hypogynous. Having the petals inserted below the carpels. (See *Flower*).

Hyponasty. The upward curving of a plant organ through increased growth on the lower side.

Hypotonic. (See *Osmosis*).

Imbricate. Overlapping — e.g. petals in a flower.

Immunity. The ability to resist attack by or the effect of a parasite.

Incompatibility. Inability to function together. The term may be applied to

the stock and scion of a graft (See *Propagation*), to a pollen grain and stigma if the pollen is unable to develop on that stigma (See *Pollination*), and to many other phenomena.

Indehiscent. Not splitting. (See *Fruit*).

Independent Assortment. (See *Heredity*).

Indigenous. Native to a given area — not introduced.

Indusium. Flap of tissue protecting the sporangia on the underside of fern fronds. (See Plate 31).

Inferior Ovary. Ovary or gynaecium that is below the insertion of the petals.

Inflorescence. Flowers are sometimes borne singly on a stem (e.g. tulip) but more frequently they occur in heads called inflorescences, of which there are two basic patterns. In the racemose pattern the main growing point of the stem goes on growing, or at least does not end in a flower. The flowers are produced laterally and if they are stalked (e.g. bluebell) the inflorescence is called a *raceme*. If the flowers are sessile on the main axis the inflorescence is called a *spike*. A branched raceme is called a *panicle*. An *umbel* is a special raceme in which the main axis stops growing after a time and all the flower stalks develop at one level. A *corymb* is superficially similar to an umbel but it is a raceme in which all the flowers reach one level because of differential growth of their stalks.

The cymose pattern differs in that the main stem does end in a flower after branching. A *dichasium* is a cyme which gives off two branches before flowering. The branches do the same (e.g. stitchwort). A *monochasium* or monochasial cyme is one which gives off only one branch before flowering.

Flowers of the family Compositae are very specialised. The dandelion 'flower' is really a collection of tiny flowers (florets) on a flat disc or *capitulum*. Each floret contains sex

INFLORESCENCE

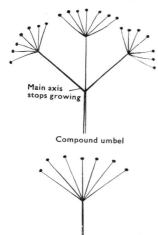

Main axis stops growing

Compound umbel

Simple umbel

All the flower stalks in an umbel come from the same level. Simple umbels are rare: most umbels are compound.

organs and is a true flower. The calyx is represented by fine hairs which develop later and carry away the fruit. Each dandelion floret has a flat blade or *ligule* but thistles have only tubular florets. Daisies have both types — the outer florets have coloured ligules while the inner ones are tubular and produce pollen and nectar. (See *Flower; Floret* and Plates 48 and 49).

Insectivorous Plant. One that supplements its nitrogen supply by digesting small insects that become trapped on its leaves. Examples include the sundew, Venus fly trap, and the various pitcher plants. (See Plates 50, 51, and 110).

Integument. Covering of the ovule (q.v.). Becomes the seed coat. (See Plate 29).

Inter-. Between.

Intercalary Meristem. A group of growing cells that is situated not at the tip of an organ but somewhere along its length, for example at a node. The easy way in which horsetail stems break is due to a layer of unstrengthened intercalary meristem at each node.

Interfascicular Cambium. Cambium that develops from parenchyma cells between the vascular bundles of a stem at the start of secondary thickening (q.v.).

Internode. Region between nodes or joints on a stem (q.v.). (See Plate 101).

Introrse. (Of anthers) Shedding pollen towards the centre of the flower.

Intra-. Within.

Inulin. A polysaccharide food storage material built up of groups of fructose molecules.

Invertase. Enzyme splitting sucrose molecule into fructose and glucose.

Involucre. A protective flap covering the archegonia of liverworts (See *Hepaticae*). Also the group of bracts protecting the developing composite flower.

Iridaceae. Family of flowering plants belonging to the order Liliiflorae and containing the irises, crocuses, and gladioli. They are perennial herbs with corms, bulbs, or rhizomes. The leaves are not divided into blade and petiole. The perianth is formed of two petaloid whorls. There are three stamens and the ovary develops into a capsule. (See Plate 126).

Irregular. (See *Zygomorphic*).

Irritability. A property of all living things — the ability to react to changes in the surroundings.

Isobilateral Leaf. One that is the same on both sides — eg. the vertical leaf of irises and certain other plants. Most leaves are dorsiventral (q.v.)

Plate 61

MENDELISM (=HEREDITY)

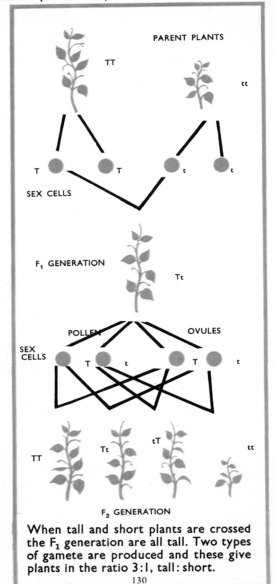

PARENT PLANTS

TT

tt

T T t t

SEX CELLS

F₁ GENERATION

Tt

POLLEN   OVULES

SEX
CELLS   T   t   T   t

TT   Tt   tT   tt

F₂ GENERATION

When tall and short plants are crossed
the F₁ generation are all tall. Two types
of gamete are produced and these give
plants in the ratio 3:1, tall: short.

MERISTEM

Diagrammatic shoot tip showing the apical meristem or growing point.

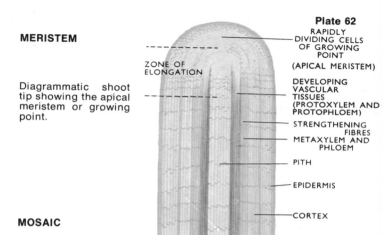

Plate 62
RAPIDLY DIVIDING CELLS OF GROWING POINT (APICAL MERISTEM)

ZONE OF ELONGATION

DEVELOPING VASCULAR TISSUES (PROTOXYLEM AND PROTOPHLOEM)

STRENGTHENING FIBRES

METAXYLEM AND PHLOEM

PITH

EPIDERMIS

CORTEX

MOSAIC

Tobacco leaves affected with tobacco mosaic virus. Many viruses produce these blotched effects on leaves and are thus called mosaic viruses.

Isogamy. The fusion of gametes that are physically alike. This phenomenon is found in some lower plants but is not common.

Isomerous. (Of a flower) Having equal numbers of parts — petals, sepals, etc.

Isotonic. (See *Osmosis*).

Juncaceae. Family of monocotyledons belonging to the order Liliiflorae. This family contains the rushes — perennial herbs with long, narrow leaves often mistaken for grasses. The flowers have a perianth but are usually small and greenish brown — another feature causing the rushes to be mistaken for grasses, although they are not arranged

in spikelets. The flowers are normally arranged in closely bunched cymose inflorescences. (See Plate 126).

Jurassic Period. Division of the geological time scale (q.v.).

Keel. Boat-shaped lower petal or petals of pea-flowers and certain others. (See Plate 118).

Labiatae. Family of dicotyledons belonging to the order Tubiflorae (q.v.). Most are herbs and typically have a square stem with opposite decussate leaves. The corolla is tubular and zygomorphic. The flowers are normally arranged in groups very close to the stem and they give the impression

LABIATAE

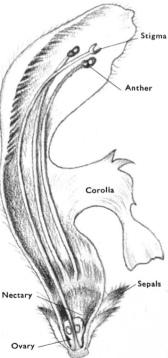

Floral diagram and half flower of white deadnettle *(Lamium)*.

of being whorled around the stem. These features make the family easily recognisable. Many of the members are characterised by particular aromatic oils. Mint, lavender, thyme, bugle, and dead nettle are examples of the family. (See Plate 128).

Lamarckism. An evolutionary theory, (now disproved) put forward by the French scientist Lamarck (1744–1829). According to this theory, characters that are acquired during an individual life-time are inherited. It was extremely difficult for biologists to accept this for the sex-organs in which the gametes form are quite unaffected by most physical changes in the rest of the organism. Weissman dealt Lamarckism a crushing blow by cutting the tails of generation after generation of mice without once obtaining a tail-less individual in a litter.

Lamella. A thin plate, e.g. the gill of a toadstool. (See *Fungi*).

Lamina. The blade of a leaf.

Lanceolate. (Of a leaf). Elongated like a willow leaf but not *linear* as a grass leaf. (See Page 136).

Latex. A thick white fluid that exudes from cut surfaces of certain plants—rubber, dandelion, spurge, and others—and rapidly coagulates. It is contained in special branching tubes and is believed to be a reservoir for unwanted material, although proteins and other food materials are often found in it. The latex of several plants is economically important.

Layering. (See *Propagation*).

Leaf. Leaves are the plant's 'food factories' in which the vital process of photosynthesis is carried out. A typical leaf consists of a stalk called the *petiole* and a flat blade called the *lamina*. If there is no stalk the leaf is said to be *sessile*. Leaves arise from the nodes of the stem and are arranged in such a way that no leaf is completely over-

shadowed by another on the same stem. They thus intercept the maximum amount of light. The angle between the leaf and the stem is called the *axil* and it normally contains a bud. The attachment to the stem varies considerably among species and the leaf base may even surround the stem. Leaves that arise in a group from a short underground stem as in the dandelion are called radical leaves.

The first leaves of a young seed plant are the cotyledons or seed leaves of which there are one (monocotyledon) or two (dicotyledon). They are usually different from ordinary leaves and do not always come above ground when the seed germinates.

The veins that run across the leaf are the vascular strands carrying water and food materials. In dicotyledonous plants they form a network but in most monocotyledonous plants they run parallel to each other. Monocotyledonous leaves are usually long and fairly narrow—grasses, irises, etc. The leaf shapes of dicotyledonous plants vary enormously according to the arrangement of the veins and the development of the lamina between them. If the margin of the leaf is smooth the leaf is said to be *entire* but more frequently the edge will be saw-edged (*serrate*) or toothed (*dentate*) to some extent—the lamina does not develop completely between the major veins or branches. This condition reaches its peak in *compound leaves* where each major vein has its own separate lamina or leaflet. If there is one primary vein—a continuation of the petiole—the compound leaf is *pinnate* as in the rose leaf. When there are several primary veins each with a leaflet, as in the horse chestnut, the leaf is *palmate*. There are a great many variations in shape, many with special names. (See Page 136).

At the base of the petiole there are often outgrowths called *stipules*. These may be green and leaf-like or they may be tiny scales, or even spines.

Internally, the petiole is like a small stem, with vascular and strengthening tissues. The lamina of the leaf is

Plate 63

E

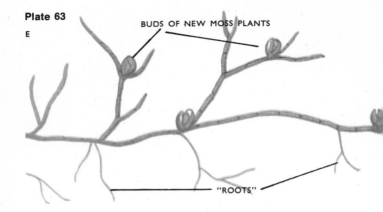

BUDS OF NEW MOSS PLANTS

"ROOTS"

The actual moss plant is the gametophyte generation. It bears sex organs (A) which produce the sex-cells. Male cells are released and they enter the female archegonia, fusing with the female cells to form zygotes. Each zygote develops into a capsule (B) which is the sporophyte generation and which grows up on a stalk (C). Spores develop inside the capsule and when they are ripe the lid of the capsule falls to reveal numerous teeth (D) which bend and release the spores. Each spore grows into a branched thread or *protonema* (E) from which many tiny moss plants grow.

MUSCI

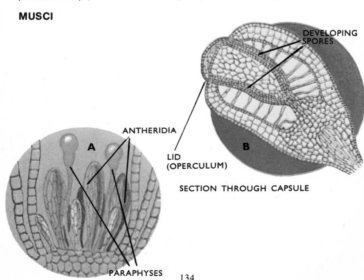

DEVELOPING SPORES

ANTHERIDIA

LID (OPERCULUM)

SECTION THROUGH CAPSULE

PARAPHYSES

134

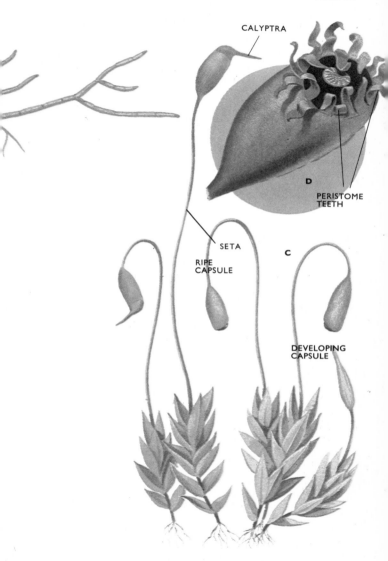

Plate 64

CALYPTRA

PERISTOME
TEETH

D

SETA

RIPE
CAPSULE

C

DEVELOPING
CAPSULE

135

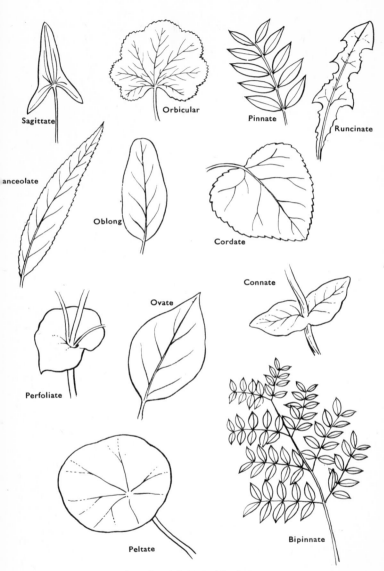

A variety of named leaf shapes.

covered with a waxy, non-cellular cuticle which is normally thicker on the upper surface than on the lower. The epidermis may be hairy or glabrous. Scattered all over the under-surface and appearing occasionally on the upper surface are tiny pores called *stomata* (singular: *stoma*), through which water vapour, oxygen, and carbon dioxide pass. The stomata are bounded by special guard cells which are sensitive to the humidity of the air and control the opening of the stomata and hence the loss of water from the leaf (See *Transpiration*). Beneath the upper epidermis is the *palisade layer* of rectangular cells containing many chloroplasts in which photosynthesis takes place. The *spongy tissue* under-neath the palisade layer contains irregular cells and many air spaces which connect with the stomata. The xylem of the veins is on top of the phloem and there is usually some strengthening tissue on each side of the veins. The xylem vessels open into the spongy tissue and release water. Leaves that stand erect (e.g. iris) usually have palisade layers on both sides of the spongy tissue and stomata are equally distributed on both sides. Such leaves are said to be *isobilateral*.

Leaves are periodically replaced in all plants—even in evergreens and tropical trees, but in these cases the leaves are not all shed at once. Only the deciduous trees lose all their leaves at one time. When a leaf is to be replaced an *abcission layer* (q.v.) forms at the base of the petiole and the cells other than the vascular strands break down. The vascular strands snap when disturbed by wind, etc. and the leaf falls, leaving a scar on the stem. Leaf fall is thus a living process in-volving the formation of special tissues: dead branches do not shed their leaves. The rich colours assumed by many leaves before they fall are associated with chemical changes accompanying the removal of food material from the leaves.

Leaves are often modified and perform special functions. Many plants that live in regions of irregular rainfall have thick fleshy leaves that act as water stores. Bulbs are composed of special leaves full of food reserves. Tendrils may be modified leaves—those of the sweet pea are the modified terminal leaflets. The pitchers of various insect-eating plants are well-known leaf modifications. (Plates 50, 51, and 101). Many spines, bud-scales, and even petals are all modified leaves. Occasionally leaves are completely absent, in which cases the stem takes over the photosynthetic activity. In the grass pea the petioles become ex-panded and look and act like leaves. (See Plates 52–56, 103, and 105).

Leaf Fall. (See *Leaf; Abcission Layer*).

Leaf Scar. Scar left on a stem when a leaf falls (See Plate 101).

Leaf Sheath. The modified base of a leaf that wraps around the stem in grasses and some other mono-cotyledons.

Leaf Trace. The strand of conducting tissue running to a leaf from the vascular cylinder.

Legume. Fruit (q.v.) of members of the Leguminoseae. Also applied (especially in agricultural circles) to a plant of this family. (See Plates 57–59).

Leguminosae. Family containing peas, beans, clovers, vetches, and many other plants with characteristic-shaped flowers. The fruit is always a pod or legume that opens by splitting along both sides. (See Plates 57–59 and 118 and 128).

Lemma. Small bract which, with a *palea*, encloses individual grass flower within a spikelet. (See *Gramineae*) and (Plate 43).

Lenticel. Small pore in the bark of woody stems, allowing gaseous inter-change. (See *Bark; Cork*) and (Plate 5).

Leucoplast. Colourless plastid con-cerned with starch storage.

137

Plate 65

MUSHROOM

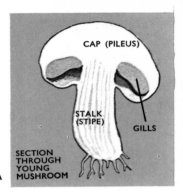

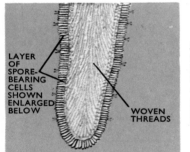

LAYER OF SPORE-BEARING CELLS SHOWN ENLARGED BELOW

WOVEN THREADS

SECTION OF A GILL

B

The life cycle of the common mushroom. The gills (A) underneath the cap are covered by a layer of spore-bearing cells (B and C). Spores are shed and they grow into hyphae which join in pairs (D) and produce new fruiting bodies (E and F).

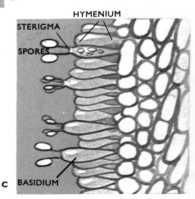

138

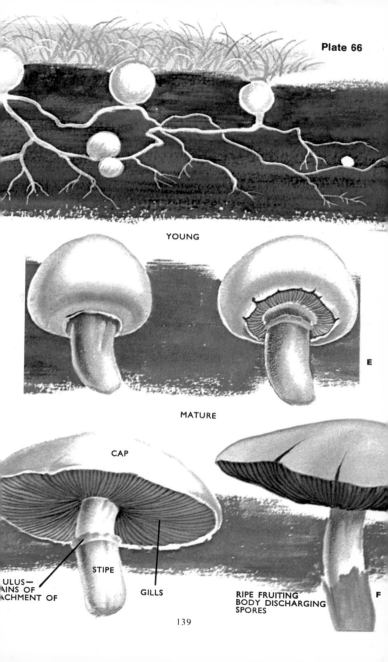

Plate 66

YOUNG

E

MATURE

CAP

ULUS—
AINS OF
ACHMENT OF

STIPE

GILLS

RIPE FRUITING
BODY DISCHARGING
SPORES

F

139

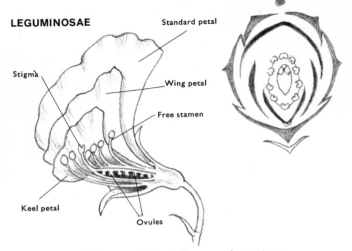

LEGUMINOSAE

- Standard petal
- Stigma
- Wing petal
- Free stamen
- Keel petal
- Ovules

Half flower and floral diagram of sweet pea.

Lianes. Tropical climbing plants with thin woody stems that twine around the other vegetation.

Lichens. Extremely common plants which are in fact symbiotic associations between certain fungi and algae. The dual nature of lichens was first realised in 1867 by a Swiss naturalist called Schwendener. The fungus is usually an ascomycete while the alga is a green or blue-green species. Although the algae concerned often live alone, the fungi have never been found growing separately. The fungus is the major partner in a lichen and its interwoven threads control the form of the plant. This may be encrusting (*crustose*), leaf-like (*foliose*), or branched (*fruticose*). The algae may be scattered throughout the lichen or restricted to certain zones. In either case they are in close contact with the fungal threads which absorb moisture from the air. The fungal hyphae also release acids that attack the rock or soil on which the lichen grows and provide nutrient salts. The algae manufacture organic food from the water,
carbon dioxide, and mineral salts. Some of this food is taken by the fungus 'in return for' the shelter it affords the algae.

Lichens grow extremely slowly and can be found in many harsh conditions – hot deserts, tundra regions, and bare rock faces, including old buildings. They can withstand greater changes of temperature and humidity than any other form of life. Their main enemy appears to be air-pollution for they are far less common in built-up areas.

Reproduction is effected in two ways. Tiny structures called *soredia* form on the surface. They consist of a few fungal hyphae wrapped round a few algal cells and they are carried away by wind to a new area. The fungus partner also releases spores – formed in brightly coloured cups on the surface. There is no alga in the spores and it is believed that the two partners join up later, although attempts to 'make' lichens in the laboratory have failed. It may be that the alternate drying and wetting, heating and cooling, of the natural habitat are needed to initiate the formation of the lichen.

LILIIFLORAE

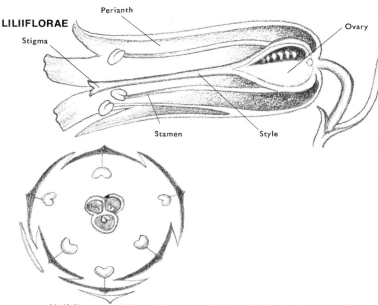

Half flower and floral diagram of bluebell *(Endymion)*.

Lichens play an important part in the first colonisation of rock faces and the formation of soil. They are also important food plants in the tundra regions—the so-called 'reindeer moss' is a lichen of the genus *Cladonia*. (See *Symbiosis* and Plates 59 and 60).

Life Cycle. The series of changes undergone by an organism or series of organisms in the cycle from seed to seed or from sexually mature individual to sexually mature individual in the next generation. As plants exhibit an *alternation of generations* (q.v.) the life cycle includes two distinct plants in many cases. (See Plate 33 and Page 16).

Lignin. A complicated mixture of carbohydrates and other substances that is deposited in the cell-walls of xylem and sclerenchyma tissues, giving them strength and rigidity. A mature tree may be 30% lignin.

Ligule. 'Collar' at base of grass leaf where it joins leaf sheath. Also the strap-shaped projection of the florets of many composite flowers. (See Plates 34 and 43).

Liliaceae. Large family of monocotyledons whose flowers are normally made up of two petaloid whorls, each whorl of three segments, and regularly arranged. The stamens are also in two whorls, opposite the perianth segments to which they may be attached. The flower is hypogynous and the fruit—usually a capsule or berry—contains many seeds. Examples include lily of the valley, asparagus, Solomon's seal, fritillary, tulip, bluebell (English), onion, and the vast numbers of cultivated lilies. (See *Liliiflorae*).

Liliiflorae. Order of monocotyledons including tulips, lilies, daffodils, irises, and rushes. Most are herbs with bulbs,

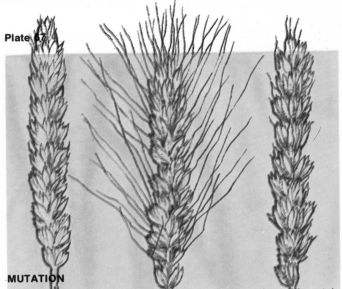

Plate 67

MUTATION

Mutations can be induced by treatment of an organism with certain chemicals or radiation. These wheat varieties were all produced by artificial mutation.

NUCLEIC ACID

Model of part of a DNA molecule showing the extremely complicated structure.

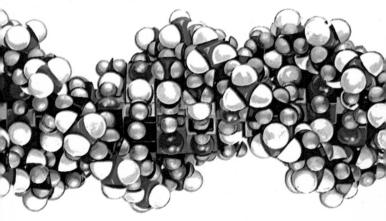

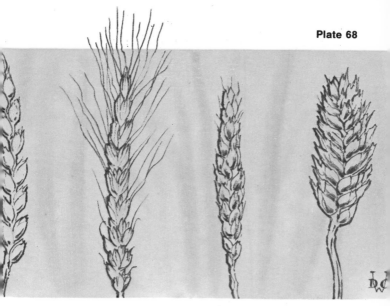

Plate 68

NUCLEIC ACID (Cont)

An electron micrograph of strands of DNA.

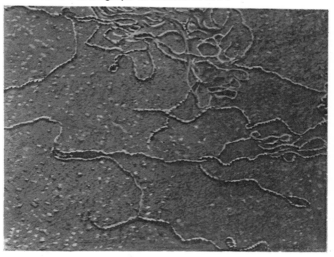

143

corms, or rhizomes. The perianth is of two whorls which are usually both petaloid. It is rare for the two whorls to be unalike. The leaves are normally upright and linear. (See *Amaryllidaceae; Liliaceae; Iridaceae; Juncaceae*) and (Plate 126).

Linear. (Of a leaf). Long and narrow, as a grass leaf.

Linkage. The association of *genes* (q.v.) on one chromosome so that the features they produce in the organism will tend to appear together. This is because complete chromosomes are normally passed on to the next generation and, if one gene goes, so will those linked to it. (See *Heredity*).

Littoral. Inhabiting the region of the sea-shore and shallows.

Liverwort. (See *Hepaticae*).

Locus. The position of a given gene (q.v.) on a certain chromosome.

Lodicules. Tiny structures in grass flowers representing the perianth. (See *Gramineae*) and (Plate 43).

Lomentum. A type of fruit (q.v.).

Lower Plants. Rather vague term embracing all plants other than those that bear seeds, although ferns are sometimes excepted too.

Lumen. The cavity of a cell or vessel.

Lycopodiales. Division of Pteridophyta, represented now by small clubmosses and related plants, but also including huge extinct trees such as *Lepidodendron* of Carboniferous times. (See Page 256) and (Plate 124).

Lysigenous Cavity. Cavity formed by disintegration of a cell and normally containing secretions produced by that cell before its disintegration. The oil glands in the leaves of citrus trees are of this type.

Maltose. A disaccharide sugar formed

during the breakdown of starch, especially during the germination of seeds.

Marsh. A region of wet ground supporting typical vegetation such as marsh-marigold, rushes, and water mint. The soil is of mineral matter and, unlike a fen or bog, there is no accumulation of peat.

Medullary Ray. Plates of parenchyma tissue running vertically between vascular bundles or between patches of secondary vascular tissue. (See *Stem*) and (Plate 99).

Megasporangium. (See *Sporangium: Spore*).

Megaspore. (See *Spore*).

Megasporophyll. (See Sporophyll).

Meiosis. A type of nuclear division during which the number of chromosomes per nucleus is halved. This division occurs at some time during the life cycle of any organism that reproduces sexually, normally during the formation of sex-cells. Without meiosis, the number of chromosomes in a cell would double with each new generation, giving rise to an impossible state of affairs. In meiosis the pairs of *homologous chromosomes* (q.v.) come together. They then separate, one of each pair going to each end of the cell. A new nuclear membrane forms around the chromosomes and the cell divides into two. The two new cells then divide again but this time the chromosomes themselves divide into two identical halves so that the number is not reduced further in the four new cells. Thus, one original cell gives rise to four sex-cells. (See *Mitosis; Gene; Chromosome; Heredity*).

Mendelism. (See *Heredity*).

Meristem. A region of active cell division. The new cells give rise to the permanent tissues — parenchyma, xylem, etc. Primary meristems are those

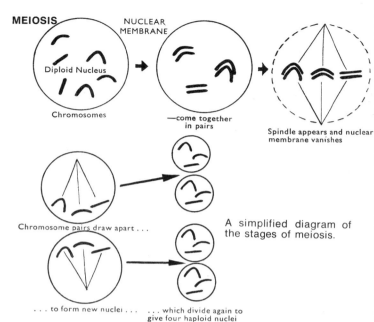

MEIOSIS

NUCLEAR MEMBRANE

Diploid Nucleus

Chromosomes

—come together in pairs

Spindle appears and nuclear membrane vanishes

Chromosome pairs draw apart . . .

A simplified diagram of the stages of meiosis.

. . . to form new nuclei . . .   . . . which divide again to give four haploid nuclei

that have existed since the origin of the plant—e.g. the meristems of the growing points and of the cambium in the vascular bundles. Secondary meristems develop from parenchyma tissues, e.g. at the start of secondary thickening (q.v.), in the formation of bark, or in response to wounding.

Mesophyll. Internal tissue of a leaf (q.v.).

Mesophyte. Any plant that grows in average conditions—i.e. not a hydrophyte or a xerophyte.

Mesozoic. Era of geological time. (See *Geological Time Scale*).

Metabolism. The sum total of processes—respiration, photosynthesis, etc.—that go on in an organism.

Metachlamydeae. (= *Sympetalae*).

Division of dicotyledons in which the petals, if present are normally united into a tube. (See *Archichlamydeae* and *Angiospermae*).

Metaphase. A stage in nuclear division. (See *Meiosis; Mitosis*).

Metaxylem. (See *Xylem*).

Micell. Tiny elongated particle, somewhat crystalline and found in many structural materials such as cellulose. Made up of bundles of long molecules.

Micro-. Minute.

Microbe. Term used to refer to a microscopic organism—especially one that causes disease (germ).

Micron. One thousandth of a millimeter—written **μ**.

Plate 69

OSMOSIS

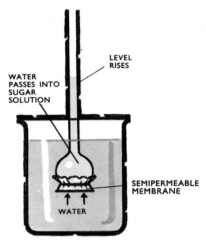

When a concentrated solution is separated from a more dilute one by a semi-permeable membrane water molecules pass into the concentrated solution and tend to even out the difference in concentration between the two sides of the membrane. This process is called osmosis.

PARASITE

Fungi are the most important plant parasites and cause many diseases such as apple scab and potato blight shown here. (See also Plate 15.)

Plate 70

PARASITE (Cont)

The mistletoe is a partial parasite on apple and otner trees from
which it obtains water and minerals by tapping the xylem with
its suckers.

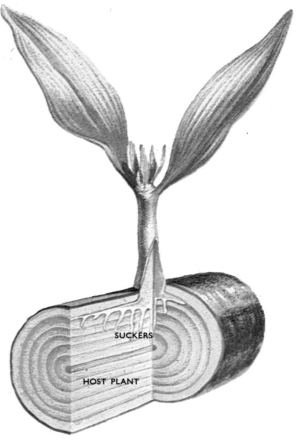

SUCKERS

HOST PLANT

Micro-organism. Any tiny organism, e.g. bacteria, that can be seen only with a microscope.

Micropyle. Tiny opening in the *ovule* (q.v.) through which the pollen tube enters prior to fertilisation. (See Plate 29).

Microsome. Microscopic particle of which there are thousands in the protoplasm of each cell. They are probably concerned with enzymatic action.

Microspermae. (See *Orchidaceae*).

Microsporangium. Structure in which microspores are formed. (See *Spore*).

Microspore. (See *Spore*).

Microsporophyll. (See *Spore; Sporophyll*).

Mildew. Term often used to refer to any fungal growth that covers its substrate with fine hyphae. More strictly, however, mildews are certain types of ascomycete fungi that are parasitic on the leaves of higher plants. (See *Fungi*).

Miocene. Division of the Tertiary Period. (See *Geological Time Scale*).

Mitochondria. Tiny particles in cells (q.v.), that appear to be concerned with cell respiration.

Mitosis. Nuclear division chief feature of which is that the new nuclei receive identical chromosomes and genes to those of the parent cell. This is the normal process of division that take place every time new cells are formed in an organism. Before the nucleus begins to divide the chromosomes duplicate themselves exactly, forming pairs of *chromatids,* and then during the dividing process one of each pair of chromatids goes to each new nucleus. After the nucleus has divided, the cell itself divides. (See *Gene; Chromosome; Heredity*).

Monadelphous. Monadelphous stamens

are those whose stalks are joined to form a tube, as in lupins.

Monocarpic. Having a single carpel.

Monochasium. A type of *inflorescence* (q.v.).

Monochlamydeous. With only one set of perianth segments — petals or sepals e.g. marsh marigold with petal-like sepals.

Monocotyledon. Widely used term denoting a member of the class Monocotyledoneae.

Monocotyledoneae. One of the two classes of flowering plants. The main feature distinguishing this class from the Dicotyledoneae is the presence of only a single seed leaf (cotyledon) in the seed. The veins of the leaves tend to run parallel to each other and the floral parts are normally arranged in threes (dicotyledonous flowers are arranged in fours or fives). Grasses and sedges, lilies, daffodils, and orchids are among the important monocotyledonous plants.

Monoecious. Having separate male and female flowers, but both on the same plant. (See *Dioecious*).

Monokaryon. A fungal hypha whose cells each contain one nucleus. (See *Dikaryon*).

Monopodial Branching. A form of branching in which the main axis of the plant goes on growing and never ends in a flower. In sympodial branching the main axis does not go on growing — it dies away or ends in a flower and growth is continued by side shoots. (See *Inflorescence)* and (page 152).

Monosaccharide. A type of sugar — such as glucose or fructose — whose molecule cannot be split into other smaller sugar molecules. (See *Disaccharide; Polysaccharide*).

Moor. A region or community dominated by heather and other acid-loving

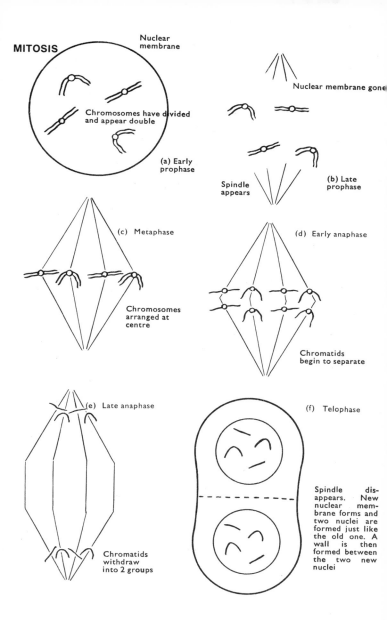

A simplified diagram of the stages of mitosis in a plant cell.

Plate 71

PARASITE (Cont)

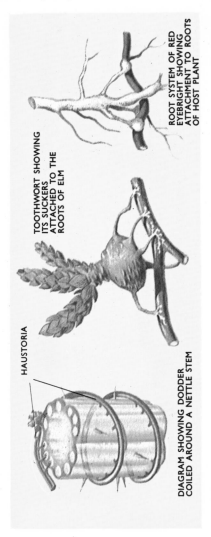

ROOT SYSTEM OF RED EYEBRIGHT SHOWING ATTACHMENT TO ROOTS OF HOST PLANT

TOOTHWORT SHOWING ITS SUCKERS ATTACHED TO THE ROOTS OF ELM

HAUSTORIA

DIAGRAM SHOWING DODDER COILED AROUND A NETTLE STEM

There are many degrees of parasitism. The dodder (left) is a complete parasite, obtaining all of its food from the host plant by putting suckers into the stem. The toothwort (centre) is also a complete parasite whose roots penetrate the roots of various trees to obtain food. The eyebright (right), however, has chlorophyll of its own and obtains only water and dissolved salts from the roots of the host plant. It makes its own organic food and is thus only a partial parasite.

Plate 72

PEAT

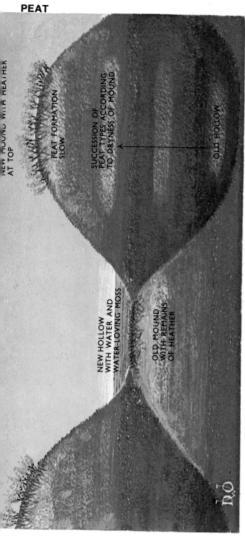

NEW MOUND WITH HEATHER AT TOP

PEAT FORMATION SLOW

SUCCESSION OF PEAT TYPES ACCORDING TO DRYNESS OF MOUND

OLD HOLLOW

NEW HOLLOW WITH WATER AND WATER-LOVING MOSS

OLD MOUND WITH REMAINS OF HEATHER

Peat bogs are typically covered with mounds, and mounds become hollows and *vice versa* many times over in the course of time. The diagram is an attempt to show how this happens. Clumps of peat-forming moss grow up and get drier as they get higher. Moss gives way to heather and other slow-growing plants at the top and in the meantime new moss begins to grow in the newly-formed hollows. Because the moss carries its water supply up with it for some way, these new moss clumps grow up above the old heather-topped mounds which thus become damp hollows again and the cycle restarts.

151

MONOPODIAL BRANCHING

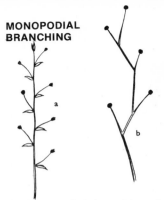

a) Monopodial branching, in which the main axis goes on growing and flowers are produced on side shoots. In sympodial branching the main axis ends in a flower and growth is continued by one side branch b) or by two side branches c). The process is then repeated.

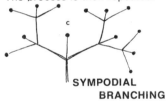

SYMPODIAL BRANCHING

plants growing on damp or dry peat. Many regions of upland Britain, once covered by blanket bog, are now covered by moors since erosion of the peat has allowed it to dry out too much for the continuance of bog vegetation. Moors are always acidic in character. (See *Bog; Peat*).

Mor. An infertile soil containing much acid, unrotted plant remains — characteristic of sandy heaths. (See *Mull*).

Morphology. The study of external form.

Mosaic. One of a number of important plant diseases caused by virus infection. (See *Virus*) and (Plate 62).

Moss. (See *Musci*).

Mould. Name given to many fungi that cover their substrates with hyphae and fruiting bodies — e.g. *Mucor* and *Penicillium*. (See *Fungi*).

Mucor. A very common phycomycete fungus that grows on a variety of decaying organic material — fruit, bread, etc. The tiny black sporangia standing up above the white mycelia have given it the name of 'pin-mould'. (See *Fungi*) and (Plate 39).

Mull. A rich soil with plenty of well rotted vegetable matter — e.g. woodland soil. (See *Mor*).

Multicostate. (Of leaves) Having several main veins — e.g. ivy, and most monocotyledons. (See Plate 52).

Multilocular. (Of an ovary) Having several separate seed-containing cavities.

Musci. Mosses — a class of green plants which, together with the liverworts, makes up the Bryophyta. The moss plant is the haploid or gametophyte generation of the life cycle and it carries the sex organs. There are distinct leaves and stems. The leaves are only one cell thick except in the centre and they contain many chloroplasts. The outer region of the stem is also green. In the centre of the stem there are longer, water-conducting cells and from the base of the stem a number of rhizoids develop.

Sex-organs arise at the tips of the stems and are surrounded by leaves. Male organs *(antheridia)* are club-shaped while the female *archegonia* are flask-shaped. Male cells are released in damp conditions and are attracted by the mucus exuded by the archegonia. The female cells are fertilised and the resulting embryos begin to grow. The lower part (the foot) embeds in the tissue of the moss and the upper part grows up and swells at the tip. This swelling develops into the spore-chamber or capsule which is green and can photosynthesise. This

152

capsule and its stalk—in fact everything that develops from the embryo—is the sporophyte generation of the plant and is really quite a separate part from the rest of the plant. It needs water and salts from the haploid moss plant but is less dependent on it than the liverwort sporophyte generation is dependent on the thallus. Capsules are found at all stages of development throughout the summer.

The moss capsule is far more complicated than that of the liverwort. There is a central column of cells surrounded by the spore tissue. Outside this is another layer of cells and then an air space, the whole structure being surrounded by a thick epidermis and covered by an operculum or lid. Spores develop after meiosis so that they have only one set of chromosomes. When the spores are ripe the cells of the capsule shrivel and the operculum falls away revealing a series of radiating teeth fixed at the edge of the capsule. These teeth are sensitive to moisture and in dry weather they curl up and expose the spores. Light air movements are sufficient to scatter the spores and when the air gets damp the teeth absorb water and close the capsule.

The spores can be carried long distances by the wind and then, when a spore falls on suitable ground, it puts out a tiny thread at each end. One thread develops into a fine root or rhizoid and the other, which is green, branches over the soil surface. It is called a *protonema*. From various points on this thread new moss plants arise and are thus clumped together in patches.

Mosses are widely distributed and there are a great many species. Most of them grow in damp places but the clumping habit enables some of them to conserve water and grow in very exposed places. (See *Alternation of Generations; Hepaticae; Peat*) and (Plates 63, 64, 74 and 123).

Mushroom. Common name given to members of the genus *Psalliota* of the fungus family Agaricaceae. Mushrooms do not differ much from other members of the family which are normally referred to as toadstools. The genus *Psalliota* is fairly typical of the whole family. The gills under the cap are covered with minute spores which fall when ripe and are scattered by the slightest breeze. They germinate in suitable damp soil to form slender hyphae. These join together in pairs and then multiply rapidly, becoming densely intertwined to produce new fruiting bodies (mushrooms). The cultivated mushroom is slightly different in that the cells have twice as many nuclei as the wild variety and the hyphae do not have to join before fruiting bodies can be formed. This is, of course, of great commercial value as a given quantity of spores can produce twice as many mushrooms. (See *Fungi*) and (Plates 65, 66 and 106).

Mutant. A gene or characteristic differing from the normal through having undergone *mutation* (q.v.)

Mutation. A sudden change in a gene or chromosome that leads to the appearance of new features in the organism possessing it. Because they are controlled by genes, these new features can be inherited. Most mutations are harmful and the organisms do not normally survive but some are useful and make the organism more successful. The organisms survive and these useful mutations will be passed on to succeeding generations. Harmful mutations will normally be lost as the organisms possessing them will fail to breed. (See *Natural Selection*).

Mycelium. Mass of tangled threads or hyphae of a fungus. (See *Fungi*).

Mycetozoa. (See *Myxomycetes*).

Mycology. The study of fungi.

Mycorrhiza. An association between a fungus and the roots of a higher plant. The majority of orchids have mycorrhizae and so do many heathland plants such as heathers and pine

Plate 73
PEAT (Cont)

Large tracts of north-west Europe are covered by peat but old tree-stumps in the peat show that the bogs have not always been there. There must have once been a drier climate (A) but as it grew wetter the trees died (B) without being replaced and blanket bog gradually developed (C).

Plate 74

PEAT (Cont)

(Top) Detail of bog surface with mounds of *Sphagnum*.

(Bottom) *Sphagnum* moss has large open cells which hold water and make the plant spongy to touch. The plant grows continuously upward but decay at the bottom balances the new growth and the living carpet is of constant thickness.

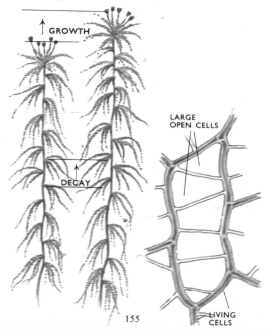

GROWTH

DECAY

LARGE
OPEN CELLS

LIVING
CELLS

155

trees. Endotrophic mycorrhizae are those in which the fungal threads actually penetrate the root cells – as in most orchids. Ectotrophic mycorrhizae, such as those of beech and pine roots, cover the fine branches of the roots and appear to replace the root hairs as organs of water absorption. Both fungus and higher plant benefit somewhat from the arrangement and, in fact, many higher plants are completely dependent on the fungi for proper growth. (See *Symbiosis*).

Mycotrophic. Having a mycorrhiza.

Myxomycetes. Group of strange, simple organisms known as slime fungi, although they are not closely related to true fungi. Indeed, zoologists often claim that the 'myxies' are animals. This is because part of the life cycle is spent in the form of a naked (without cell walls) mass of protoplasm called the plasmodium which creeps along by amoeboid movement and ingests particles of food. Spores are formed, however, in the manner of typical plants. Slime fungi abound in decaying tree-stumps and other rotting materials from which the plasmodium can be seen exuding at the appropriate time. Some attack living plants – the clubroot disease of cabbages is caused by a slime fungus of the genus *Plasmodiophora*. (See *Fungi*) and (Plate 121).

Myxophyceae (=Cyanophyceae). (See *Algae*).

Nastic Movement. A movement that is caused by a stimulus yet is independent of the direction of that stimulus. Examples are the opening and closing of flowers in response to changes in temperature and light intensity, and the familiar folding of *Mimosa* leaves when the plant is touched. (See *Tropism*).

Natural Selection. A naturally-occurring mechanism which Darwin suggested as the basis of evolution and which is now widely held to be so. Darwin's theory appeared in print in 1859 as the famous 'Origin of Species' although he had previously lectured on his findings and those of Wallace who arrived independently at a similar theory at about the same time. Darwin witnessed the 'struggle for existence' among living things. Most of them produce many offspring but only a few survive. The others succumb to predators and disease: in other words there is 'survival of the fittest'. Darwin also noticed that individuals of a species all vary slightly. Such variations make some individuals more suited to their surroundings than others. Those best suited are more likely to survive and to reproduce and therefore the favourable variations will be passed on to the next generation. In this way a species gradually changes and becomes ideally suited to its surroundings. The latter are always changing however and so natural selection works continuously to produce new forms and, eventually new species.

Although Darwin's theory showed clearly how natural variation could be the basis of evolutionary change, there was no explanation of how the variations occurred or how they were inherited. Later work on genetics, however, has shown how the natural variations can come about and also how sudden changes may lead to the appearance of new characteristics. (See *Heredity; Mutation*).

Nectar. A sweet, insect-attracting fluid produced by many flowering plants. Nectar is produced in nectaries which are placed in such a way that the insects have to brush against the stamens and stigmas in order to reach the nectar. The insects thus pollinate the flowers in the process. Sucrose is the commonest sugar in most nectars, followed by fructose and glucose. In the production of honey, bees remove most of the water from nectar and, by enzyme action, convert most of the sucrose into glucose, fructose and various more complex sugars.

Nitrification. A series of stages in the *nitrogen cycle* (q.v.) by which certain bacteria convert organic nitrogenous material into nitrates available for plant use.

Nitrogen Cycle. Nitrogen is one of the essential elements of life, being a major constituent of protein. In the form of nitrates, nitrogen is absorbed by plants and used to build up proteins. These are consumed by animals and converted to other proteins in the body. Upon the death of the organisms, the organic substances decay and bacteria convert the proteins back to nitrites and nitrates which can be used again by plants. This is the basis of the nitrogen cycle. A few bacteria, notably those forming nodules in the roots of leguminous plants, can convert free nitrogen into nitrates. Nitrates are also formed during thunderstorms: the energy of lightning causes oxygen and nitrogen to combine. The compound so formed dissolves in the rain water and falls to earth as a very dilute solution of nitric acid. This acts on minerals in the soil to form nitrates. But the formation of nitrates in this way is offset by the activity of certain bacteria that break down protein and release free nitrogen to the air. This is all part of the nitrogen cycle. (See Page 160).

Nitrogen Fixation. The conversion of atmospheric nitrogen into nitrates and organic nitrogen-containing compounds. Only certain bacteria can do this. Some of them live symbiotically in the roots of leguminous plants which thus benefit from the organic substances elaborated by the bacteria. (See *Nitrogen Cycle*).

Node. Region of a stem where leaves arise. Nodes are separated by internodes and are often swollen. (See Plate 101).

Nucellus. Nutritive tissue in *ovule* (q.v.)

Nucleic Acid. A complex compound made up of chains of chains of pentose sugar molecules linked to molecules of phosphate and nitrogen-containing molecules called bases. Nucleic acids occur in the chromosomes and in the cytoplasm of the cell. The genes are, in fact, chains of nucleic acid put together in various ways, and they control the features of the cells by controlling the types of protein that are made in the cells. (See Plates 67 and 68).

Nucleo-proteins. Important substances formed by the combination of nucleic acids and proteins.

Nucleus. The controlling body within the cell of an organism. The nucleus controls the activity of the cell by controlling the manufacture of protein within the cell. The nucleus is also the seat of reproduction and it contains the chromosomes (q.v.) which contain the 'instructions' needed to produce new cells just like the parent cells. (See *Cell*).

Nut. A type of *fruit* (q.v.) which usually contains only one seed and which has a hard woody outer wall that does not split open. The seed is not released until the fruit wall rots. The hazel nut is a typical example.

Nutation. The twisting growth exhibited by the tip of a stem or any other plant organ. A speeded-up film of the tip shows a continuous rotation as it grows. This is not to be confused with the twining behaviour of climbing plants.

Nyctinasty. The opening and closing of flowers and leaves in response to alternating day and night. (See *Nastic Movement*).

Oblong. A particular leaf shape. (See Page 136).

Oligocene. Division of the Tertiary Period. (See *Geological Time Scale*).

Onagraceae. Family of plants including the willowherbs, the evening primrose, and the woody *Fuchsia*.

Oogamy. The fertilisation of a relatively large immobile female cell — the oosphere — by a small, mobile male

Plate 75

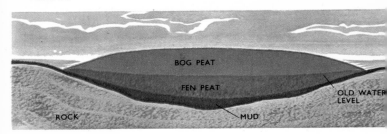

PEAT (Cont)

Raised bog (above) and blanket bog seen in section.

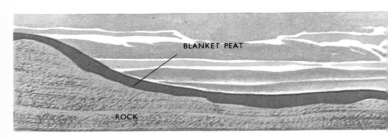

PHOTOSYNTHESIS

A diagram of a chloroplast summarising its role in photosynthesis.

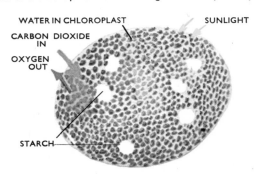

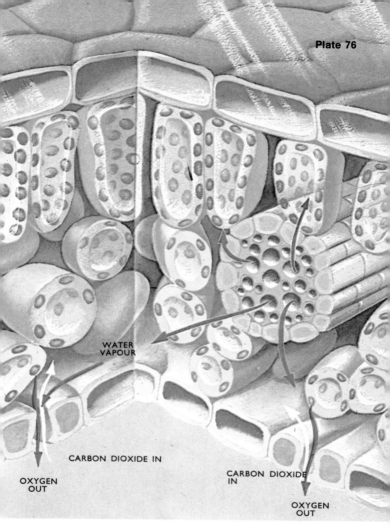

Plate 76

WATER
VAPOUR

CARBON DIOXIDE IN

CARBON DIOXIDE
IN

OXYGEN
OUT

OXYGEN
OUT

PHOTOSYNTHESIS (Cont)

Block diagram of part of a leaf showing the entry of carbon dioxide through the stomata and its passage into the leaf cells. Oxygen— produced during photosynthesis—also passes out through the stomata. Water (blue arrows) is shown passing from the xylem into the leaf cells and spaces. Some of it combines with carbon dioxide during photosynthesis but much of it evaporates away through the stomata. (See Transpiration.)

159

NITROGEN CYCLE

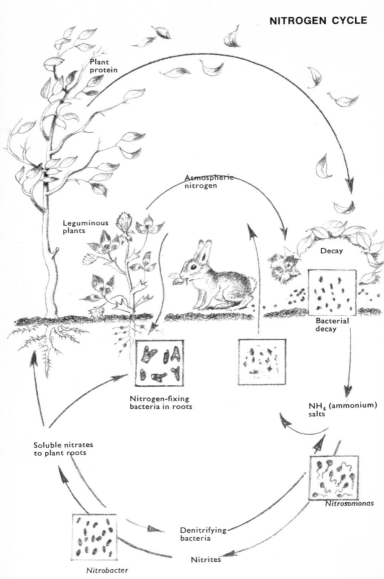

Plant protein

Atmospheric nitrogen

Leguminous plants

Decay

Bacterial decay

Nitrogen-fixing bacteria in roots

NH_4 (ammonium) salts

Soluble nitrates to plant roots

Nitrosomonas

Denitrifying bacteria

Nitrobacter

Nitrites

A simplified diagram of the nitrogen cycle.

gamete. It is a feature of many lower plants – algae and fungi. (See Plate 40).

Oogonium. Organ in which oospheres are formed.

Oosphere. Relatively large, non-mobile female gamete of many lower plants. (See *Oogamy*).

Oospore. Fertilised oosphere with a thick outer wall – a resting stage.

Operculum. A lid, such as covers moss capsules and fruits such as that of the poppy. (See Plates 35 and 63).

Orbicular. A particular leaf shape. (See Page 136).

Orchidaceae. Large, widespread family of monocotyledonous plants – orchids. The flowers are very irregular due to the suppression of some parts and the overgrowth of others. There are 6 perianth segments, often with a spur. There are elaborate mechanisms to ensure pollination by insects. The majority of orchids have mycorrhizal associations with fungi. Many are epiphytic – growing on the branches of tropical trees – and many more are saprophytes. Because of the very tiny seeds of orchids the group is sometimes called the Microspermae. (See Plate 78).

Order. A grouping used in classification (q.v.) containing one or more related families. Order names in botany frequently end in – ales.

Ordovician Period. Division of the *Geological Time Scale* (q.v.).

Organ. Any part of an organism that plays a certain role within that organism – e.g. a stamen.

Orthotropous. (See *Ovule*).

Osmosis. The phenomenon whereby, when a solution is separated from a weaker one by a semi-permeable membrane such as a piece of Cellophane, water (or other solvent) moves

through the membrane into the stronger solution in an effort to equalise the strengths of the two solutions. It would appear that the membrane allows solvent molecules to pass but not solute molecules – hence 'semi-permeable'. If a thistle funnel containing a strong sugar solution and covered with Cellophane is inverted in a beaker of water as shown on Plate 69 water will pass into the funnel and the solution will rise up the tube for some distance. The pressure needed at the top of the tube to stop the rise is equal to the osmotic pressure of the solution and is greater for more concentrated solutions. Cell-membranes are all more or less semi-permeable and so osmosis occurs widely in nature. It is responsible for the passage of water into and out of many tissues. A solution less strong than another – i.e. with a lower osmotic pressure is said to be *hypotonic*. *Hypertonic* solutions have higher osmotic pressures than a reference solution. Solutions which have equal osmotic pressures are said to be *isotonic*. (See Plate 69).

Ostiole. Tiny opening through which spores are released from the fruiting bodies of various fungi. (See Plate 122).

Ovary. The hollow region of a carpel or a number of joined carpels in which the ovules are found.

Ovate. A particular leaf shape. (See Page 136).

Ovule. Structure found only in flowering plants, conifers, and a few other strange plants, that contains the female sex-cell and that develops into a seed after fertilisation of the sex-cell. In flowering plants the ovule is protected within the carpel to which it is attached by a stalk – the *funicle*. In conifers and other gymnosperms the ovule lies naked on the scale of the cone. The typical flowering plant ovule has two coats or integuments surrounding a layer of nutritional tissue – the *nucellus*. Within this is the embryo-sac (equivalent to the megaspore of lower

Plate 77

MALE CONE

LAST YEAR'S FEMALE CONE

MATURE CONE

MICROPYLE

SCALE (SPOROPHYLL)

FEMALE CELLS

NUCELLUS

PROTHALLUS

OVULE

SCARS OF OLD SPURS

SPURS WITH NEEDLES

Pine shoot in spring: at the tips of the upper shoots are the young red female cones. The green cones were pollinated the previous year and now contain fertilised ovules. The brown cone is two years old and is now shedding seeds. (Inset) Section of an ovuliferous scale and mature ovule of female cone.

PINUS

162

POLLINIUM

The pollinia of an orchid and a diagram showing how they bend forward when attached to a bee and come to be in the right position to hit the stigma of the next orchid visited by the bee. In some orchids the pollinia actually attach themselves to the bee's tongue.

Plate 78

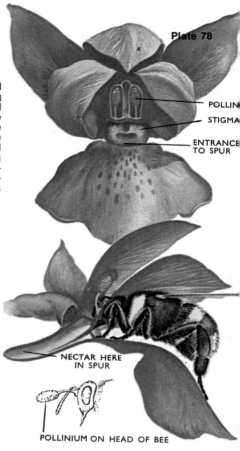

POLLIN

STIGMA

ENTRANCE TO SPUR

NECTAR HERE IN SPUR

POLLINIUM ON HEAD OF BEE

Various pollen grains showing the great variations in shape.

LBERRY

OAK

BIRCH

POLLEN

H

WILLOWHERB

PINE

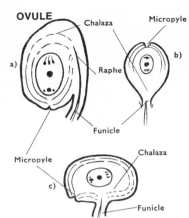

OVULE

The three main types of ovule:
a) anatropous; b) orthotropous;
c) campylotropous.

plants — see *Spore*) containing the female cell. The integuments are pierced at the tip by a tiny hole — the micropyle — through which the pollen tube enters prior to fertilisation.

Many ovules are arranged so that the micropyle is close to the funicle (*anatropous* condition) but in some plants the ovule is straight (*orthotropous* condition). In the anatropous condition the funicle is connected for most of its length with the integument, forming the *raphe*. The *chalaza* is that region of the ovule where the vascular strand of the funicle enters it. The *amphitropous* ovule is intermediate between the orthotropous and the anatropous types, there being a small amount of fusion of funicle and integument. The *campylotropous* ovule is twisted perpendicularly to the funicle but there is no fusion with the funicle. (See Plates 29 and 30).

Palaeo-. Ancient.

Palaeobotany. The study of fossil plants.

Palaeocene. Division of the Tertiary Period. (See *Geological Time Scale*).

Palaeontology. The study of fossils.

Palaeozoic. Era of geological time. (See Geological Time Scale).

Palea. One of the small bracts enclosing an individual grass flower. (See *Gramineae*) and (Plate 43).

Palmate. A palmate leaf is one with several lobes from a central point. e.g. horse-chestnut. (See Plate 52).

Palynology. Pollen analysis — the study of the associations of pollen grains in deposits of peat from which deductions can be made about the plants living when the peat was formed, and hence, the climate at the time.

Panicle. A type of *inflorescence* (q.v.) made up of a number of branched racemes.

Papaveraceae. Plant family containing poppies and their relatives. They are characterised by two sepals which fall off as the flowers open, and four petals. (See Plate 127)

Papilionaceae. Alternative name for *Leguminosae* (q.v.).

Papilionaceous. Having flowers like the pea-flower. Belonging to the family Papilionaceae (Leguminosae).

Pappus. Tuft of fine hairs that are attached to fruits of the Compositae family — dandelions, daisies, etc. It is formed from the calyx of each floret and aids distribution. (See Plates 34 and 35).

Paraphysis. Sterile hair-like process found in many lower plants, such as mosses, among the sex organs. (See Plate 63).

Parasite. An organism that lives *in close association* with another — often inside it — and takes food from it without giving anything in return. The organism that is attacked is called the host but it is not normally killed — at least not until the parasite has completed that part of its life cycle that takes place in the host.

Many fungi are parasites and cause serious diseases, both in other plants and in animals. (See Plates 14–16). A few flowering plants are parasitic – e.g. the dodder and the toothwort. The dodder entwines itself on clover and other plants and obtains all its food by penetrating the host tissues with special organs called *haustoria*. The dodder has no roots. The toothwort obtains its food by penetrating the roots of other plants – especially hazel trees.

A number of plants, although green and able to make food by photosynthesis, are partial parasites in that they obtain their water supplies, but not their whole food, from other plants, The eyebright and the mistletoe are examples. (See Plates 69–71).

Parenchyma. A tissue made up of large thin-walled, living cells, separated by air spaces and making up the bulk of herbaceous plants – the cortex, pith, and medullary rays. (See *Stem; Root*).

Parthenocarpy. The development of fruit without prior fertilisation. This happens normally in some plants such as banana and the fruits then have no seeds. Fruit development can be induced artificially in certain plants by dusting the flowers with hormones.

Passage Cells. Cells in the endodermis of plant roots that remain unthickened. (See *Root*).

Pathogen. A disease-causing *parasite* (q.v.).

Pathology. The study of disease.

Peat. Partly decayed plant material that accumulates wherever waterlogging or acidity slows down the processes of bacterial decay. Fen peat, formed under slightly alkaline conditions, tends to be black and well decomposed but bog peat, which is formed under acid conditions is a brownish colour and the plant fragments are clearly visible. Bog peat is composed largely of the remains of

Sphagnum moss. This plant lives under acid conditions and forms a living blanket over large tracts of country where rainfall is high. Growth at the tip is balanced by death at the base and large thicknesses of partly decayed material build up. Coal passed through a stage similar to peat before the great pressures to which it has been subjected in the earth converted it to its present state. (See *Bog; Fen*) and (Plates 72–75).

Pedicel. Stalk of an individual flower.

Peduncle. Stalk of an inflorescence. In the case of solitary flowers the peduncle is also a pedicel.

Peltate. (Of a leaf). Flat, with the stalk attached below – e.g. Nasturtium leaf. (See Page 136).

Penicillium. A genus of mould fungi (ascomycetes) found on many organic substrates and famed for the production of penicillin. (See *Fungi*) and (Plate 90).

Pentose Sugar. A monosaccharide sugar whose molecule has five carbon atoms. Ribose, which is an important constituent of nucleic acids, is a typical example. Many plant polysaccharides are made up of chains of pentoses.

Perennation. The survival of a plant from one year to the next by means of vegetative organs such as corms or rhizomes.

Perfect. When applied to a flower this term means that the flower has all the typical organs – i.e. it is hermaphrodite.

Perfoliate. Condition of a leaf on which the lamina is extended round the stem so that the stem appears to be growing through the leaf. (See Page 136).

Perianth. The outer, non-sexual part of a flower. In dicotyledonous plants it is normally in two parts – the calyx of sepals and the corolla of petals – but in monocotyledonous plants all the perianth segments are the same. In

Plate 79

Plate 80

POLLINATION

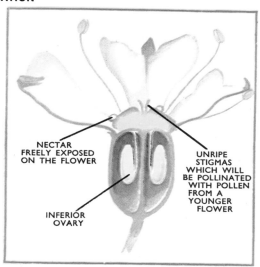

NECTAR FREELY EXPOSED ON THE FLOWER

UNRIPE STIGMAS WHICH WILL BE POLLINATED WITH POLLEN FROM A YOUNGER FLOWER

INFERIOR OVARY

Some flowers, such as the umbellifer enlarged above, have freely exposed nectar and many types of insect pollinate the flowers as they feed on the nectar (opposite).

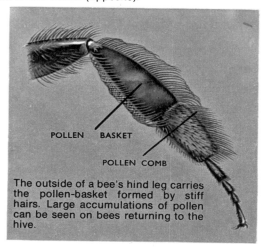

POLLEN   BASKET

POLLEN COMB

The outside of a bee's hind leg carries the pollen-basket formed by stiff hairs. Large accumulations of pollen can be seen on bees returning to the hive.

some flowers the perianth is missing altogether. (See *Flower*).

Periblem. That tissue in the growing point of a vascular plant whose cells give rise to the cortex. (See *Growing Point* and *Histogen*).

Pericarp. Wall of the carpel after it has developed into a *fruit* (q.v.).

Periclinal Wall. A cell wall lying parallel to the surface of the plant in that region.

Pericycle. Layer of tissue just inside the endodermis of a *root* (q.v.).

Periderm. The products of the cork cambium. (See *Bark*).

Perigynous. Condition of a flower in which the receptacle is flattened or cup-shaped and the petals are inserted at the edge, i.e. around the gynaecium of carpels. Examples include blackberry and plum. (See Plate 18).

Perisperm. In some plants the nucellus of the ovule (q.v.) is not completely replaced by endosperm and the remaining part is called the perisperm. (See *Seed*).

Peristome. Name for the group of hygroscopic teeth in the capsule of a moss. (See *Musci*) and (Plate 63).

Perithecium. Fruiting body of various ascomycete fungi, embedded in a mass of hyphae and opening to the exterior by a tiny pore through which the spores escape. (See *Fungi; Ascomycetes*).

Permeability. The rate at which any substance can diffuse through a given type of membrane is the permeability of that membrane to that substance.

Permian Period. A division of the geological time scale (q.v.).

Peroxidase. An enzyme that occurs particularly in plants, oxidising materials by removing hydrogen and combining it with hydrogen peroxide.

Persistent. Remaining. Used especially of the calyx when it remains after flowering and protects the fruit.

Petal. Conspicuous part of the majority of flowers (q.v.).

Petiole. Leaf stalk.

pH. An index figure denoting the degree of acidity or alkalinity of a solution. pH 7 is neutral: lower figures denote acidity and higher ones alkalinity.

Phaeophyceae. Class of algae (q.v.) whose members contain the brown pigment xanthophyll which masks the green colour of their chlorophyll. These plants are the brown seaweeds so common around almost all coasts. Their sizes and shapes vary enormously from the long oarweeds to tiny plants that live attached to other seaweeds. A selection of brown algae is shown on Plates 91–94.

Phanerogam. Old name given to seed-bearing plants because their reproductive organs are clearly visible (Greek *phaneros* = visible). This distinguished them from cryptogams such as ferns and mosses whose reproductive processes were not understood for a long time (Greek *kruptos* = hidden). Phanerogams are normally now called spermatophytes.

Phellem. (See *Phellogen*).

Phelloderm. (See *Phellogen*).

Phellogen. Cork cambium, an actively dividing layer within the bark of a tree which produces cork (phellem) on the outside and parenchymatous tissue (phelloderm) on the inside. In this way the outer layers of the tree keep pace with the increase in girth. (See *Bark; Cork; Stem*) and (Plates 2–5).

Phenology. The study of periodicity in plants, e.g. the cycle of opening and closing of flowers and the annual cycle of flowering.

Phenotype. The visible appearance of an organism with respect to one or more characters, as opposed to the genetic constitution *(Genotype)*. A certain genotype may give rise to several phenotypes according to the environment in which they live. Also a given phenotype may be produced by different genotypes: an heterozygous organism will exhibit the same features as a homozygous one possessing dominant genes. (See *Gene*).

Phloem. Tissue through which organic food materials are conducted in vascular plants. In the flowering plant it is made up of elongated cells called *sieve-tubes* each of which is perforated on the end walls so that the food materials in solution can pass through. Each sieve-tube has a *companion cell* alongside it and the companion cell appears to regulate the activity of the sieve-tube, for, although the phloem tubes are alive, they have no nuclei. There is usually a good deal of ordinary parenchyma tissue among the sieve-tubes as well. The phloem tissue of gymnosperms and pteridophytes does not have typical sieve-tubes. The phloem cells are elongated but the sieve plates are normally found on the side walls and not the end walls. The cells are irregular and not neatly placed side by side so the food materials can still move along within the phloem. There are no companion cells in the phloem of gymnosperms and pteridophytes. In temperate and cold regions many plants stop growth for a certain period each year. As growth slows down in autumn the sieve-tubes become blocked with a substance called callose. In some plants completely new phloem tubes are formed each season — the older blocked ones being squashed and forced towards the outside of the stem (See *Bark*). In others, however, the callose plug dissolves in spring and the tube continues for another season. (See Plate 99).

Photo-. Concerning light.

Photonasty. Non-directional response

PHLOEM

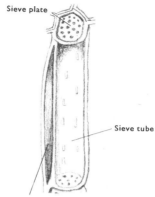

Sieve plate

Sieve tube

Companion cell

to light, e.g. opening of flowers when the sun rises.

Photoperiodism. The reaction of plants to length of day. This varies from one species to another, for example some plants will not flower unless they receive at least 12 hours light per 24 hours. These are known as long-day plants. Others — short-day plants — will flower only if subjected to less than 12 hours light in each 24 hours. Many plants will flower under any conditions of light but age and temperature also play a part.

Photosynthesis. The process whereby green plants manufacture sugars from water and carbon dioxide. No other organism can do this and green plants are therefore the primary food producers in the world — all animals depend ultimately on plants, either by feeding directly on them or by feeding on other animals that themselves feed on plants.

In photosynthesis, water and carbon dioxide are combined using the energy of sunlight. The green chlorophyll plays a vital part in the absorption of this sunlight and the utilisation of its energy. Photosynthesis takes place mainly in the leaves of the plant and

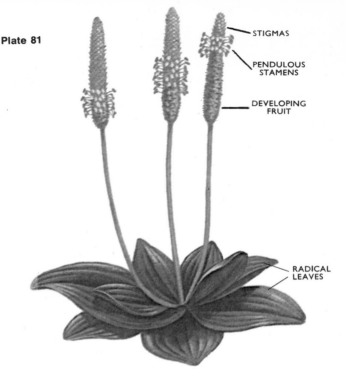

Plate 81

STIGMAS

PENDULOUS STAMENS

DEVELOPING FRUIT

RADICAL LEAVES

The flowers of a plantain spike ripen from the bottom upwards and the stamens ripen after the stigmas. The mature stamens are thus always below the ripe stigmas and the chance of self-pollination is reduced.

POLLINATION (Cont)

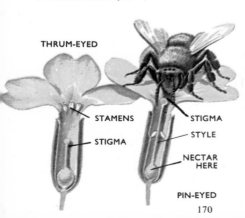

THRUM-EYED

STAMENS

STIGMA

STIGMA

STYLE

NECTAR HERE

PIN-EYED

Thrum-eyed and pin-eyed primroses — an example of dimorphism and heterostyly. Bees collect pollen from one type at just the right level on their tongues to transfer it to the stigma of the other type.

Plate 82

PROPAGATION

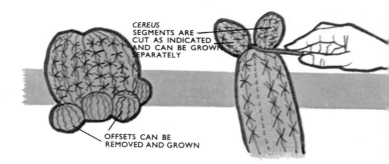

CEREUS SEGMENTS ARE CUT AS INDICATED AND CAN BE GROWN SEPARATELY

OFFSETS CAN BE REMOVED AND GROWN

(Top) The taking of cuttings and offshoots is one of the commonest methods of propagation and is suitable for many types of plant. The removed pieces take root when put into suitable soil.

(Bottom) Layering is another method, used especially for carnations. Partially-cut shoots are pegged down until they take root, when they can be removed from the parent plant.

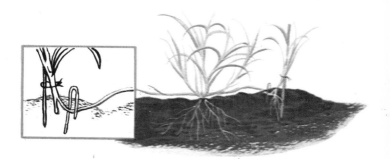

only during the hours of daylight. Water is absorbed through the root of the plant and carbon dioxide is absorbed from the air through the stomata on the leaf surface.

The process of photosynthesis can be summarised by the equation:
$$6CO_2 + 6H_2O + energy \rightarrow C_6H_{12}O_6 + 6O_2$$
which in words is: carbon dioxide plus water plus energy gives glucose plus oxygen. Although this process cannot take place without chlorophyll, the latter is not used up in the process, in other words, chlorophyll is a catalyst.

The above equation summarising the process of photosynthesis is actually very much simplified for, although the starting and end products are shown, there are many intermediate stages not shown here. (See Plates 75 and 76).

Phototaxis. Movement of whole organisms in response to light. (See *Taxis*).

Phototrophic. Feeding by photosynthesis.

Phototropism. Movement or bending of part of a plant in response to light. (See *Tropism*).

Phycocyanin. One of the pigments found in red algae (Rhodophyceae).

Phycoerythrin. A pigment found in red algae (Rhodophyceae).

Phycomycetes. Class of *fungi* (q.v.) in which the threads or hyphae are not divided into cells. Many members live in water while others are important parasites of higher plants. These fungi reproduce asexually by releasing thousands of tiny spores or by cutting off the ends of threads which are full of nuclei and which grow into new threads. They also reproduce sexually by the fusion of threads. Examples include *Pythium, Empusa,* and *Mucor.* (See Plates 15, 39, 40, and 121).

Phylloclade. (=*Cladode* q.v.).

Phyllode. Flattened petiole taking over the role of the leaf, as in the grass pea. (See Plate 55).

Phyllotaxy (=*Phyllotaxis*). The arrangement of leaves on the plant stem. In *spiral* phyllotaxy the leaves are arranged one to each node and are said to be *alternate,* although a particular leaf is not necessarily on the opposite side of the stem from the one below it. A line round the outside of the stem and passing through the bases of the leaves would be a spiral and it may have to go several times around the stem before joining two leaves exactly above one another. The other type of phyllotaxy is *whorled* or *cyclic.* Two or more leaves develop at each node. If there are only two, they are said to be *opposite* and in this case, each pair is usually at right angles to the pairs above and below — the *opposite decussate* arrangement. If more than two leaves arise at each node the arrangement is said to be *verticillate.* (See Page 69).

Phylogeny. The evolutionary relationships of a group of organisms.

Physiology. The study of living processes such as respiration.

Phyto-. Concerning plants — e.g. phytopathology — the study of plant diseases.

Phytoplankton. The assemblage of minute plants that float in their millions near the surface of the seas and lakes.

Pileus. The cap of a toadstool. (See Plate 65).

Piliferous Layer. Region of root epidermis bearing root hairs. (See Page 196).

Pinna. Leaflet of a compound leaf.

Pinnate. A pinnate leaf is a compound leaf with a single main axis — the rhachis — and a number of separate leaflets attached to it. If the leaflets on the rhachis are themselves divided into leaflets, the leaf is said to be *bipinnate.* (See Page 136).

Pinnatifid. A simple, unicostate leaf such as the oak leaf, in which the incisions do not reach more than about half-way into the main vein, is said to be *pinnatifid*. (See Plate 52).

Pinus. Generic name of the pine — a typical coniferous tree. (See *Coniferales*) and (Plate 77).

Pistil. Uncommon term referring to the complete female part of a flower. (=*Gynaecium*).

Pistillate. A pistillate flower is one containing carpels but no stamens — i.e. a female flower.

Pit. An unthickened region of a cell wall which is for the most part thickened by lignin. The pits allow water to pass from cell to cell. They

PIT

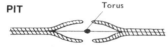

Torus

Section through a bordered pit. Pressure on one side will force the torus across and out of the cell with the high pressure.

are especially important in the water-conducting xylem tissues. These sometimes have special types of pit called *bordered pits*. These can be closed by a central thickened lump — the *torus* — on the pit membrane. In this way, pressure build-ups can be localised because pressure in one vessel or tracheid will force the pits to close (see diagram). (See *Xylem*).

Pith. Central core of stems that have their vascular tissues in a cylinder. Pith normally consists of parenchyma cells which play a part in food storage.

Placenta. Region of ovary wall to which ovules are attached.

Placentation. The arrangement of the ovules in the ovary. When the ovary consists of several joined carpels

there are several ways in which the ovules can be attached.

Plagiogeotropism. The growth of a plant organ in such a way that its main axis is neither vertical nor horizontal. Most root branches exhibits this phenomenon.

Plankton. The floating plant and animal life in the upper layers of seas and lakes. It consists mainly of minute plants and animals.

Plantaginaceae. Family of plants containing the plantains. The leaves are usually radical and the small green flowers are arranged in spikes. The hanging stamens scatter pollen to the wind. (See Plate 81).

Plasma-membrane. Extremely thin membrane surrounding all cells just inside the cell wall. Also bordering vacuoles inside the cells. The membrane is semi-permeable and lets only certain substances pass into the protoplasm.

Plasmodium. Mass of naked protoplasm found at certain stage in the life cycle of Myxomycetes (q.v.). (See Plate 121).

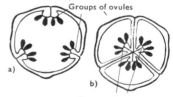

Groups of ovules

Groups of ovules

PLACENTATION

Two types of placentation. Both ovaries have been formed by the fusion of three carpels. In a) the inner walls have disappeared and the ovary is unilocular — with a single chamber. Placentation is parietal. In b) the ovary is trilocular and placentation is axile.

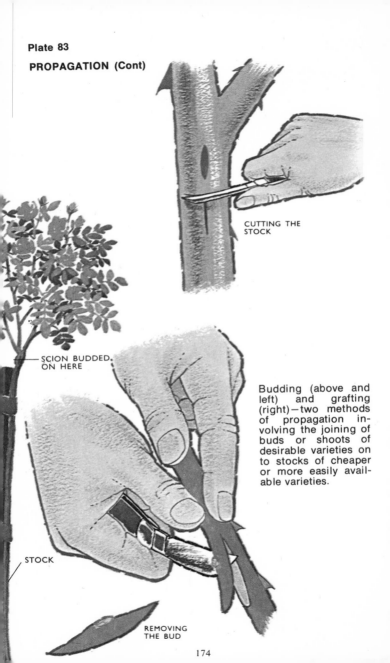

Plate 83

PROPAGATION (Cont)

CUTTING THE
STOCK

SCION BUDDED
ON HERE

STOCK

REMOVING
THE BUD

Budding (above and left) and grafting (right)—two methods of propagation involving the joining of buds or shoots of desirable varieties on to stocks of cheaper or more easily available varieties.

174

Plate 84

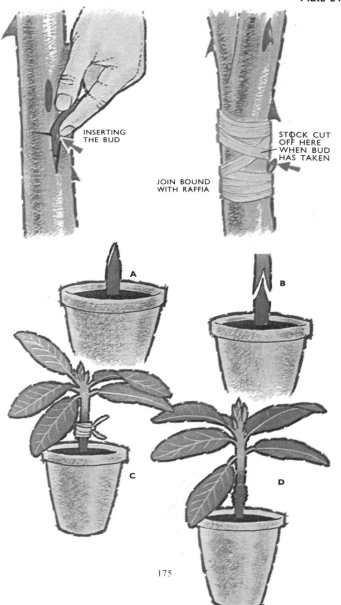

INSERTING
THE BUD

STOCK CUT
OFF HERE
WHEN BUD
HAS TAKEN

JOIN BOUND
WITH RAFFIA

A

B

C

D

175

Plasmolysis. When a cell is put into a solution of greater osmotic pressure than the cell sap, water is withdrawn from the vacuole and the protoplasm shrinks away from the wall in response to the reduced pressure in the central vacuole. This phenomenon is called plasmolysis. It is reversible up to a point but if the protoplasm shrinks away too much it cannot return and the cell dies.

Plastid. Tiny body of which large numbers are found in the protoplasm of plant cells. Some (leucoplasts) are colourless and are concerned with starch storage. Others contains chlorophyll and are called chloroplasts. Chromoplasts contain other pigments such as carotene and xanthophyll — they are found mainly in flowers and fruits.

Pleistocene Epoch. Division of the Geological Time Scale (q.v.).

Plerome (See *Histogen*).

Pliocene Epoch. Division of the Geological Time Scale (q.v.).

Plumule. The shoot of an embryo seed plant — the part that will grow into the stem and produce the true leaves. (See *Seed: Germination)* and (Plate 41 and Page 204).

Pod. (= *Legume* q.v.).

Podsol. A type of soil found in regions of high rainfall, especially on sandy ground. Rainfall exceeds evaporation and iron and other minerals tend to be washed down from the surface layers. These minerals are deposited lower down as a *hard pan* which is dark in colour — in contrast to the pale colour of the leached surface layer. The leached surface layer is acidic and, as the hard pan is impervious to water, bog vegetation often develops.

Pollen. The mass of male spores produced by seed plants. Each pollen grain, when it reaches a receptive stigma, puts out a pollen tube which grows towards the ovule. Two male gametes are formed within the tube and one of them fuses with the female cell. (See *Pollination: Fertilisation)* and (Plates 29 and 78).

Pollen Analysis. (See *Palynology*).

Pollen Sac. The cavity of the anther in which pollen is formed. (See Plate 34).

Pollen Tube. (See *Pollen: Fertilisation)* and (Plate 29).

Pollination. The transference of pollen from stamens to stigma: the first stage in the process whereby the male cells gain access to the female egg-cells of seed-bearing plants. All parts of the flower may play a part in pollination but the main organs concerned are the *stamens* and the *stigma*.

Each stamen consists of a *filament* and a pair of *anthers* which are the pollen-producing sacs. When the pollen grains are ripe the anther walls split and expose them. The stigma is the receptive surface of the carpel and may or may not be on a stalk — the *style*. When pollen falls upon a style of the same species the process of fertilisation begins.

When seeds are produced after the transference of pollen from one flower to another (*cross-pollination*) the resulting plants are often stronger than if the pollen and ovule had both come from a single flower (*self-pollination*). It is not surprising, therefore, that most flowers have some way of avoiding self-pollination and ensuring cross-pollination. Those flowers which are adapted to ensure cross-pollination will produce stronger and more successful offspring which in turn will be adapted for cross-pollination. Most flowers contain both stamens and carpels but a number of plants have flowers of one sex only. Some species (e.g. willow) even bear the male and female flowers on different plants. In these cases self-pollination is impossible. Where there are organs of both sexes in a flower, self-pollination is avoided by separating the anthers and stigmas in space or time. In an upright flower the anthers may be below the stigmas and vice versa in a hanging flower so that pollen will not fall on the stigmas. The most frequent device is that whereby the stamens ripen before the stigma is ready to receive pollen. This is known as *protandry*. The reverse condition (*protogyny*) occurs in some flowers whose stigmas mature before their stamens shed any pollen. A number of plants whose flowers are not structurally adapted to prevent self-pollination are *self-sterile*. The pollen can fall on the stigma but it cannot fertilise the ovule because there appears to be a chemical barrier to its further development: the pollen and stigma are *incompatible*.

Although cross-pollination is preferable, self-pollination is better than no pollination at all and in many cases the stamens and stigma bend towards each other before the flower dies so that self-pollination may occur if cross-pollination has failed. A number of plants (including the sweet violet) produce special flowers late in the season which always pollinate themselves – in fact they do not even open; the pollen passes direct from stamen to stigma and ensures that at least some seed will be produced.

Wind-pollination (*anemophily*) occurs in many trees and all grasses. The flowers are typically borne in catkins or the stamens are provided with long filaments. In both cases even slight air movements release pollen. The pollen is light and produced in large quantities for wind pollination is wasteful – very little reaches the female stigmas. The latter are usually large and feathery in wind-pollinated plants so that the maximum amount of pollen may be trapped. Petals are often absent. The flowers are normally inconspicuous although well exposed. The hazel tree produces its male flowers in hanging catkins. The female flowers are tiny structures with branched red stigmas. Separation of the flowers in this way ensures cross-pollination. Grass flowers have very long filamentous stamens which hang well below the stigma and thus the risk of self-pollination is reduced. Plantains produce spikes of protogynous flowers. The lowest flowers open first and expose their stigmas. As the latter wither, the hanging stamens appear, but these rarely pollinate the younger flowers on the same spike since the stamens are always below the stigmas. Wind pollination is undoubtedly the most primitive mechanism.

Insect pollination (*entomophily*) is by far the commonest method of pollen transference. Many flowers are unspecialised and can be pollinated by almost any insect, but the more specialised flowers can be pollinated by only a few species of insect. The elaborate associations between flowers and insects are not coincidental. They are the results of evolutionary forces which have been acting ever since insects first began to feed at flowers.

The early wind-pollinated flowers must have been attractive to insects in some way – probably on account of the large amount of pollen they produced, for pollen has a high food value. Those flowers which were visited regularly by insects would have been pollinated efficiently and would have produced offspring in larger numbers than the wind-pollinated plants. These offspring too would have been attractive to insects. and from this stage the many refinements of insect-pollinated flowers must have arisen. The insects too have evolved special structures which enable them to gather pollen and nectar (and therefore to pollinate) more efficiently. The 'pollen basket' and the fine feathery hairs of honey bees illustrate this.

Entomophilous flowers are usually brightly coloured and scented. They normally contain a sweet liquid – *nectar* – as well as pollen, but some flowers (e.g. dog rose) are 'pollen flowers' – they produce extra pollen as insect food but no nectar. The

177

Plate 85

ROOT

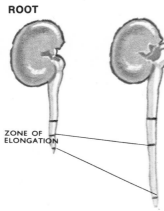

ZONE OF ELONGATION

The tips of roots and stems are the actual sites of cell division where masses of tiny new cells are formed. A short way behind the tip these cells begin to enlarge. This is the *zone of elongation* where most of the growth takes place. That growth occurs mainly in this region can be shown by marking a root with dye. The divisions become separated most rapidly just behind the tip. Growth substances produced at the tip control the rate of elongation of the cells.

An enlarged root tip showing the cap and the growth region (below line). The soil particles are compressed by growth pressure.

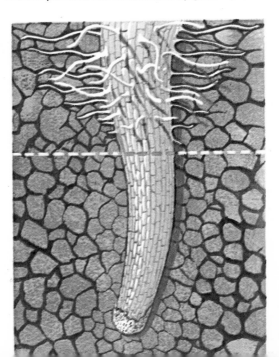

Plate 86

ROOT (Cont)

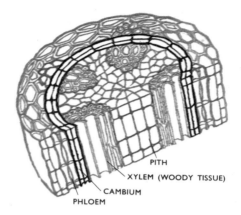

(Top) Diagrammatic section of a buttercup stem. Fleshy or her-baceous plants contain a small amount of woody material in their vascular bundles whose ring-like arrangement gives strength and flexibility to the stems.

(Bottom) The woody tissues of the root are concentrated in the centre and give the root a cable-like strength—ideal for anchorage.

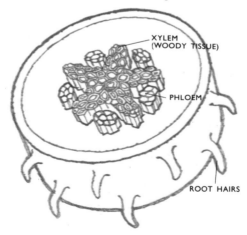

pollen of entomophilous flowers is sticky and adheres to the bodies of insects. Because of the more efficient pollination mechanism less pollen is produced than in the wind-pollinated flowers.

Bees are the most important pollinating insects. In their search for pollen and nectar they visit large number of flowers — usually all of the same species on one journey — and pollinate them. The relatively long 'tongue' *(proboscis)* of bees enables them to find nectar which is *concealed* (e.g. in spurs formed by petals). Bees visit flowers which are blue, purple, yellow and sometimes white but rarely visit red flowers. Experiments have shown that the insects are attracted by colour from a distance and then by both colour and scent when they are close to the flower. The dark lines on petals *(honey guides)* are believed to guide the insect to the nectar and the stamens and stigma. Butterflies and moths are also important pollinating agents. Butterflies visit all types of flower, chiefly red and white ones. Their long tongues can reach nectar in tubular flowers. Night-flying moths hover in front of flowers and reach the nectar with their very long tongues. The flowers are usually white or yellow and strongly scented (e.g. honeysuckle). Their stamens and stigmas protrude from the flower, touching the hovering moth. Other insects which frequently visit flowers include flies and beetles. These are not specialised for reaching concealed nectar and are normally found on 'open' flowers such as those of the family Umbelliferae. Heads of flowers are frequently covered with insects which feed upon the exposed nectar. The flowers are markedly protandrous and the insects transfer pollen from the younger flowers in the centre of the head to the outer, older flowers whose stigmas are ripe. Flowers of the family Compositae are also visited by various types of insect.

Water carries pollen of some aquatic plants. The pollen grains have tiny floats which carry them along on the surface until they reach a flower at the surface of the water. Birds are common agents of pollination in the tropics (e.g. humming-birds). The flowers are usually red and produce large amounts of nectar. Bats may be pollinators of some flowers, again especially in the tropics. Other animals may effect pollination during their wanderings but they are not regular pollinators. (See *Fertilisation*) and (Plates 78–81).

Pollinium. A sticky mass of pollen grains which are the entire products of an anther and which are transferred to another flower all in one mass. Typical of orchids. (See Plate 78).

Poly-. Many.

Polyadelphous. Having stamens united in several groups. (See *Monadelphous; Diadelphous*).

Polygonaceae. Family of plants including knotweed and rhubarb.

Polymorphism. Existence of a species in two or more forms. The common milkwort *(Polygala)*, with pink and purple flowered varieties, is a good example of a polymorphic flower.

Polypetalous. Having separate or free petals.

Polyploid. Having three or more times the haploid number of chromosomes in the cells. (See *Chromosome*).

Polysaccharide. Substance such as starch or cellulose whose molecules are composed of many linked monosaccharide molecules (sugars). (See *Monosaccharide; Disaccharide*).

Polysepalous. Having free sepals.

Pome. A false fruit formed largely from the receptacle, e.g. apple. (See *Fruit*).

Posterior. The side of a flower nearest the main axis of the stem.

Precambrian. Convenient name for the whole of geological time before the beginning of the Cambrian Period some 600 million years ago. (See *Geological Time Scale*).

Prickle. (See *Emergences*).

Primary Meristem. Meristematic tissue that develops as such in the embryo and remains so throughout life. (See *Meristem*).

Primordial Meristem. (= Promeristem).

Primulales. Order of plants including the primulas and the scarlet pimpernel (Family Primulaceae). The order in-

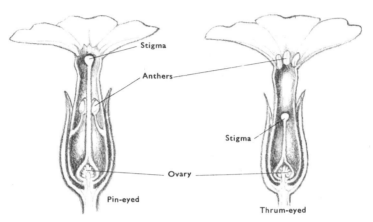

Pin-eyed

Thrum-eyed

PRIMULALES

Half flowers and floral diagram of primrose *(Primula)*.

Plate 87

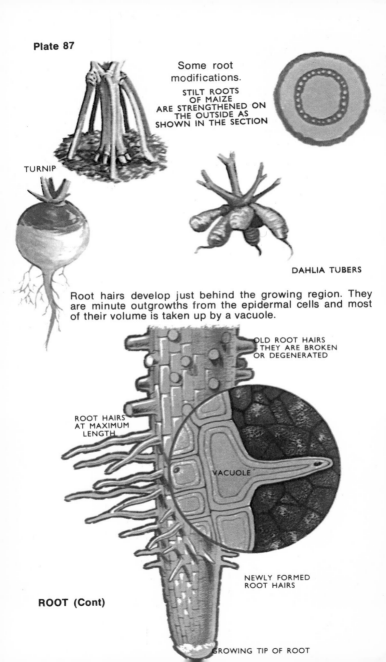

Some root modifications.

STILT ROOTS OF MAIZE ARE STRENGTHENED ON THE OUTSIDE AS SHOWN IN THE SECTION

TURNIP

DAHLIA TUBERS

Root hairs develop just behind the growing region. They are minute outgrowths from the epidermal cells and most of their volume is taken up by a vacuole.

OLD ROOT HAIRS THEY ARE BROKEN OR DEGENERATED

ROOT HAIRS AT MAXIMUM LENGTH

VACUOLE

NEWLY FORMED ROOT HAIRS

ROOT (Cont)

GROWING TIP OF ROOT

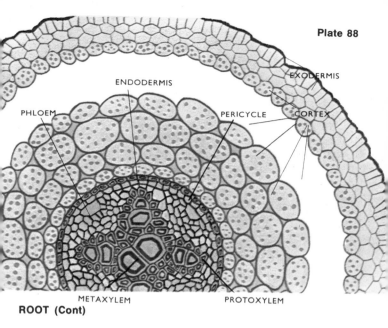

Plate 88

ENDODERMIS

EXODERMIS

PHLOEM

PERICYCLE

CORTEX

METAXYLEM

PROTOXYLEM

ROOT (Cont)

Cross section of part of a young dicotyledonous root showing the arrangement of the tissues and (below) diagram showing how branch roots develop internally and grow out through the cortex. When they appear outside the parent root they are behind the root hair region.

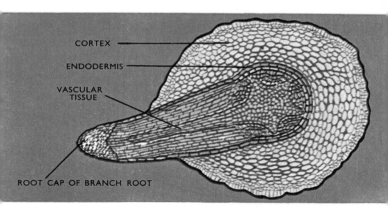

CORTEX

ENDODERMIS

VASCULAR TISSUE

ROOT CAP OF BRANCH ROOT

cludes both shrubs and trees as well as the familiar herbs. There are usually 5 sepals and 5 petals, the stamens being joined to the petals. The flowers are normally hypogynous and the fruit is a capsule.

Procambium. Elongated cells in the stem or root, just behind the growing point which give rise to the first vascular tissues — the protoxylem and protophloem.

Proliferation. Active cell division.

Promeristem. Actively dividing tip of growing point.

Propagation. Propagation means increase by any means but the gardener normally restricts the term to increase by vegetative means — i.e. other than sowing seed. One of the commonest methods is the taking of *cuttings*. This involves cutting a piece of stem (with some plants it can also be done with roots or even leaves) and putting it into moist but well-aerated soil until it takes root and begins to grow as a new plant. The speed of root growth varies with the species but the gardener has been helped in recent years by the development of rooting hormones which encourage root growth.

Layering is a form of propagation allied to cutting and which is used especially for carnations. A shoot is partly cut and the cut region is pegged into the soil until it takes root. The rooted portion is then detached from the parent plant.

Although taking cuttings is suitable for propagating small plants, it would take a long time for cuttings to grow into fair-sized trees and shrubs. Nurserymen therefore use different methods for these plants. These methods, known as *budding* and *grafting*, involve joining a bud or a shoot (the *scion*) of the desired variety on to the stem of another cheaper or more readily available variety (the *stock*). The stock must, of course, be healthy and must normally be closely related to the scion. Roses are normally

budded on to wild briar stocks and cherry varieties are grafted on to stocks of wild cherry. Scion and stock must be securely bound together until they are completely united. The vital thing is that the cambium — the ring of living cells just under the bark — of the scion is in contact with that of the stock, for only the cambium can produce new cells to knit the two parts together. This happens quickly: water and dissolved salts pass from the stock into the scion which grows quite well. When the scion has taken properly the upper part of the stock is removed so that all new shoots come from the scion and the flowers and fruit are of the desired variety. Although the new plant grows as a complete individual, the original stock and scion retain their individual characteristics: shoots (*suckers*) coming from the stock are of no use and must be removed. (See *Vegetative Reproduction*) and (Plates 82–84).

Prophase. First stage in nuclear division. (See *Meiosis; Mitosis*).

Protandrous. Having anthers that ripen and shed pollen before the stigmas of the flower are receptive. Self-pollination is thus unlikely. (See *Protogynous*).

Protein. Proteins are extremely complicated substances whose molecules consist of long chains of amino-acids and may have molecular weights of several million. All protein molecules contain carbon, hydrogen, oxygen, and nitrogen, and many contain sulphur and phosphorus as well. The number of different proteins is astonishing — every living species of plant and animal has some characteristic proteins not found in any other living organism. Proteins and water are the basic components of protoplasm which itself is the basis of life. Proteins also form part of the hereditary material carried on the chromosomes of cell nuclei — they are combined with other substances in the nuclei and are called nucleoproteins. As well as their roles in the structure of organisms, proteins are also used very widely as food stores – many seeds and other storage organs contain valuable protein stores.

Proteolytic enzyme. An enzyme that breaks down protein.

Prothallus. The gametophyte or sexual generation of ferns and related plants which is quite separate from and different from the spore-bearing sporophyte generations. (See *Pteridophyta; Alternation of Generations*) and (Plates 20 and 31).

Protista. Uncommon term for all single-celled organisms.

Protogynous. Having stigmas that ripen before the stamens of the flower shed their pollen. Self-fertilisation is thus unlikely. (See *Protandrous*).

Protonema. Fine branching thread that grows from a moss spore and that bears the buds from which the moss plants develop. (See *Musci*) and (Plate 63).

Protoplasm. The substance of all living cells, usually divided into cytoplasm and nucleoplasm – the latter being confined within the membrane of the nucleus. Protoplasm is not a single substance but a very complicated mixture of organic and inorganic materials in which chemical changes are continuously taking place. The composition of protoplasm varies therefore, not only between species and between cells performing different functions, but also in individual cells at different times. The main component is water in which are dissolved or suspended numerous inorganic salts, proteins, and lipids. Electron microscopy indicates that there is a delicate system of fibres and channels within the protoplasm. (See *Protein*).

Protoplast. A plant cell excluding the cellulose wall – the living part.

Protostele. (See *Stele*).

Protoxylem. (See *Xylem*).

Psilophytales. Extinct order containing the oldest known plants. (See Page 256) and (Plate 124).

Psilotales. Order of plants distantly related to ferns and containing two strange forms – *Psilotum* and *Tmesipteris*. (See Page 256) and (Plate 124).

Pteridophyta. A large division of the plant kingdom including ferns, horsetails, club-mosses, and a few other forms as well as numerous fossil groups. They are non-flowering plants and show a well-marked alternation of generations (q.v.). The haploid generation or prothallus is independent of the sporophyte and in some cases is green and able to make its own food. In other cases it remains underground and feeds saprophytically. The sporophyte normally has a well-developed vascular system. (See *Filicales; Lycopodiales; Equisetales*) and (Page 256).

Pubescent. Clothed with soft, short hair.

Pyrenoid. Structure found in the chloroplasts of various algae and concerned with starch metabolism.

Quadrat. A square frame or the area enclosed by it used for studying the vegetation of a particular habitat. The frame (normal size is 1 metre square) is thrown at random and the numbers of the various plants it encloses are counted.

Quaternary Period. Most recent division of the Geological Time Scale (q.v.).

Raceme. Type of inflorescence (q.v.).

Rachis. Main axis of an inflorescence or a pinnate leaf. (See Plate 52).

Radical. Concerning the root or crown of a plant. Radical leaves arise from the crown and are close to the ground – e.g. dandelion, plantain. (See Plate 81).

Plate 89

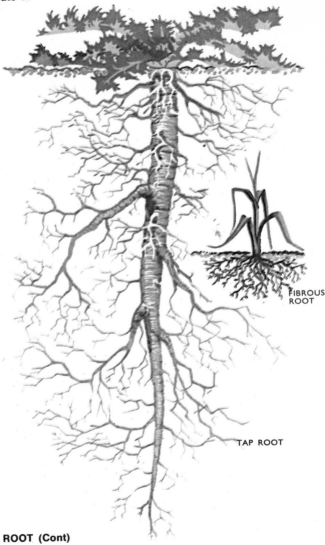

FIBROUS
ROOT

TAP ROOT

ROOT (Cont)

The tap root system of a thistle and the fibrous system of a grass.

Plate 90

SAPROPHYTE

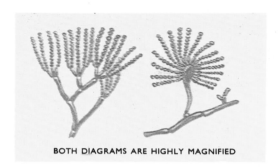

BOTH DIAGRAMS ARE HIGHLY MAGNIFIED

Plants that obtain nourishment from dead organisms. (Above left) The mould *Penicillium* and (right) *Aspergillus*, a mould that attacks leather and stored grain. Both thrive in damp conditions. (Below) A bracket fungus commonly found on decaying trees.

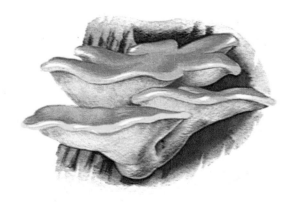

Fruiting head
of buttercup—
a cluster or
etaerio of achenes

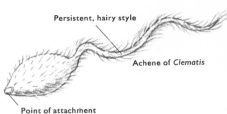

Persistent, hairy style

Achene of *Clematis*

Point of attachment
to receptacle

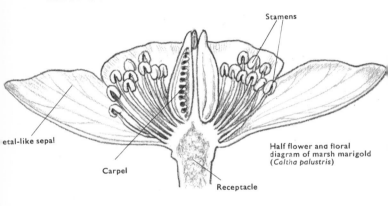

Stamens

etal-like sepal

Carpel

Receptacle

Half flower and floral
diagram of marsh marigold
(*Caltha palustris*)

RANUNCULACEAE

Some features of the family Ranunculaceae.

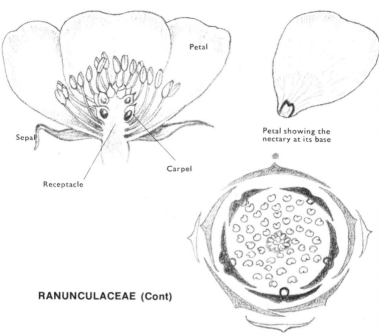

Labels on diagram:
Petal
Sepal
Receptacle
Carpel
Petal showing the nectary at its base

RANUNCULACEAE (Cont)

Half flower and floral diagram of buttercup *(Ranunculus)*.

Radicle. The root of an embryo seed plant. (See Plate 42).

Ranales. Order of plants containing the families Ranunculaceae (buttercups), Nymphaeaceae (water lilies), and a few other families. Most members are herbaceous. The flowers are regular as a rule and hypogynous. Carpels are free and give rise to fruits of various types.

Ranunculaceae. Large family of di-cotyledons including the buttercups, *Clematis*, anemones, *Delphinium*, and hellebores. The stamens and carpels are usually arranged spirally on the receptacle. In some species – e.g. the marsh marigold – the petals are lacking and the sepals are petaloid. There is wide variation in flower shape – from

the regular buttercup to the highly irregular *Delphinium*. Many plants of this family contain poisonous alkaloids (q.v.). (See *Ranales*).

Raphe. That part of an anatropous ovule composed of the fused funicle and integument. (See *Ovule*) and (Plate 29).

Ray Floret. Floret with a ligule – i.e. the outer floret of a daisy. (See *Floret*).

Receptacle. Apex of flower stalk on which the parts of the flower are inserted. (See *Flower*) and (Plate 34).

Recessive. (See *Gene*).

Reduction Division. (=*Meiosis*).

Plate 91

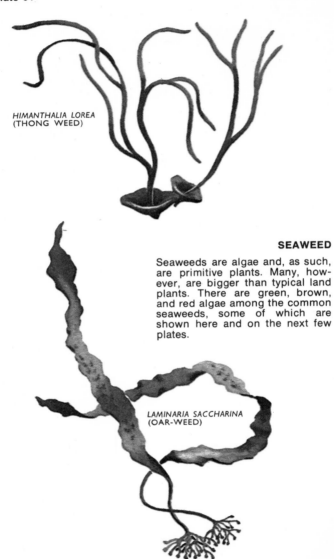

HIMANTHALIA LOREA
(THONG WEED)

SEAWEED

Seaweeds are algae and, as such, are primitive plants. Many, however, are bigger than typical land plants. There are green, brown, and red algae among the common seaweeds, some of which are shown here and on the next few plates.

LAMINARIA SACCHARINA
(OAR-WEED)

Plate 92

SEAWEED (Cont)

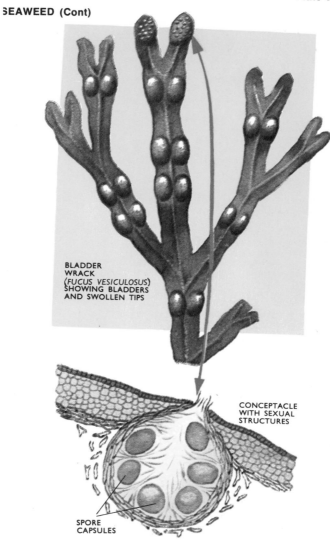

BLADDER
WRACK
(*FUCUS VESICULOSUS*)
SHOWING BLADDERS
AND SWOLLEN TIPS

CONCEPTACLE
WITH SEXUAL
STRUCTURES

SPORE
CAPSULES

Regular. (=*Actinomorphic*).

Respiration. All living processes require energy and this is obtained by oxidation of food materials within the tissues of the organism. In the majority of plants this process depends on the presence of free oxygen which is absorbed from the air (aerobic respiration). The chemical reaction which releases the energy is called respiration. In actual fact there is not one reaction but a series of complicated reactions involving numerous enzymes and intermediate stages. The net result, however, can be shown as:

food + oxygen = carbon dioxide + water + energy

This reaction holds good for both plants and animals. Glucose is a commonly used food material. Its oxidation can be shown chemically as follows:

$C_6H_{12}O_6 + 6O_2 = 6CO_2 + 6H_2O + energy$

In other words glucose is combined with oxygen to release carbon dioxide and water and energy. The glucose broken down in respiration is that that is formed in the process of photosynthesis. In fact the process of respiration adds up to photosynthesis in reverse although the stages and actual processes are different. Unlike the process of photosynthesis, respiration goes on all the time.

A number of bacteria are able to use other chemical reactions to obtain energy (they are *chemosynthetic*). They are not dependent upon free oxygen and this form of respiration is called anaerobic.

Resting Cell. A cell not in the process of dividing, although it is likely to be very active in other ways.

Reticulate Thickening. (See *Xylem*).

Rhachis. (See *Rachis*).

Rhizoid. Simple root of bryophytes and fern prothalli consisting of only a few cells.

Rhizome. Horizontal underground stem which acts as a food store and as a means of vegetative reproduction. (See *Stem*) and (Plate 102).

Rhizomorph. Root-like structure of fungus made up of compacted hyphae. Absorbs food material and also passes it from place to place in the fungus.

Rhodophyceae. Class of algae in which the red phycoerythrin is the dominant pigment. These are the red seaweeds and they are widely distributed, although normally at greater depth than the brown ones. Examples are shown on Plates 93 and 94. (See *Algae*) and (Page 240).

Rhoedales. Order of plants containing the cabbage and poppy families — Cruciferae and Papaveraceae. (See Plate 127).

RNA. Ribonucleic acid. (See *Nucleic Acid*).

Rogue. A plant that through mutation differs from other individuals of the same species around it.

Root. The main functions of a root are to anchor the plant and to absorb and transport water and dissolved salts.

Normally, roots grow downwards under the influence of gravity and away from light. This reaction enables a sprouting seed to get a hold on the soil. There are two basic patterns of root growth — the *tap-root* system (e.g. thistle) and the *fibrous* system found, for example, in grasses. The tap-root system is an extension of the primary root (*radicle*) of the young seedling, but in fibrous systems this primary root is quickly replaced by numerous fine roots from the base of the stem. All roots which do not grow as branches from the primary root are called *adventitious* roots.

At the tip of all roots there is a mass of cells — the *root-cap* — which protects the growing point during its passage through the soil. The cells of the root-cap are produced by the actively dividing cells of the growing point. As the outer parts of the root-cap wear away, fresh cells replace them. The old cap cells may also lubricate the tip as it grows downward. Cells formed just behind the tip lengthen rapidly and push the tip further into the soil with considerable force. The growing region is followed by the *root-hair* region. The hairs are minute outgrowths of the *exodermal* cells and are the main organs of water absorption. They occupy only a limited region. Hairs in the growing region would be sheared off as the root pushed downward. Each hair has only a brief existence and as the hairs die off they are replaced with new ones further down. The hair region is thus kept at a more or less constant size. Branches—if any—occur behind the root-hair region.

The root contains the same sort of tissues as the stem but the strengthening tissues of the root are centrally placed, reflecting the pulling strain suffered by the root as opposed to the bending strain imposed on the stem. The inner layer of the wide cortex is called the *endodermis*. The walls of this layer—except for a few cells called *passage cells*—become thickened with a corky substance. Within the endodermis is the *stele* whose outer layer is of parenchyma cells and is called the *pericycle*. The protoxylem is on the outside of the xylem tissue (*exarch* condition) which is star-shaped as a rule. Monocotyledons usually have more 'arms' than dicotyledons. A central *pith* occurs in some species.

Secondary growth (with very few exceptions) occurs only in dicotyledons. A strip of parenchyma inside the phloem becomes active, forming a *cambium* which grows and makes contact with the pericycle. A continuous wavy ring of cambium is thus formed and the secondary tissues are produced from this. Opposite the xylem groups a ray of parenchyma is produced instead of vascular tissue. If secondary growth is excessive (e.g. in trees) the whole pericycle becomes active and produces a layer of cork outside the stele. The cortex then dies away leaving this corky covering.

In the stem, buds develop from the outer tissues close to the tip. But if this happened in the root the buds would be torn off as the main root moved through the soil. Root branches develop internally behind the growing region and are said to be *endogenous*. Branches develop before secondary thickening begins. Cells of the pericycle opposite the protoxylem groups become active and produce a growing point just like that of the main root. This new tip grows through the cortex just as the main root grows through the soil. When it breaks out of the parent root the vascular connections are complete and the region is behind that of the root-hairs. The degree of branching is associated with the size and habit of the plant. Large trees have thick, spreading roots for firm anchorage.

Between the root and the stem is a region called the *hypocotyl* where the vascular tissues change from the root arrangement to that of the stem, but they are *continuous all the way through*.

Roots are often modified for food storage. Man has made use of such stores in plants like carrots, turnips and beet. These are tap-roots, but adventitious roots also serve as storage organs. Dahlia 'tubers' and various orchid roots are examples. The food may be stored in the cortex or the phloem. The climbing roots of ivy are adventitious—arising all the way along the stem—so also are the roots on strawberry runners. Some tropical orchids which grow on tree-trunks have spongy roots exposed to the air. The roots absorb moisture and may contain chlorophyll too. Maize plants and many others have *stilt* roots which develop from nodes on the stem and provide extra support. *Prop* roots are admirably shown in the banyan tree. Roots develop in the horizontal branches and grow into the soil. They form solid supports for the spreading branches. Some swamp-growing plants, such as the mangrove, develop *breathing-roots*. The swampy soil is poor in oxygen and some root branches

Plate 93

PELVETIA CANALICULATA
(CHANNELLED WRACK)

SEAWEED (Cont)

DELESSERIA SANGUINEA

ELACHISTA GROWING ON
FUCUS

ASCOPHYLLUM NODOSUM
(KNOTTED WRACK)

CHONDRUS CRISPUS

194

Plate 94

FUCUS SERRATUS
(SAW-EDGED WRACK)

CORALLINA

ULVA LACTUCA
(SEA LETTUCE)

grow upwards into the air. Oxygen diffuses into these and into the rest of the root system. (See Plates 85–89 and 96).

Root Cap. Protective layer at tip of root. (See *Root*) and (Plates 87 and 88).

Root Hair. Organ of water absorption. (See *Root*) and (Plate 87).

Root Nodule. Swelling found on the root of leguminous plants caused by the presence in the tissues of certain bacteria (e.g. *Rhizobium*). These bacteria are able to convert free nitrogen into an available form and are thus of great value to the plant. (See Plate 57).

Root Pressure. Pressure generated in the root forcing water into the xylem vessels and up the stem. It can be shown to exist by cutting a stem a short way above ground and watching the flow of water.

Rosaceae. Large family of dicotyledons belonging to the order Rosales. The members are herbs, shrubs, or trees with regular perigynous or epigynous flowers. Sepals and petals normally number 5 and the stamens normally 10, 15, or 20. The carpels vary widely in number and are free in the majority of species. Fruits are achenes, follicles, drupes, or pomes. Some flowers may be confused with those of the family Ranunculaceae but in these cases the stipules of the rosaceous leaves will distinguish them. Members of the Rosaceae include rose, blackberry, plum, apple, hawthorn, *Spiraea, Geum,* and strawberry. (See Plates 18 and 128).

Rosales. Order of dicotyledons containing the families Rosaceae (q.v.), Saxifragaceae (saxifrages), and Crassulaceae (stonecrops).

ROOT HAIR

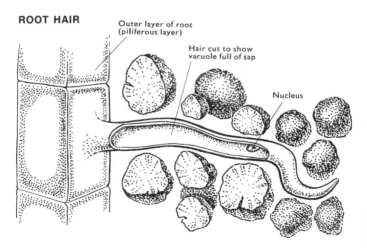

Outer layer of root (piliferous layer)

Hair cut to show vacuole full of sap

Nucleus

Drawing to show the way in which a root hair penetrates between the soil crumbs. The sap in the root hair is stronger than the soil solution and so water from around the soil crumbs moves into the root hair by osmosis (q.v.).

Rubiales. Order of dicotyledons containing the families Rubiaceae (bed-straws) and Caprifoliaceae (honey-suckle, elder, and guelder rose).

Ruderal. A plant typically occurring on waste land or land subject to disturbance by man—roadsides, rubbish dumps, bombed sites, etc. Examples include dandelion, stinging nettle, and plantains. (See *Weed*).

Sagittate. Arrow-shaped—especially of leaves. (See Page 136).

Salicaceae. (See *Salicales*).

Salicales. Order containing the sallows and willows and poplars, (family *Salicaceae*). They are trees or shrubs. The flowers of poplars are borne in hanging catkins while those of willows are borne in upright catkins. The male and

ROSACEAE

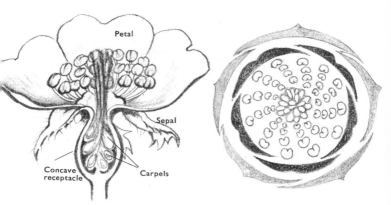

Half flower and floral diagram of rose *(Rosa)*.

Runcinate Leaf. Pinnatifid leaf with a triangular terminal lobe and with the other lobes pointing backwards. (See page 136).

Runner. Horizontal stem growing above ground and serving as an organ of vegetative reproduction—as in the strawberry. (See *Stem*).

Rust. One of the many important parasitic fungi of the class Basidiomycetes. Rusts cause serious diseases of cereals and other plants. (See *Diseases of plants; Fungi;* Page 108) and (Plate 14).

Saccharomyces. (=*Yeasts*, q.v.).

female catkins are carried on different trees and they normally appear before the leaves. Poplars are wind-pollinated while willows are pollinated by insects. (See Page 200) and (Plate 127).

Saltation. (=*Mutation*). Term used especially of fungi.

Samara. Type of fruit (q.v.).

Saprophyte. An organism that obtains its food from dead organic material. Many bacteria, the majority of fungi, and some flowering plants live in this way. (See *Fungi* and Plate 90).

Sapwood. Outer region of xylem of

Plate 95

SECONDARY THICKENING

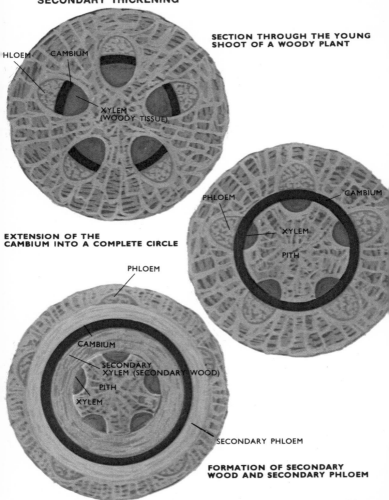

SECTION THROUGH THE YOUNG
SHOOT OF A WOODY PLANT

HLOEM

CAMBIUM

XYLEM
(WOODY TISSUE)

EXTENSION OF THE
CAMBIUM INTO A COMPLETE CIRCLE

PHLOEM

CAMBIUM

XYLEM

PITH

PHLOEM

CAMBIUM

SECONDARY
XYLEM (SECONDARY WOOD)

PITH

XYLEM

SECONDARY PHLOEM

FORMATION OF SECONDARY
WOOD AND SECONDARY PHLOEM

Young shoots of trees have their vascular bundles arranged in a
ring. Before secondary wood is formed the cambium spreads to
form a circle. Secondary tissues eventually obscure the original
positions of the vascular bundles.

198

Plate 96

SECONDARY THICKENING (Cont)

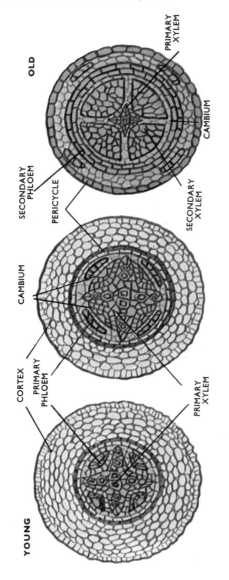

Stages in the development of secondary tissues in a root.

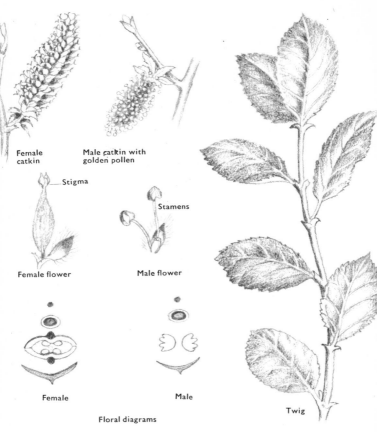

Female catkin

Male catkin with golden pollen

Stigma

Female flower

Stamens

Male flower

Female

Male

Floral diagrams

Some features of the sallow or pussy willow *(Salix).*

trees—the active region of water conduction. The heartwood in the centre is very compact and the vessels are crushed and unable to carry water.

Sarraceniales. Family of herbaceous dicotyledons which are insectivorous, catching insects and digesting them with juices from gland cells. The family includes the pitcher plant *Sarracenia* and the sundews *(Drosera).* (See Plate 110).

Saxifragaceae. (See *Rosales*).

Scalariform Thickening. (See *Xylem*).

Scape. Leafless flowering stem of plant with radical leaves—e.g. dandelion. (See Plate 13).

Schizocarp. Type of fruit (q.v.).

Scion. That portion of a plant which is grafted on to another plant. (See *Propagation*).

Sclereid. A woody cell (See *Sclerenchyma*).

Sclerenchyma. Tough mechanical tissue of plants composed largely of long fibres, thickly lignified and containing no protoplasm. Sclerenchyma frequently surrounds vascular tissue and the bundles of fibres in some plants are so tough that they are used to make ropes and other materials— hemp, sisal, linen, etc. The hard 'stones' found in pears and some other fruits are composed of sclerenchyma cells, although these are not elongated as the fibres are.

Sclerotium. Hard, compact mass of fungal hyphae, often with a sort of 'skin', that can remain inactive for long periods and then start into growth.

Scrophulariaceae. Family of dicotyledons containing foxgloves, speedwells, snapdragons, and a variety of other plants. Most are herbs and a number are semiparasites (e.g. eyebright). The flowers are irregular and very varied. The petals are united into a tube, at least at the base. The fruit is normally a capsule containing many small seeds. (See *Tubiflorae*) and (Plate 128).

Scrub. A community dominated by shrubs and bushes.

Scutellum. Name given to the seed leaf of grasses.

Seaweeds. Algae living around the shore, and sometimes far out to sea. They may be green, brown or red. (See *Algae; Chlorophyceae; Phaeophyceae; Rhodophyceae*) and (Plates 91-94).

Secondary Meristem. One that develops from parenchyma tissue by the readoption of the ability to divide. E.g. cork cambium and the cambium that forms at the site of a wound and produces cells to heal the wound. (See *Meristem; Cambium; Bark*).

Secondary Thickening. The laying down of extra strengthening and conducting tissue in a plant necessitated by increase in size. It happens in most dicotyledons, but especially in those with persistent aerial parts. It occurs in both stem and root by the reactivation of parenchyma which becomes meristematic and begins to form more xylem and phloem. (See *Root; Stem*) and (Plates 95 and 96).

Seed. Reproductive structure of flowering plants, conifers, and a few other plants such as seed ferns. The seed is formed from the fertilised ovule and contains an embryo and a food reserve. The seed coat (testa) is formed from the integument of the ovule. The embryo consists of a radicle (root), plumule (stem), and seed leaves (cotyledons). Gymnosperms have several seed leaves but flowering plants have either one or two. In flowering plants a special tissue called endosperm develops in the seed. This is a food reserve but it does not always persist into the mature seed. The food material may be absorbed rapidly into the cotyledons as in the runner bean seed. The seed is then called non-endospermous. But if the endosperm remains as a food store until the seed germinates, the seed is called endospermous. The castor oil bean is an endospermous seed. Seeds can usually be distinguished from fruits (q.v.) by the fact that seeds have only one scar—where the ovule stalk was attached. (This is easily noticeable when shelling peas from a pod.) Fruits, on the other hand, have two scars—one from the flower stalk junction, and one where the style or stigma was attached. (See

Plate 97

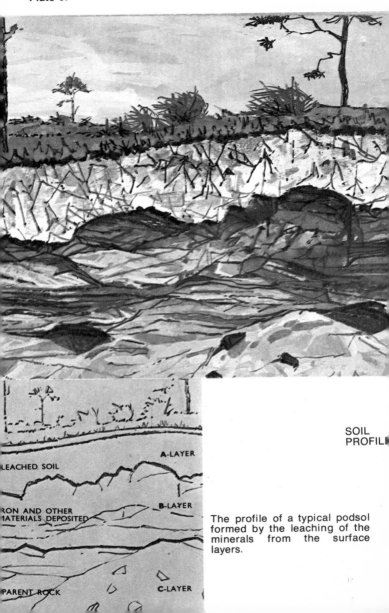

SOIL PROFILE

LEACHED SOIL

A-LAYER

IRON AND OTHER MATERIALS DEPOSITED

B-LAYER

PARENT ROCK

C-LAYER

The profile of a typical podsol formed by the leaching of the minerals from the surface layers.

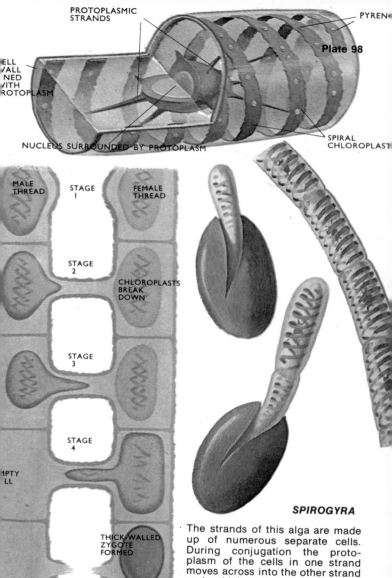

PROTOPLASMIC STRANDS

PYREN●

Plate 98

●ELL
●ALL
●NED
●ITH
●ROTOPLASM

NUCLEUS SURROUNDED BY PROTOPLASM

SPIRAL CHLOROPLAST

MALE THREAD

STAGE I

FEMALE THREAD

STAGE 2

CHLOROPLASTS BREAK DOWN

STAGE 3

STAGE 4

●PTY
●LL

THICK-WALLED ZYGOTE FORMED

THE STAGES OF CONJUGATION

SPIROGYRA

The strands of this alga are made up of numerous separate cells. During conjugation the protoplasm of the cells in one strand moves across into the other strand and thick-walled zygotes are formed. These grow into new strands.

Fertilisation; Germination; Spore) and (Plates 35–37).

Segregation. Separation of alleles (genes) into different gametes. (See *Heredity*).

Sere. (See *Succession*).

Serrate. (Of a leaf). With a toothed edge, like a saw. (See *Dentate*).

Sessile. Without a stalk.

SEED

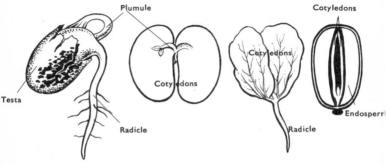

The bean (left) is a non-endospermous seed: the food reserve is contained within the swollen cotyledons. The castor oil seed is an endospermous seed: the food reserve is in the endosperm around the thin cotyledons.

Seismonasty. Response to vibration. It is well shown by the leaves of *Mimosa* which fold up and droop when the plant is knocked.

Selaginella. Moss-like plant related to club mosses but differing from them in being heterosporous. (See *Lycopodiales*).

Self Fertilisation. Fertilisation of an ovule by a male gamete from the same flower.

Self Pollination. Pollination of a stigma by pollen from the same flower.

Self Sterility. Inability to be fertilised by a gamete from the same flower. (See *Pollination*).

Sepal. One of the outermost parts of a flower (q.v.). Usually green and protective in function. Sepals form the calyx.

Seta. Stalk — especially of a capsule of a moss or liverwort. (See Plate 64).

Sex Chromosome. One of a pair of chromosomes (q.v.) that control sex determination. They are found in only a limited number of plants of course for the majority of plants are hermaphrodite and all alike.

Sexual Reproduction. Reproduction involving the joining of two gametes or sex-cells whether they be from the same or different individuals. (See *Asexual Reproduction*).

Short-day Plant. (See *Photoperiodism*).

Shrub. A woody plant, typically branching at or near the base and not developing much of a trunk. Of limited height.

Sieve Plate. Perforated end of sieve tube — one of the components of phloem tissue that conducts food materials through the plant. (See *Phloem*).

Sieve Tube. (See *Phloem*).

Silicula. Type of fruit (q.v.).

Siliqua. Type of fruit (q.v.).

Silurian Period. Division of Geological Time Scale (q.v.).

Siphonostele. (See *Stele*).

Slime Fungi. (=*Myxomycetes*).

Smut. Parasitic fungus of the class Basidiomycetes. They commonly cause diseases of cereals — producing masses of sooty black spores on the leaves or flowers.

Soil Profile. Vertical section through

SOLANACEAE

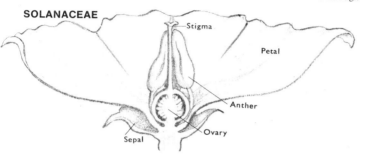

Stigma

Petal

Anther

Ovary

Sepal

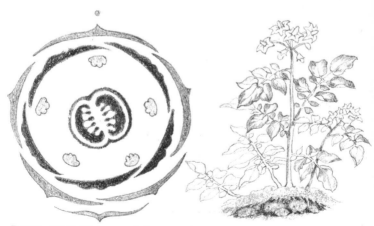

Potato plant *(Solanum tuberosum)*, together with a half flower and floral diagram.

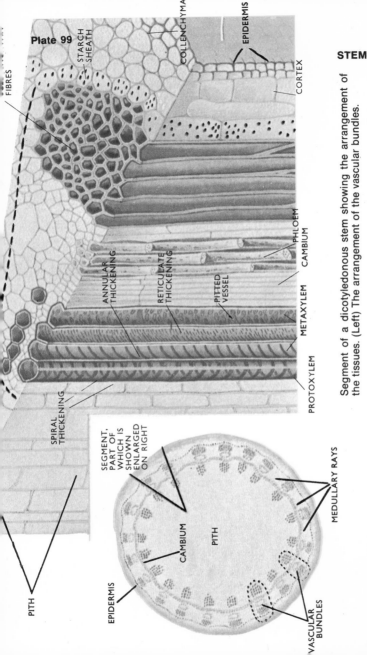

Plate 99

STEM

Segment of a dicotyledonous stem showing the arrangement of the tissues. (Left) The arrangement of the vascular bundles.

FIBRES

STARCH SHEATH

COLLENCHYMA

EPIDERMIS

CORTEX

ANNULAR THICKENING

RETICULATE THICKENING

PITTED VESSEL

PHLOEM

CAMBIUM

METAXYLEM

PROTOXYLEM

SPIRAL THICKENING

PITH

SEGMENT, PART OF WHICH IS SHOWN ENLARGED ON RIGHT

CAMBIUM

PITH

EPIDERMIS

MEDULLARY RAYS

VASCULAR BUNDLES

Plate 100

STEM (Cont)

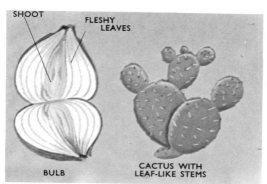

SHOOT
FLESHY LEAVES

BULB

CACTUS WITH LEAF-LIKE STEMS

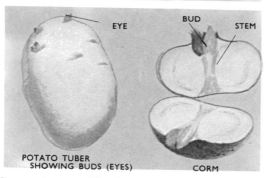

EYE

BUD   STEM

POTATO TUBER SHOWING BUDS (EYES)

CORM

Some stem modifications and (below) the arrangement and structure of the vascular bundles in a monocotyledonous stem.

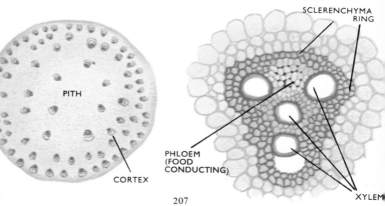

PITH

CORTEX

SCLERENCHYMA RING

PHLOEM (FOOD CONDUCTING)

XYLEM

207

the soil showing the various layers such as humus, top-soil, sub-soil, and parent rock below. The profile of a chalky soil on the downs is very different from that of a wood or a podsol (q.v.).

Solanaceae. Family containing the potato and tomato as well as the deadly nightshade. (See *Tubiflorae* and Page 205).

Solitary Flower. One borne alone on an unbranched axis. (See *Inflorescence*) and (Plate 49).

Soredia. (See *Lichens*).

Sorus. Group of sporangia on a fern frond. (See Plate 31).

Spadix. Thick, fleshy flowering spike of *Arum* and other lilies.

Spathe. Large bract protecting a spadix. The name is also applied to the membranous covering protecting the unopened flowers of daffodils and related plants. (See Plate 126).

Species. The smallest normally-used category of classification (q.v.). The members of a species are generally very much alike and can all be interbreed. They cannot, however, cross with other species and produce normal fertile offspring. This ensures that the species remains distinct, although genetic variations can occur within the species. The variations will be 'smoothed out' by cross breeding in any given area but, if a species covers a wide range, the variations in one area will probably be somewhat different from those found at the other end of the range. The plants differing in this way are called *sub-species*. At first these sub-species can produce fertile plants if they pollinate each other but if they remain separated and unable to cross with each other, the differences may increase to such an extent that the two sub-species cannot fertilise each other even if pollen is artificially transferred from one to the other. The

original species has then evolved along two different lines and produced two separate species.

Spermatium. Non-mobile male gamete found in a few algae and fungi.

Spermatophyta. All the seed-bearing plants — flowering plants and the conifers, together with a few others.

Spermatozoid. Motile, flagellated male gamete, common among lower plants.

SPATHE

The fleshy flowering spike or spadix of *Arum* (cuckoo-pint or lords-and-ladies), surrounded by its protective spathe. The flower is pollinated by small flies which are attracted by the smell and trapped for a while in the base of the spike.

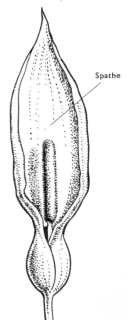

Spathe

Spermogonium. Structure in which fungal spermatia are formed.

Sphenophyllales. Extinct group of Pteridophyta (q.v.) including *Sphenophyllum*. (See Plate 23).

Spike. Type if inflorescence (q.v.) in which individual flowers are attached directly to main axis without stalks.

Spindle. Phenomenon observed during nuclear division. (See *Meiosis; Mitosis*).

Spiral Thickening. (See *Xylem*).

Spirogyra. A very common alga of the class Chlorophyceae. Its green strands are found in almost every pond and stream. Each strand consists of a chain of tiny cells all of which look alike and can act as a single separate plant. The most noticeable feature of the cells is the spiral chloroplast which gives the plant its name. The chloroplast coils round the cell close to the cell wall and the nucleus is suspended in the centre of the large vacuole. The cells divide rapidly when food and warmth are available and the strands grow in length. If a strand is broken, each part can continue to grow just as if nothing has happened and so large masses can quickly accumulate. *Spirogyra* also reproduces by *conjugation*. Neighbouring strands come close together and projections from one strand grow out and join with the other so that the two strands resemble a ladder (Plate 98). By this time the contents of the cells have shrunk and the cell contents of one strand move across into the opposite cells and join with the protoplasm there. The fused masses of protoplasm produce thick walls around themselves and these walled structures are called *zygospores*. They are released when the old cell walls break up and they fall to the bottom of the pond. They are resistant to cold and drought and can be blown about by the wind if the pond dries up. When they reach suitable conditions again they germinate by sending out a strand of cells just like one of the original strands. This type of reproduction takes place when conditions are not very favourable for growth and so the species is not destroyed when its habitat temporarily freezes or dries up. (See *Algae*) and (Plate 98).

Spontaneous Generation. The idea, squashed by Pasteur, that living things, especially micro-organisms such as fungi and bacteria, arose spontaneously from dead organic material. Pasteur showed conclusively that the micro-organisms associated with dead and decaying matter originated from spores in the air and that spontaneous generation does not occur.

Sporangiophore. Special hypha of fungi carrying the spore-containing sporangium. (See Plate 39).

Sporangium. Structure in which asexual spores are formed. Found in groups on fern fronds and represented by the ovule of seed plants. (See Plate 31).

Spore. A true spore is a non-sexual reproductive body produced by the sporophyte generation (See *Alternation of Generations*) of a plant after meiosis. Spores are thus haploid and they develop, without pairing, into the gametophyte generation of the plant. Spores are produced by all plants but they are most obvious in fungi and ferns.

Fungal spores are released from the fruiting bodies and grow into new hyphae whose nuclei must join at some stage before a further generation of spores can be produced. The asexual zoospores produced by the haploid thallus of many algae and fungi are not true spores for they are not part of the alternation of generations.

Mosses and liverworts produce spores in capsules which are the sporophyte stage of the life-cycle. The spores develop into new moss plants which bear sex organs. Fusion of sex-cells then gives rise to new spore-bearing capsules. (See *Hepaticae; Musci*).

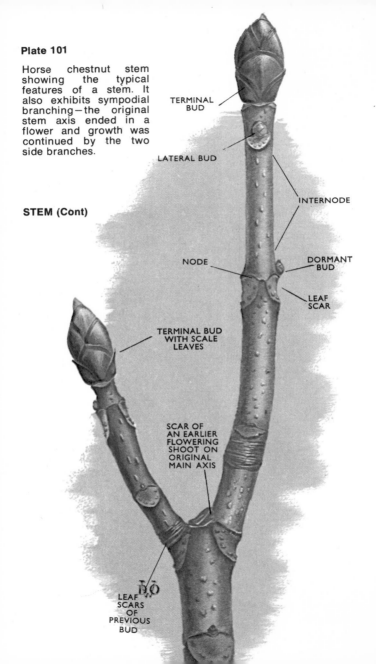

Plate 101

Horse chestnut stem showing the typical features of a stem. It also exhibits sympodial branching—the original stem axis ended in a flower and growth was continued by the two side branches.

STEM (Cont)

TERMINAL BUD

LATERAL BUD

INTERNODE

NODE

DORMANT BUD

LEAF SCAR

TERMINAL BUD WITH SCALE LEAVES

SCAR OF AN EARLIER FLOWERING SHOOT ON ORIGINAL MAIN AXIS

LEAF SCARS OF PREVIOUS BUD

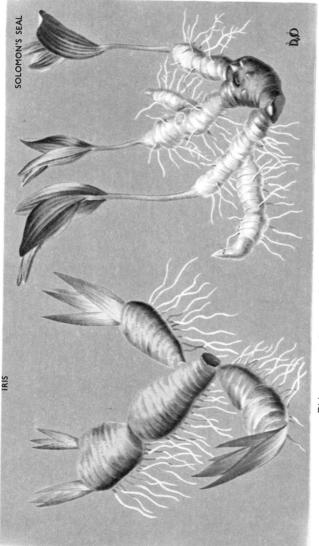

SOLOMON'S SEAL

IRIS

Rhizomes—underground storage organs—are modified stems.

Fern spores are formed in sporangia which are normally situated on the fronds. The spore grows into a prothallus which bears sex-organs. In most cases the spores are all alike and the prothalli formed all produce both male and female sex-organs. There are, however, a number of species in which two different types of spore are formed. One – the *microspore* – gives rise to prothalli with male organs while the larger *megaspore* develops into a prothallus with female organs. (See *Filicales*).

This is taken a stage further in seed-bearing plants – two types of spore are always formed and only the microspore (the pollen grain) is released. The megaspore remains within its sporangium (the ovule) and there produces a number of cells which represent the prothallus. One of the nuclei is the female cell which fuses with a male cell formed in the pollen grain (See *Fertilisation*). The new sporophyte embryo then develops within the sporangium of the previous sporophyte generation and the whole structure forms a *seed* (q.v.).

The thick-walled resting cells produced by many lower plants are not true spores because they are not an essential stage in the life-cycle.

Spore Mother Cell. Diploid cell in a sporangium which, by a meiotic division, gives rise to four spores.

Sporogonium. Sporophyte generation of bryophytes – the capsule in which spores are formed. (See Plate 64).

Sporophyll. Modified leaf bearing sporangia. In ferns and other pteridophytes the sporophylls are often otherwise-normal leaves. In gymnosperms – conifers and others – the sporophylls are small and aggregated into cones. The carpels and stamens of flowering plants are the equivalents of sporophylls. In those plants which produce separate megaspores and microspores, the sporangia and sporophylls are similarly referred to as mega- and micro-. (See *Spore; Sporangium*) and (Plates 21, 77 and 125).

Sporophyte. Stage in the life cycle which produces spores and whose nuclei are diploid. (See *Alternation of Generations*).

Sport. Abnormal individual or part of an individual arising from a mutation (q.v.).

Spur. Slender, hollow projection of a petal, often containing nectar. (Plate 78).

Stamen. Male part of flower (q.v.) consisting of filament and pollen-producing anther.

Staminate. Having stamens but no carpels – a male flower such as a hazel catkin.

Staminode. Sterile, non-pollen-producing stamen.

Statocyte. Cell containing starch granule or other solid particle that is free to move in the cell under the action of gravity. It is believed that the mechanism is responsible for some geotropic responses in plants.

Statolith. The solid particle in a statocyte (q.v.).

Stele. Central cylinder or core of vascular and strengthening tissues in a root or stem. The simplest arrangement is the protostele which consists of a solid central core of xylem surrounded by a ring of phloem – as in roots and certain fern stems. In the siphonostele the xylem and phloem form concentric cylinders surrounding a central pith. The dictyostele, found in certain fern stems, is broken up into a network of strands by numerous leaf gaps very close together. There is a central pith and so the dictyostele is a modified siphonostele.

Stem. Stems perform two basic functions: they support the leaves and flowers and they carry water and food from place to place within the plant. The typical flowering plant stem is

Parenchyma

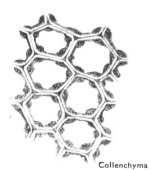

Collenchyma

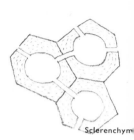

Sclerenchyma

Three important plant tissues seen in cross section.

cylindrical and may be soft (*herbaceous*) or woody. It is usually branched and leafy. The point at which a leaf joins the stem is called the *node*. There are several nodes on a stem, each separated by leafless *internodes*. Each node has one or more leaves, each of which has a bud in its basal angle (*axil*). These *axillary* buds often remain dormant, but may produce a branch, especially if the main stem is damaged. Buds are in fact miniature stems which have not yet elongated and whose leaves are clustered together around the tip (the *growing point*). It is in winter that buds are most noticeable. The outer leaves are modified as protective scales around the young stem. When these scale-leaves fall off in spring they leave rings of scars on the stem. The age of a woody twig can be established by counting these scar patches. The main axis of a plant may continue to grow throughout life, giving off branches laterally. This is the *racemose* or *monopodial* branching habit, well illustrated in larches and 'Christmas trees'. The *cymose* or *sympodial* branching habit differs in that the

main stem apex does not continue through life. It ends in a flower or dies away and a lateral bud assumes the main position each year.

The stem contains conducting and supporting tissues which are basically similar in all parts of the plant but the arrangement of the tissues differs in stems and roots. The arrangement also differs between monocotyledons and dicotyledons. A typical dicotyledon stem is described here.

A section of an internode cut a short distance from the tip shows the mature primary structure. The *epidermal cells* are regular and have a waxy cuticle on the outside. The cortex cells are simple and of the type known as *parenchyma*. In the outer cortical region the cells have thicker walls for extra support and are known as *collenchyma* cells. The inner layer of the cortex is the *starch sheath* whose cells have starch deposits within them. Inside this sheath is the *stele*, made up of *vascular tissue* and *pith*. The conducting (vascular) tissue is arranged in *vascular bundles,* each with a number of *sclerenchyma* fibres on the outside. These are elongated cells

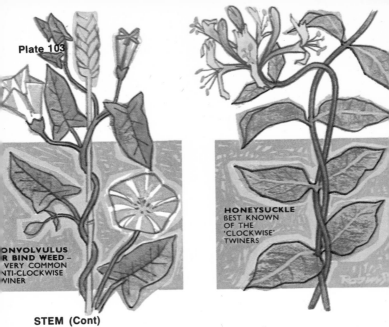

Plate 103

CONVOLVULUS OR BIND WEED – VERY COMMON ANTI-CLOCKWISE TWINER

HONEYSUCKLE BEST KNOWN OF THE 'CLOCKWISE' TWINERS

STEM (Cont)

Clockwise and anti-clockwise twining stems.

The upper leaflets of the sweet pea are modified into climbing tendrils.

TENDRILS (MODIFIED LEAFLET)

NORMAL LEAFLET

TENDRIL STEM IS WINGED, INCREASING PHOTOSYNTHETIC SURFACE

LEAF-LIKE STIPULES

Plate 104

SUCCESSION

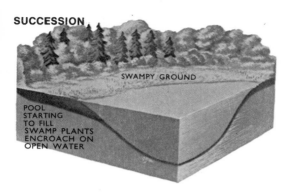

SWAMPY GROUND

POOL STARTING TO FILL SWAMP PLANTS ENCROACH ON OPEN WATER

A

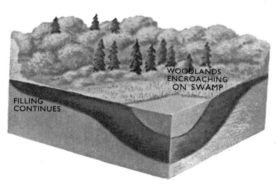

WOODLANDS ENCROACHING ON SWAMP

FILLING CONTINUES

B

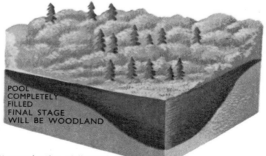

POOL COMPLETELY FILLED FINAL STAGE WILL BE WOODLAND

C

Stages in the obliteration of a pool.

215

whose walls have been impregnated with various chemicals known collectively as *lignin*. The fibres have no protoplasm: they are tough and elastic, enabling the plant to withstand bending by the wind. The *phloem* (q.v.) is the tissue through which manufactured food is transported. *Cambium* is the name given to the actively dividing cells or *meristems* in the centre of the bundle. These play an important part in secondary growth. The inner part of the bundle consists of the water-conducting tissue — *xylem* (q.v.). The pith and the *medullary rays* between the bundles are normally of simple parenchyma.

Monocotyledon bundles are irregularly arranged and contain no cambium. Strengthening may occur near the outside of the stem and the bundles are frequently surrounded by sclerenchyma fibres.

The growing point of a stem is right at the tip and consists of rapidly-dividing, unvacuolated, meristematic cells. Growth takes place just behind the tip where the new cells develop vacuoles and lengthen rapidly, producing an elongation of the stem. As the cells lengthen they begin to change in character (*differentiate*). The outer cells develop into epidermal cells and very quickly tiny leaves arise and cover the growing point. Other cells give rise to the cortex, while certain columns of cells retain their ability to divide and are known as the *procambial strands*. In the elongating region the first conducting tissues (*protoxylem* and *protophloem*) are formed from the procambial strands. The vascular tissues lengthen very rapidly and form the conducting strands. At about the same time the first strengthening tissues develop on the outside of the phloem. The procambial strands continue to produce vascular tissue beyond the elongating region until only a narrow band of cambium remains.

Secondary thickening occurs to some degree in most dicotyledons and is especially marked in those with perennial aerial parts. It involves the laying down of extra vascular and strengthening tissue necessitated by the increased size of the plant. Some of the cells of the medullary rays become active again and join with the cambium of the vascular bundles to form a meristematic ring. Secondary xylem and phloem are then formed. The xylem tissues build up inside the cambium and force it and the phloem further from the centre. A tree trunk consists mainly of xylem tissue, with a thin layer of phloem near the outside. In areas with well-marked seasons the xylem shows *annual rings*. In the spring, when the sap is rising, the xylem consists mainly of large vessels, but in autumn there is a high proportion of fibres. In cross-section spring and autumn wood are very different, producing the ringed effect. Secondary phloem does not build up a thick layer because the cells are unthickened and are sooner or later crushed by the pressure of the expanding xylem tissue. This tension usually breaks down the epidermis too and its protective function is taken over by the *phellem*. This is a corky tissue formed from a layer of cortex which becomes meristematic. The phellem is a dead tissue and cuts off food from all tissues outside it. These tissues also die and as a whole they form the *bark*.

Stems frequently perform other functions in addition to or instead of their basic ones. The chief modifications are concerned with food storage and vegetative reproduction. *Runners* are long thin stems which spread over the ground surface and produce new plants some distance from the parent. Strawberries reproduce rapidly in this way. Horizontally-growing underground stems are termed *rhizomes*. They may be food stores, as in irises, or merely reproductive shoots, as in some grasses. Potatoes are swellings (*tubers*) arising on the underground parts of the stem. They serve as food stores and reproductive organs. These underground stems can be distinguished from roots by the presence of scale leaves and buds. *Corms* are special types of underground stems. They are swollen with food reserves and carry a number of scale leaves. One or more buds are developed in the axils of the leaves and these buds produce the flowering shoots. The base of each new shoot forms a new corm. *Bulbs* are small underground stems with a number of fleshy scales in which food material is stored. In both corms and bulbs the flowering shoot is fully formed underground and grows rapidly when environmental conditions are suitable. Next year's shoot develops in the axil of one of this year's leaves.

Climbing stems are fairly common. They may climb by coiling round a support (e.g. runner bean), by using tendrils (e.g. vine) or they may scramble over the vegetation using hooked prickles (e.g. blackberry). Protective spines often occur as stem modifications (hawthorn) or as stem outgrowths (rose). Stems are in some cases modified to perform as leaves. Butcher's broom has very leaflike branch stems and its leaves are tiny scales. The stems of cacti also act as leaves (and water stores too). Stems acting as leaves are called *cladodes* or *phylloclades*. (See Plates 95, and 99–103).

Sterigma. Tiny stalk bearing one or more spores in fungi. (See Plate 65).

Sterile. (1) Unable to reproduce sexually. (2) Uncontaminated by living organisms.

Stigma. Surface of carpel receptive to pollen grains – may be sticky or feathery. (See *Flower*) and (Plate 81).

Stipe. Stalk – especially of toadstools and of algae. (See Plate 66).

Stipule. Outgrowth of the base of a leaf-stalk. Often leaf-like but sometimes modified as spines. (Plate 53).

Stock. Plant on to which another is grafted or budded. (See *Propagation*).

Stolon. Modified stem growing horizontally above ground and rooting at the nodes. (See *Stem; Vegetative Reproduction*).

Stoma. Tiny opening in plant epidermis – especially of leaves – through which gaseous interchange with air takes place. (See *Leaf*) and (Plate 54).

Stone Cell. Tough woody cell composed of sclerenchyma (q.v.) and found singly or in groups in various parts of plants. Pear fruits contain large numbers of them.

Stonewort. Member of the order Charales, grouped with the algae for convenience although their position is unclear. They live in water and the main axis of the plant has distinct nodes from which branches arise.

Strobilus. A cone or cone-like group of sporophylls. (See Plate 21).

Stroma. Dense mass of fungal hyphae in which fruiting bodies are produced.

Style. Elongation of carpel carrying stigma into a more prominent position. Not present in all species of flowering plant. (See Plate 81).

Suberin. Complicated mixture of fatty acid derivatives responsible for the impervious nature of cork.

Suberisation. Deposition of suberin.

Sub-species. (See *Species*).

Succession. The progressive changes in the vegetation of a habitat from first colonisation to the attainment of the climax associated with the prevailing climate. (See Climax Vegetation). A hillside after a landslip will first be colonised by lichens and mosses, then by grasses and other herbs, finally by shrubs and trees. Ponds gradually become filled as reeds and other water plants die and accumulate on the bottom, allowing terrestrial plants to encroach. Any particular example of a succession is called a *sere*. (See Plate 104).

Plate 105

THORN

DWARF
BRANCH

HAWTHORN THORNS ARE DWARF STEMS

SPINOSE
LEAVES
ON DWARF
BRANCH

DWARF
BRANCH
(THORN)

GORSE
LEAVES AND
BRANCHES FORM
SPINES AND THORNS

GOOSEBERRY
SPINES ARE OUTGROWTHS
OF LEAF BASE

COPRINUS PLICATILIS

Plate 106
TOADSTOOL

SHAGGY INK-CAP

TRICHOLOMA SULPHUREUM

▲ MOREL

FLY AGARIC

▼ PUFF-BALL

Succulent. Fleshy—of fruits, or of xerophytic plants with water stores.

Sucker. Shoot arising from a root or underground stem, usually some way away from the main stem. It develops its own roots and becomes a separate plant. It is thus an organ of *vegetative reproduction* (q.v.).

Sucrose. Cane sugar—a food reserve found in many plants. It is a di-saccharide and before use in the plant its molecule is split into a molecule of glucose and one of fructose.

Superior Ovary. Ovary or gynaecium which is above the insertion of the petals of the flower (hypogynous condition).

Suspensor. String of cells formed in early development of seed plant embryo and from which the embryo proper develops.

Symbiont. One of the partners in symbiosis (q.v.).

Symbiosis. A close association between two organisms, of different species, which benefits both individuals. There are many examples in the animal world and many more in which animals associate with plants. Several coelenterates—corals, sea-anemones, etc.—have green algae living in their tissues. The algae are of no food value to the animals and it has been shown that the oxygen they release bears no relationship to the needs of the animal but it appears that the algae use up the waste materials produced by the animal tissues. This is of benefit to the animal and the algae get shelter and food in return.

Leguminous plants usually harbour certain bacteria in nodules on their roots. These bacteria are able to convert free nitrogen into nitrates which the plant can use. In return they gain shelter and food from the leguminous plant. The associations between fungi and the roots of higher plants are also good examples of symbiosis. (See

Mycorrhiza). But the most striking examples of symbiosis in plants are the *lichens* (q.v.). These strange plants that seem to be able to grow almost everywhere are actually made up of fungi and algae. The algae live within the mass of fungal hyphae that make up the body of the lichen.

Sympetalae. Sub-division of flowering plants (Dicotyledonae) in which the petals are united. (=*Metachlamydeae*).

Sympetalous. With united petals.

Sympodial Branching. (See *Monopodial Branching*) and (Plate 101).

Synangium. Group of united sporangia.

Syncarpous. With joined carpels.

Syngamy. The union of gametes.

Systematics. The study of classification according to phylogenetic relationships.

Tapetum. Layer of nutritive cells surrounding spore mother cells in a sporangium.

Tap Root. (See *Root*) and (Plate 89).

Taxis. Movement of a complete organism in response to a stimulus, e.g. chemo-taxis in response to a chemical stimulus. (See *Tropism*).

Taxonomy. The science of naming living organisms and classifying them. (See *Systematics*).

Telophase. A stage in nuclear division. (See *Meiosis; Mitosis*).

Tendril. Modified stem or leaf which is thin and used for climbing by twining or adhesion. (Plate 103).

Tepal. Name given to segment of perianth when there is no distinction into petals and sepals—e.g. tulip.

Terpene. A type of unsaturated hydro-carbon which is a common constituent of plant oils and resins.

Tertiary Period. Division of Geological Time Scale (q.v.).

Testa. Seed coat. (See *Seed*).

Tetrad. A group of four spores all formed from one spore mother cell.

Tetradynamous. (Of an androecium). Having four long stamens and two short stamens—as in the family Cruciferae.

Thallophyta. Large division of the plant kingdom containing the most primitive plants—algae, fungi, and lichens, and also the bacteria and slime fungi although these are not clearly related to other thallophytes. The body of thallophytes is simple in that it is not divided into root, stem, and leaf, although, as in the case of various sea-weeds, it may be very large. This simple body is called a thallus. (See *Algae; Fungi; Lichens; Bacteria*) and (Pages 245-252).

Thallus. Simple plant body of the Thallophyta (q.v.).

Thermonasty. Movement of a plant organ in response to a non-directional heat stimulus—e.g. the opening of flowers when brought into a warm room.

Thiamin. Vitamin B_1, also called aneurin. This important vitamin is synthesised by most green plants.

Thigmotropism. Curvature of a plant organ in response to tactile stimuli. E.g. the curving of a tendril around a support.

Thorn. A sharp, woody structure, strictly one that is a modified stem as in the hawthorn. Other pointed structures, such as those of the acacia which are modified stipules, are called spines. Thorns are sometimes called stem-spines. The prickles of roses are

not modified organs but outgrowths of the stem and are called *emergences*. (See Plate 105).

Tissue. A mass of cells all of the same or similar type and performing the same function in the body. Examples are phloem tissue conducting food materials through the plant and sclerenchyma tissue providing support.

Toadstool. Common name given to fungi of the family Agaricaceae and other stalked fungi which are of characteristic shape. They are basidiomycete fungi. (See *Fungi; Mushroom*) and (Plates 65, 66 and 106).

Tonoplast. Protoplasmic membrane bordering the vacuole of a cell.

Torus. (See *Pit*).

Trace Element. Element that is required in minute amounts for correct plant growth. Lack of a trace element leads to deficiency disease while too much of it can produce deformities. Examples of trace elements needed by plants are boron and manganese.

Tracheid. A type of cell found in xylem tissue (q.v.).

Transect. A line drawn across a region and along which samples are taken to illustrate the changes in vegetation accompanying changes in some feature such as height, soil, or water table. (See Page 224).

Transfusion Tissue. Mass of mainly empty cells around the vascular strands in gymnosperm leaves, through which water reaches the photosynthetic cells of the leaves.

Translocation. The movement of organic food materials—sugars, etc.—within the plant from the manufacturing or storage regions to where it is needed.

Transpiration. The evaporation of water vapour from the surface of

Plate 107   **TRICHOME**

Plant hairs form some of the most important plant glands. The stinging cells of the nettle are special secretory structures which inject poison into marauding animals. A protective tip breaks away, leaving the needle-like point of the stinging cell exposed.

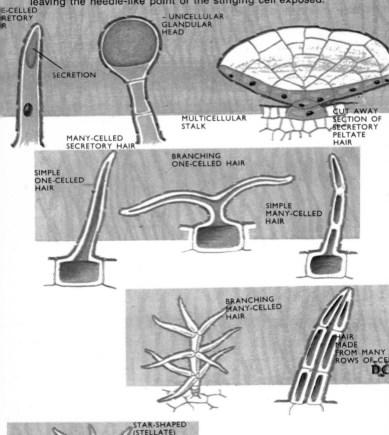

E-CELLED
RETORY
R

SECRETION

– UNICELLULAR GLANDULAR HEAD

MULTICELLULAR STALK

CUT AWAY SECTION OF SECRETORY PELTATE HAIR

MANY-CELLED SECRETORY HAIR

SIMPLE ONE-CELLED HAIR

BRANCHING ONE-CELLED HAIR

SIMPLE MANY-CELLED HAIR

BRANCHING MANY-CELLED HAIR

HAIR MADE FROM MANY ROWS OF CE

STAR-SHAPED (STELLATE) MANY-CELLED HAIR

The structure and formation of various types of plant hairs.

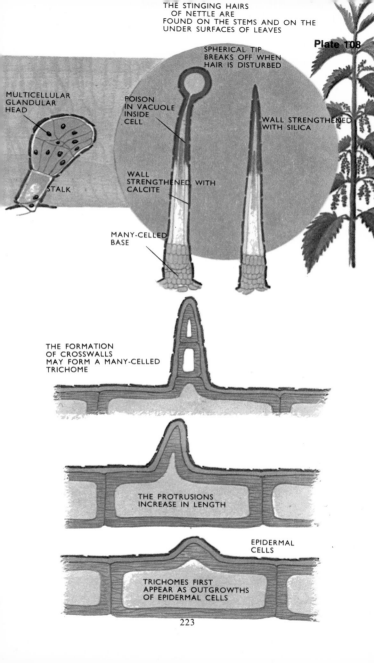

THE STINGING HAIRS
OF NETTLE ARE
FOUND ON THE STEMS AND ON THE
UNDER SURFACES OF LEAVES

Plate 108

SPHERICAL TIP
BREAKS OFF WHEN
HAIR IS DISTURBED

MULTICELLULAR
GLANDULAR
HEAD

POISON
IN VACUOLE
INSIDE
CELL

WALL STRENGTHENED
WITH SILICA

STALK

WALL
STRENGTHENED WITH
CALCITE

MANY-CELLED
BASE

THE FORMATION
OF CROSSWALLS
MAY FORM A MANY-CELLED
TRICHOME

THE PROTRUSIONS
INCREASE IN LENGTH

EPIDERMAL
CELLS

TRICHOMES FIRST
APPEAR AS OUTGROWTHS
OF EPIDERMAL CELLS

223

TRANSECT

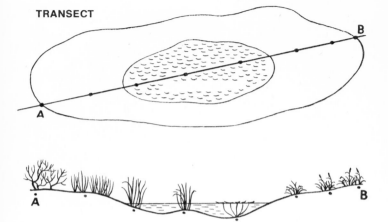

The transect across the region from A to B shows how the vegetation varies with the height above the water level.

plants. It occurs mainly through the stomata of the leaves. (See *Leaf*). The evaporation of water from the surfaces of cells near the stomata produces a 'pull' on the water around cells deeper in the leaf. This 'pull' from the thousands of stomata in the thousands of leaves is responsible – at least in part – for the upward movement of water through the plant stem. This movement up the stem and through the leaves is called the *transpiration stream*. Transpiration also has a cooling effect on the plant. Excessive transpiration – if it

TRANSPIRATION

A simple experiment to demonstrate transpiration. The pot is covered with polythene and the condensation on the bell jar can have come only from water given off by the leaves.

224

takes place faster than a plant can absorb water from the soil — causes wilting.

Triassic Period. Division of the Geological Time Scale (q.v.).

Trichogyne. Structure on the female organ of various algae and fungi through which the male gamete gains access to the female cell.

Trichome. Plant hair formed by the outgrowth of an epidermal cell. The shape, size and structure varies greatly according to function. Root hairs (Plate 87) are minute trichomes which increase the absorbing surface of the root. Trichomes are found to a greater or lesser degree on most stems and leaves. Plants growing in exposed conditions frequently have a good covering of hairs which protect them from the cold or from the drying effects of sun and wind.

Hairs may be unicellular (root hairs) or multicellular and may be branched or unbranched. They are often short lived — being required only for the protection of buds, etc. — but some are quite persistent and retain their living contents. Those whose protoplasm is lost normally look white because of the reflection of light from them.

Cell walls are normally of cellulose but they may become woody or even impregnated with silica or calcium carbonate. Such sharp, rigid hairs protect the plants from enemies such as slugs and snails. Stiff hairs, especially if hooked as in goose-grass, may assist in climbing.

Trichomes are often capable of secretion. Secretary trichomes form some of the most important glands found in the plant kingdom. The most common glandular hairs are multicellular — a number of cells forming a *stalk* and a *head*. The actual secretory cells of the structure have large nuclei and dense protoplasm. Droplets of secretion can be seen inside the living tissues of the young cells. In the mature cell the fluid usually lies between the cellulose wall and the cuticle and is released when the cuticle breaks.

The substances secreted vary with plants — resins, gums, volatile oils, mucilage. Sometimes the oils are scented and give plants their characteristic fragrance — e.g. lavender.

The *stinging hairs* of the common nettle are very special. The hair is made of a single secretory cell embedded in a multi-cellular epidermal stalk. The cell walls of the secretory cells are reinforced with calcite in the lower half and silica in the upper regions. Within the living protoplasm is a large vacuole filled with a complex chemical poison.

Quite broad at its base, the hair tapers to a point near its apex, and then expands into a small spherical tip. If the hair is disturbed by an animal the tip breaks off along a pre-determined line of weakness; the sharp tip of the stinging hair is left exposed. It penetrates a skin surface easily. The compression of the bladder-like stalk drives the poison from the main part of the secretory cell into the wound. The poison is a complex substance known to contain a *histamine* and an *acetycholine*. Inside the skin, it sets up an irritation and causes swellings and flushings of the skin surface.

Cotton fibres are really very long trichomes. Though each hair is made of only one cell it may elongate until it is over two inches long. Cotton is found covering the seeds of the cotton plant. The hairs aid wind disposal. Many other seeds are similarly equipped. (See Plates 107–109).

Triploid. Form of polyploidy (q.v.) in which the nucleus of an organism has three times the haploid number of chromosomes. (See *Chromosome*).

Tropism. A bending movement of part of a stem in response to some directional stimulus. Examples are phototropism — bending of stems in response to light — and geotropism — the downward curving of roots and the upward curving of stems in a plant laid horizontally. The stimulus in this

Plate 109
TRICHOME (Cont)

Further examples of plant hairs.

COTTON
IS
REALLY
PLANT
HAIR
COVERING
SEEDS

The sundew folds its leaves ov
when they are stimulated by
insect. (Below) Seedlings in f
light are normal: those grown
the dark are upright and spindl
side lighting causes a shoot
bend. The experiment (far rigl
shows that tropisms are initiat
by the stem tip. Shoots with the t
covered or removed do not be
towards light.

TROPISM

SEA-PURSLANE
– ITS LEAVES
ARE EQUIPPED
WITH PELTATE
HAIRS

EACH
SEGMENT
IS AN INDIVIDUAL
CELL

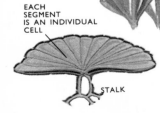

STALK

226

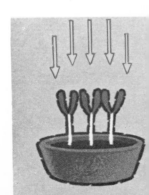

Plate 110

latter example is the downward force of gravity. The actual bending is due to differential growth caused by unequal distribution of a hormone or hormones known as *auxins*. (See Plates 2 and 110).

Truffle. Fruiting body of certain ascomycete fungi.

Tuber. Food store formed from a swollen root or underground stem. The potato is a stem tuber but dahlia tubers are modified roots. Tubers are able to grow into new plants when detached from the parent plant and are thus agents of vegetative reproduction (q.v.). (See *Root; Stem*) and (Plates 87 and 100).

Tubiflorae. A large order of dicotyle-dons, mainly herbaceous, including several families of widely varying form. The corolla is tubular—at least at the base and is 4- or 5-lobed. The stamens—equal to or less than the corolla lobes in number—are attached to the corolla. (See *Boraginaceae; Convolvulaceae; Labiatae; Solanaceae; and Scrophulariaceae*) and (Plate 128).

Tundra. Name given to the land in circum-polar regions which is frozen for most of the year but which supports a certain amount of plant life. The tundra is beyond the tree line and the plants are all small. A few stunted, creeping willows and birches are found and other flowering plants which make the tundra a brilliant mass of colour for a short period each year. Most of the

TUBIFLORAE (Family Boraginaceae)

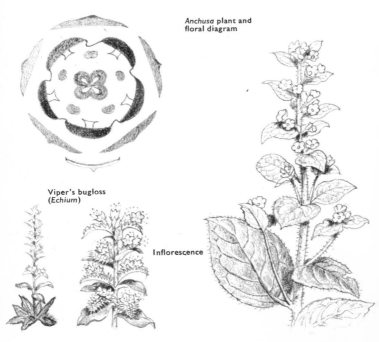

Anchusa plant and floral diagram

Viper's bugloss
(*Echium*)

Inflorescence

TUBIFLORAE (Family Scrophulariaceae)

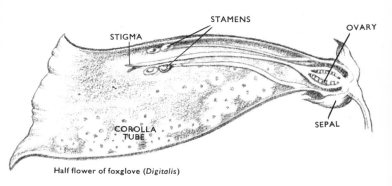

STAMENS

STIGMA

OVARY

COROLLA TUBE

SEPAL

Half flower of foxglove (*Digitalis*)

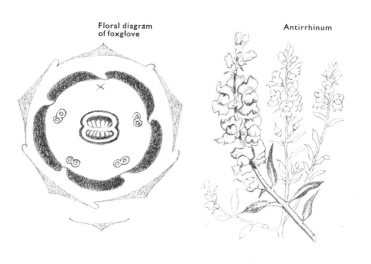

Floral diagram of foxglove

Antirrhinum

Above and opposite: some members of the order Tubiflorae.

Plate 111

TROPISM (Cont)

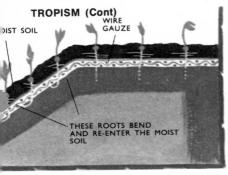

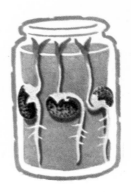

The beans in the jar show that whichever way up the seed is placed, the root will grow down and the shoot up. By growing seeds above a wire gauze, however, one can demonstrate (left) that moisture has a greater attraction for roots than gravity—the roots curve back into the moist soil instead of continuing their downward growth.

(Below) The revolving clinostat continuously alters the position of the plants with respect to gravity and there is no response. Only the stationary seedlings (bottom) respond to gravity in the normal way.

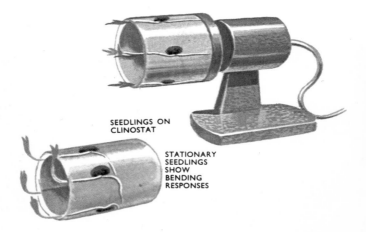

SEEDLINGS ON CLINOSTAT

STATIONARY SEEDLINGS SHOW BENDING RESPONSES

TUNDRA

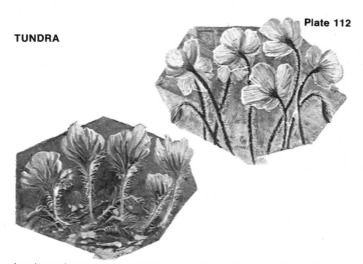

Plate 112

In winter the tundra is a frozen waste but with the melting of the ice the land becomes clothed with quick-growing colourful flowers. There are no plants of any size in the tundra regions.

TUNDRA IN SUMMER

species of plant, however, are mosses and lichens. Their growing season is very short and the plants must produce flowers and fruits (or equivalent structures) very quickly while the ground surface is unfrozen. (See Plate 112).

Turgid. In a state of turgor (q.v.).

Turgor. Condition of a plant cell in which the vacuole is full of sap and making the cell-wall rigid. If a plant loses water the cells lose their turgor and the plant becomes limp. It is rather like a car tyre — if it is fully pumped up it is firm and can support weight, but if some of the air escapes it becomes soft and floppy.

Tylose. A swelling blocking the cavity of a xylem vessel or tracheid. The vessels of the heartwood of trees are nearly all blocked in this way. The swelling develops from the cell membrane.

Umbel. A type of inflorescence (q.v.)

Umbelliferae. Large family of dicotyledons, mainly herbs, in which the inflorescence is usually an umbel or compound umbel. The flowers are epigynous and usually white. Nectar is freely exposed and the large, showy flowering heads are pollinated by many types of insect. (See Plates 79 and 80). Stems are often hollow. Examples include cow parsley, angelica, parsnip, and carrot.

Unicostate. (Of a leaf) Having a single main vein — e.g. privet, oak. (See Plate 52).

Unilocular. (Of an ovary) Having a single seed-containing cavity.

Unisexual. Flowers with only stamens or carpels in each individual are unisexual, i.e. the flowers are either male or female. Male and female flowers may both occur on one plant (e.g. hazel) or there may be separate male and female plants (e.g. willow). (See

Hermaphrodite; Monoecious; Dioecious).

Urticales. Order of dicotyledons including the nettle, hop, and elm. The 4 or 5 perianth segments are more or less united and are sepaloid. They are not normally conspicuous. (Page 236).

Vacuole. Central, fluid-filled space in a cell. Most plant cells have a single large vacuole. The sap it contains is responsible for the turgor (q.v.) of the cell.

Variation. Difference from the typical form of an organism brought about by differences in genetic constitution.

Variegation. Irregular pigmentation of leaves and flowers — e.g. the blotched effects on the leaves of many ornamental plants due to the irregular development of chlorophyll. Virus diseases are also responsible for variegated effects. (See *Mosaic*).

Variety. A plant or group of plants differing from the typical form in one or more features, and continuing to show these differences in succeeding generations. (See *Species; Polymorphism*).

Vascular Bundle. Group of conducting vessels — xylem and phloem — in the stems and leaves of angiosperms and flowering plants. (See *Stem*).

Vascular Plant. One which has a continuous system of tubes which carry water and food materials within it. Bryophytes do not have such a vascular system but all higher plants do — ferns, conifers, and flowering plants.

Vascular System. The system of xylem and phloem tubes that conduct water and food materials around the bodies of ferns and seed plants. (See *Phloem; Xylem*).

Vegetative Reproduction. Reproduction by the vegetative parts of a plant — root, stem, and leaf — not involving

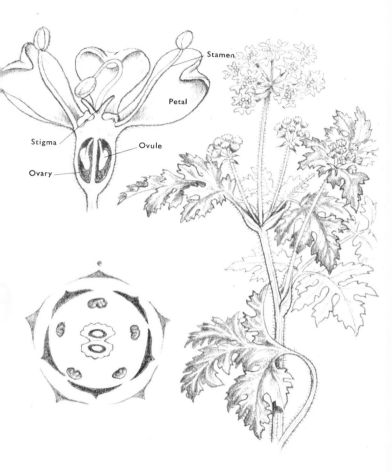

Hogweed plant *(Heracleum)*, half flower and floral diagram.

Q PDPW

Plate 113

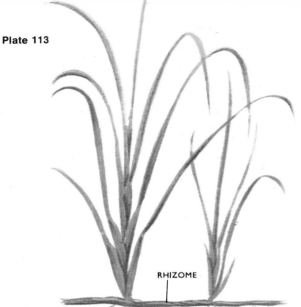

RHIZOME

CREEPING RHIZOME OF MARRAM GRASS

Some methods of vegetative reproduction.

VEGETATIVE REPRODUCTION

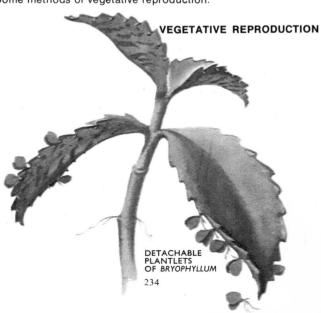

DETACHABLE
PLANTLETS
OF *BRYOPHYLLUM*

234

Plate 114

The creeping stems of witch thyme take root wherever they find suitable soil.

VIRUS

Virus particles: tobacco mosaic (A), a virus that attacks only bacteria (B), aucuba mosaic (C), and poliomyelitis virus (D) inside an infected cell. All are magnified many thousands of times.

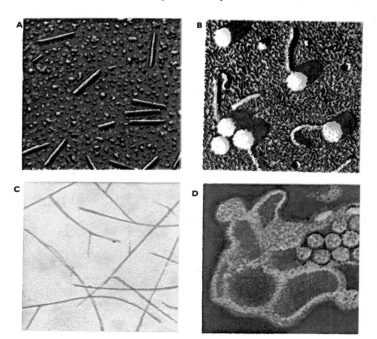

Male flower

Plant with flower clusters

Female flower

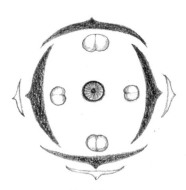

Floral diagram

Some features of the stinging nettle *(Urtica)*.

the flower or any sexual process. The simplest form of vegetative reproduction is shown by many fungi and algae. The threads of which they are composed can be broken into several pieces and yet continue to grow. Liverworts frequently produce small detachable buds called *gemmae* in shallow cups. Rain splashes wash these gemmae out and they develop into new plants on the moist soil nearby. Higher plants, especially the flowering ones have a number of special modifications concerned with vegetative reproduction and the gardener frequently takes advantage of these (See *Propagation*). Many plants that creep over the ground will take root whenever their stems touch suitable soil. *Runners* are specialised stems that develop on certain plants at certain times of the year and creep over the ground, taking root at the tips (and other nodes) and developing into new plants. These become separated when the runners decay. The strawberry is a typical example of a plant producing runners. *Rhizomes* are underground stems which not only spread the plant over an area but also store food and tide the plant over the winter. *Corms, bulbs,* and *tubers* are further examples of organs of vegetative reproduction. A number of plants, notably the wild leek and the coralroot *(Dentaria)*, produce detachable buds called *bulbils* which drop off and take root in the surrounding soil. The familiar houseplant *Bryophyllum* produces little plantlets on its leaves. These may often develop roots before falling from the parent.

The main advantage of vegetative reproduction is that it enables a species to colonise a small area very rapidly. It does not help to extend the range of a species much for the vegetative organs are not spread widely as seeds are. Another important point is that the vegetatively produced offspring are genetically the same as the parents and no variation is introduced by this method of reproduction. (See Plates 113-114).

Vein. Vascular or conducting strand of a leaf.

Velamen. Spongy tissue on the outside of the roots of various epiphytic plants responsible for absorbing rain water. (See *Epiphyte*).

Venation. The arrangement of the veins of a leaf (q.v.)

Venter. Base of an archegonium (female organ of mosses and ferns) in which the female sex cell lies.

Vernalisation. Exposure of plants to low temperatures as they germinate in order to speed up their development. It is an economically important process for many crops such as some cereal varieties which normally need to pass a winter before reaching maturity. The exposure of the germinating seed to low temperatures seems to take the place of winter and the plants mature in a single season.

Vernation. The way in which leaves are arranged in a bud and the way in which they unfold as the bud opens. There are several variations.

Verticillate. (Of leaves). Arranged in whorls of 3 or more on the stem. (See *Phyllotaxis*).

Vessel. (See *Xylem*).

Viable. Able to live and develop — especially of seeds.

Violaceae. A family of dicotyledons, containing herbs, shrubs and trees although British species are all herbs of genus *Viola*. The violets of this genus have solitary flowers as a rule, with two bracteoles on the pedicel. Pansies are also included in this family. The fruit is a capsule with 3 valves containing many seeds. (See Page 261 and Plate 127).

Virus. A minute organism of which many kinds are known. All produce disease in plants or animals — indeed

Plate 115

WEED

Some common farmland weeds.

Plate 116

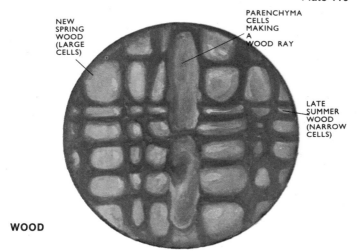

NEW
SPRING
WOOD
(LARGE
CELLS)

PARENCHYMA
CELLS
MAKING
A
WOOD RAY

LATE
SUMMER
WOOD
(NARROW
CELLS)

WOOD

Highly magnified diagram of a piece of wood showing the different sizes of xylem vessels responsible for the appearance of growth rings.

(Below) Section of an oak tree trunk. The central heartwood, coloured by gums and tannins, no longer conducts water—a function now carried out by the whiter sapwood. Phloem tissue is on the inner side of the bark. Wood rays in the oak are dozens of cells thick but in many timbers they are only one cell thick.

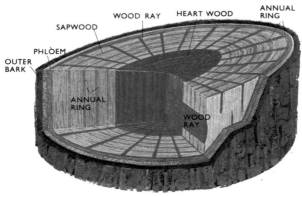

WOOD RAY HEART WOOD ANNUAL RING

SAPWOOD

PHLOEM

OUTER
BARK

ANNUAL
RING

WOOD
RAY

**SEGMENT OF
AN OAK-TREE TRUNK**

were it not for the fact that they produce disease they would almost certainly not have been discovered. There is a good deal of argument as to whether viruses are living or not: they can reproduce themselves in the cells of the host organism and yet they can be crystallised from cell extracts just like non-living substances. They appear to be little more than nucleoprotein molecules. It is not really possible to say that viruses are either plants or animals but they are often classed with the plant kingdom for convenience. Viruses pass through the pores of the finest filters — a property that can be demonstrated by filtering an extract of a diseased organism and contaminating a healthy organism with the filtrate: the healthy organism will become diseased. Among the many diseases caused by viruses are: poliomyelitis, measles, influenza, and many plant diseases known as mosaics. (See Plates 62 and 114).

Vittae. Ducts containing resins or oils, especially in fruits.

Viviparous. (Of flowers) Producing vegetative buds instead of sex organs. This happens in several members of the onion genus *Allium* where the buds, or bulbils as they are usually called, may replace some or all of the flowers in a head. The bulbils fall off and grow into new plants.

Weed. A plant growing out of place or where it is not wanted. Weeds occur on waste land, roadsides, and all disturbed ground but it is in cultivated fields that they are most obvious and important. They compete with the cultivated plants for light, water, and mineral salts. Recent research also suggests that weeds even produce in their roots substances which reduce the growth of neighbouring plants. Apart from this direct competition, weeds may harbour pests and diseases which can spread to the crop.

Weeds are characterised by their high seed production and their ability to colonise fresh ground quickly and compete effectively with other plants. Indeed, without these features, a plant would not become established as a weed. There are two main types of weed in cultivated land: small, quick-growing plants, often with several generations per year; and perennial herbs (e.g. bindweeds) with creeping rootstocks which continue to produce new plants even when broken into tiny pieces. Both of these forms can survive cultivation processes and produce a fresh crop of weeds each year.

The soil has not always been disturbed by agricultural practices, however, and it is suggested that sand dunes and cliffs might be the natural habitats from which some of our weeds have invaded agricultural land. A number of weeds, especially of agricultural land, are foreign in origin, having been introduced accidentally in consignments of grain and other seed. Freed from their natural controls, these plants quickly assumed weed status. Introduction of weeds in this way is less likely now as a result of strict regulations on seed purity. (See Plate 115).

Whorl. Circular group of leaves or floral organs all leaving the stem at one level.

Wilting. Loss of cell turgor (q.v.) through loss of water.

Wing Petal. One of the side petals of the typical pea-flower. (See Plate 118).

Wood. Dense plant tissue made up of xylem (q.v.) and sclerenchyma tissues. Also used as synonym of xylem. (See *Bark*) and (Plate 116).

Xanthophyceae. Group of yellowish green algae in which the pigment xanthophyll predominates. In form they are similar to the green algae.

Xanthophyll. One of the four major plant pigments, yellowish in colour.

Xeromorphic. Having the visible characteristics of xerophytes (q.v.).

Xerophyte. A plant capable of survival in dry conditions or regions subject to drought. Xerophytes have a number of characteristic features such as reduced leaf area, sunken stomata, thick cuticle. Many have water storage tissue which tides them over periods of drought. Some xerophytes have a remarkable ability to recover from desiccation. A number of plants, for example those of salt marshes, have characteristics similar to those of xerophytes yet they cannot withstand drought. Such plants are called *xeromorphs*. (See Plates 117 and 118).

Xylem. Tissue that conducts water and dissolved salts in the vascular plant. This tissue also provides mechanical support for the plant. The earliest xylem—the *protoxylem*—develops from the procambial strands just behind the tip of the stem or root. Metaxylem develops a little further behind the tip. As the xylem tissues become differentiated from the normal cells of the growing region, their walls become impregnated with lignin and the cells lose their protoplasm. Xylem cells are dead. There are two types of conducting tube. *Vessels* are long and are made up of several cells all joined end to end. *Tracheids* are shorter and are formed from single cells. Tracheids are not common in flowering plant stems but are the only conducting tubes in gymnosperm xylem. The walls of the tubes are thickened with lignin but the thickening is not even. In the protoxylem, which actually develops in the growing region of the stem or root, the thickening is in the form of a spiral or separate rings (*spiral* or *annular* thickening). This means that the xylem cells can still lengthen to some extent as the plant grows. The tissues of the metaxylem may have thickened bars — *scalariform* thickening — a network of thickening — *reticulate* thickening — or they may be completely thickened apart from numerous pits. Water can pass from one vessel to the next by means of the unthickened pits.

There are numerous simple parenchyma cells in the xylem and also many sclerenchyma fibres — especially around the outside of the vascular tissues. The protoxylem and metaxylem, formed from the primary cambium when the stem develops, make up the primary xylem. Secondary

XYLEM

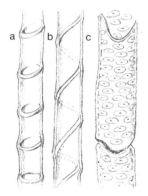

a) b) c)

Types of thickening in xylem tissues: a) annular; b) spiral; c) pitted. (See also Plate 99).

Plate 117

XEROPHYTE

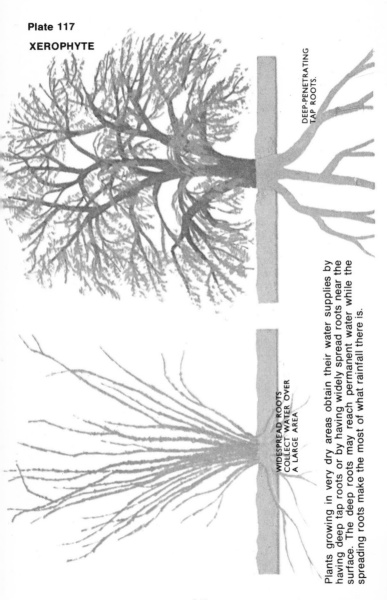

DEEP-PENETRATING TAP ROOTS.

WIDESPREAD ROOTS COLLECT WATER OVER A LARGE AREA

Plants growing in very dry areas obtain their water supplies by having deep tap roots or by having widely spread roots near the surface. The deep roots may reach permanent water while the spreading roots make the most of what rainfall there is.

Plate 118

XEROPHYTE (Cont)

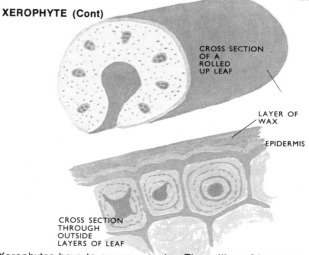

Xerophytes have to conserve water. The rolling of leaves and the presence of waxy coatings both help to reduce evaporation from leaf surfaces. In many desert-living species the leaves are reduced to spines (below).

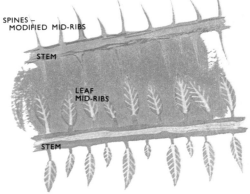

ZYGOMORPHIC

A zygomorphic or irregular flower.

243

xylem develops from secondary cambium during the process of secondary thickening. This is the process whereby the extra strengthening and conducting tissues are produced to keep pace with plant growth. The bulk of a tree trunk consists of secondary xylem. (See *Root; Stem; Pit*) and (Plates 62, 86, 88, 95, 96 and 99).

Zoospore. Haploid single-celled reproductive body, often flagellated, formed by the haploid generation of many algae and lower fungi. It is not a true spore (q.v.).

Zygomorphic. (Of a flower). Irregular, having only one plane of symmetry, such as a sweet pea. (See Plate 118).

YEAST

Yeasts in various stages of budding and division.

Yeast (=*Saccharomyces*). Simple single-celled ascomycete fungi which multiply normally by budding. Yeasts are economically important in that they produce certain enzymes capable of producing fermentation (q.v.). Yeasts convert sugars to alcohol in wine making. The baking industry uses yeast because the carbon dioxide given off during fermentation makes the dough rise. Yeasts are also important sources of vitamins. (See Plate 122).

Zygospore. Thick-walled resting stage formed in certain fungi and algae after fusion of gametes or gametangia. (See Plate 121).

Zygote. Diploid cell formed by fusion of two haploid gametes.

Zymase. The enzyme which is produced by yeast and which is responsible for the breakdown of sugar into alcohol and carbon dioxide.

The World of Plants

There are few places on Earth without plants. From the high alpine meadows to the steaming tropical forests, plants grow and play a vital part in the Balance of Nature. Plants are distinguished from the other great group of living organisms — the Animals — by the fact that they (the plants) normally contain chlorophyll and can usually manufacture food from non-living material in their surroundings. Animals cannot do this and must obtain food from plants or from other animals.

The range of plant form is enormous — from tiny single-celled organisms, seen only with the aid of the microscope, to the huge Sequoias — the Big Trees of California which may exceed 300 feet in height. Their habitats, too, range from the surface waters of the oceans to the dry desert.

Many schemes have been suggested for classifying the vast number of species of plants. Linnaeus established the *binomial system* whereby each species has a *generic* name and a *specific* name, e.g. *Ranunculus bulbosus* (the bulbous buttercup). *Bulbosus* is one species of the *genus Ranunculus*. Linnaeus also arranged his known species into groups — some of which are still used today. He has been called the 'Father of Modern Botany', but he was by no means the first to try to classify plants. One of the best

known of the earlier ones was the English botanist John Ray who lived in the seventeenth century.

There are a number of organisms which do not fit well into either plant or animal kingdoms and for convenience can be included here.

Viruses

All viruses are parasitic, i.e. they live on plants and animals, causing disease. It is doubtful if viruses would have been discovered were it not for the diseases they cause, for they are minute organisms visible only with the newest techniques such as *electron microscopy*. They cannot grow outside the host body and it is still debated whether they are living organisms. Their structure is little more than that of a collection of protein molecules. They can even be crystallised and redissolved without losing their infective power. Examples are those producing tobacco mosaic, poliomyelitis and smallpox.

Bacteria

These organisms are usually single cells without typical nuclei. They are larger than viruses but still only about one hundredth of a millimetre in size. Bacteria can be grown on artificial food materials. Many are parasitic, producing diseases such as tuberculosis and tetanus. Others are free living and play important roles in the nitrogen cycle. Example: *Azotobacter*.

see Plate 119

Plate 119

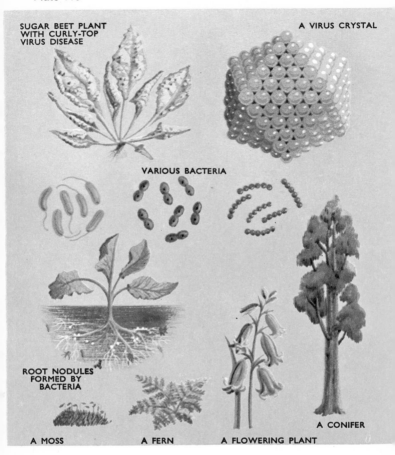

SUGAR BEET PLANT
WITH CURLY-TOP
VIRUS DISEASE

A VIRUS CRYSTAL

VARIOUS BACTERIA

ROOT NODULES
FORMED BY
BACTERIA

A MOSS

A FERN

A FLOWERING PLANT

A CONIFER

THE PLANT KINGDOM

Plate 120

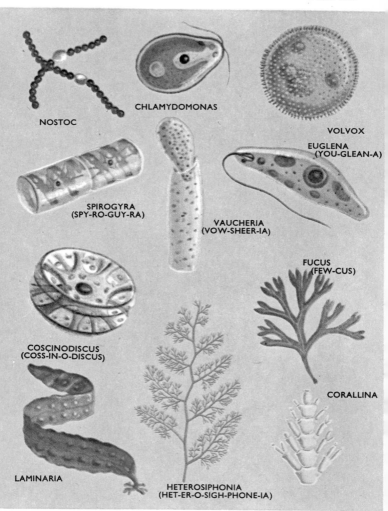

NOSTOC

CHLAMYDOMONAS

VOLVOX

EUGLENA
(YOU-GLEAN-A)

SPIROGYRA
(SPY-RO-GUY-RA)

VAUCHERIA
(VOW-SHEER-IA)

FUCUS
(FEW-CUS)

COSCINODISCUS
(COSS-IN-O-DISCUS)

CORALLINA

LAMINARIA

HETEROSIPHONIA
(HET-ER-O-SIGH-PHONE-IA)

ALGAE

The World of Plants

The Algae

The simple plants known as Algae (singular, alga) belong to the *Thallophyta* — the division of plants whose members show no separation into root, stem and leaf. Many algae are single celled organisms which exist as plankton in the surface layers of the sea and fresh water. They are provided with flagella for movement. Others consist of a simple filamentous or branched structure called a *thallus*. The majority of algae contain chlorophyll and normally live in water. Vegetative or asexual reproduction by spore formation is common, as well as sexual reproduction by fusion of cells. There are several groups of Algae.

Cyanophyceae (Sigh-anno-figh-see) (Blue-Green Algae).

In the members of this group (e.g. *Nostoc*) the green of chlorophyll is modified by a blue pigment. They exist as groups or strings of simple cells which reproduce by simple division. There is no sexual reproduction. Many species live in damp soil.

The Green Algae (**Chlorophyceae**) contain many mainly fresh-water forms whose chloroplasts are of varying shapes. *Chlamydomonas* (Clam-ee-dom-o-nas) is a tiny single-celled motile form. *Volvox* is a related form which consists of thousands of Chlamydomonas-like cells. Filamentous forms include *Spirogyra* and *Vaucheria* — the latter without cross-walls. *Euglena* is also green but belongs to the **Euglenineae** (You-glen-e-nee). There is no cellulose wall and some species even lack chlorophyll.

The diatoms (**Diatomeae**) (Die-at-o-mee) are very common planktonic organisms whose cell walls are impregnated with silica (sand) and formed of two valves. Example: *Coscinodiscus*. The chlorophyll of the Brown Algae (**Phaeophyceae**) (Figh-o-figh-see) is masked by a brown pigment. The members are mainly marine (i.e. sea-weeds) and normally have flat branched bodies. They are attached to rocks, etc., by a special 'hold-fast'. Examples include *Fucus* and *Laminaria*.

Red Algae (**Rhodophyceae**) are again mainly sea-weeds. The thallus is branched or filamentous — the individual cells often having protoplasmic connections. Examples include *Heterosiphonia* and *Corallina*. The latter, encrusted with a chalky deposit, is a common rock-pool inhabitant.

The World of Plants

Fungi

The Fungi (like the Algae) belong to the *Thallophyta* — those plants which have no division into root, stem and leaves, but just a simple body called a *thallus*. Fungi are peculiar among plants in that they lack chlorophyll. They live as parasites or saprophytes (i.e. absorbing food from living or dead organisms respectively). The fungal thallus normally consists of fine threads called *hyphae* (high-fee). These branch and grow over the substrate, forming a mycelium (my-SEAL-ium). The threads may or may not be divided up into individual cells. In their structure and reproduction many fungi resemble the algae, but the presence or absence of chlorophyll is taken as a convenient criterion to divide the Thallophyta into these two main groups. The fungi themselves are divided into several groups.

Actinomycetes

These organisms are not regarded as fungi at all by some botanists. They have many of the characters of bacteria, there often being no mycelium but just fragments of threads. Economically they are important as producers of antibiotics such as Streptomycin.

Myxomycetes

Like the actinomycetes these are border-line cases, sometimes classed as animals. They are known as Slime Fungi, for when the spores germinate each releases a mass of naked protoplasm (i.e. without a cell wall) which creeps about in the manner of an amoeba. Large numbers may unite and form a jelly-like mass *(plasmodium)* which then gives rise to fruiting bodies and spores. They are common in ditches and damp woodlands. Example: *Stemonitis.*

Phycomycetes

The members of this group are very much like algae. The hyphae are not divided up into cells. Many of the moulds and parasitic fungi belong here. Two divisions are recognised within the Phycomycetes. The first, called the *Oomycetes,* reproduce by fusion of unlike sex-cells or organs, by the asexual production of flagellated spores, or by the production of wind-dispersed *conidia* which are little more than swollen pieces of hypha. Most of the oomycetes live in water or as parasites of plants. Examples include *Saprolegnia, Peronospora, Pythium* and *Synchytrium.* The second division — the *Zygomycetes* — reproduce by fusion of parts of hyphae or by the production of non-flagellated spores. Examples include the common pin mould *(Mucor)* and *Entomophthora* which parasitises houseflies.

see Plate 121

R PDPW

Plate 121

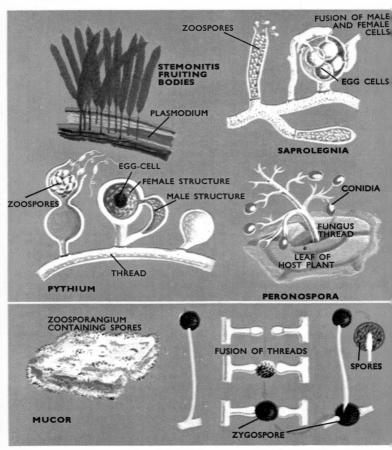

ZOOSPORES

FUSION OF MALE AND FEMALE CELLS

STEMONITIS FRUITING BODIES

PLASMODIUM

EGG CELLS

SAPROLEGNIA

EGG-CELL

FEMALE STRUCTURE

MALE STRUCTURE

ZOOSPORES

CONIDIA

FUNGUS THREAD

LEAF OF HOST PLANT

THREAD

PYTHIUM

PERONOSPORA

ZOOSPORANGIUM CONTAINING SPORES

FUSION OF THREADS

SPORES

MUCOR

ZYGOSPORE

FUNGI — MYXOMYCETES AND PHYCOMYCETES

Plate 122

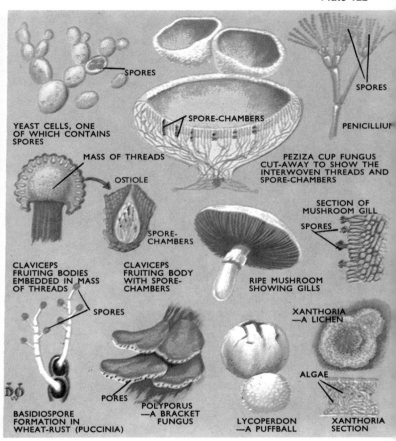

SPORES

YEAST CELLS, ONE
OF WHICH CONTAINS
SPORES

SPORE-CHAMBERS

SPORES

PENICILLIUM

MASS OF THREADS

OSTIOLE

PEZIZA CUP FUNGUS
CUT-AWAY TO SHOW THE
INTERWOVEN THREADS AND
SPORE-CHAMBERS

SPORE-
CHAMBERS

SECTION OF
MUSHROOM GILL

SPORES

CLAVICEPS
FRUITING BODIES
EMBEDDED IN MASS
OF THREADS

CLAVICEPS
FRUITING BODY
WITH SPORE-
CHAMBERS

RIPE MUSHROOM
SHOWING GILLS

SPORES

XANTHORIA
—A LICHEN

ALGAE

BASIDIOSPORE
FORMATION IN
WHEAT-RUST (PUCCINIA)

PORES

POLYPORUS
—A BRACKET
FUNGUS

LYCOPERDON
—A PUFFBALL

XANTHORIA
SECTION

FUNGI—ASCOMYCETES AND BASIDIOMYCETES

The World of Plants

The **Ascomycetes** are a group of fungi whose threads are divided into cells and which reproduce themselves in a rather special way. Spores *(ascospores)* are produced *inside* special cells called *asci,* after joining of two threads and their nuclei. The two threads look alike but act differently. Non-sexual spores are also produced, especially among the lower forms and the parasitic ones.

The yeasts such as *Saccharomyces* (Sack-arrow-my-sees) form chains of cells rather than threads. Reproduction is normally by asexual budding, but ascospores are sometimes produced inside the cells.

In the rest of the group, the spore-chambers *(asci)* develop in 'fruiting-bodies' made up of masses of interwoven threads. The fruiting body of the Plectomycetes is a closed structure which eventually breaks to release the spores. *Penicillium* is an example, but it more frequently reproduces by asexual spores. The Discomycetes (e.g. *Peziza*) produce spore-chambers in a cup-shaped body which is often brightly coloured. The Pyrenomycetes, such as *Claviceps,* bear their spore-chambers in flask-shaped structures, themselves often embedded in more masses of fungal threads.

The **Basidiomycetes** (Bas-idio-my-seat-ees) are the last large group of fungi. The spores are produced on the *outside* of special cells called *basidia.* As in the Ascomycetes, the threads are divided into cells. The Heterobasidiomycetes are all parasites — the rusts and smuts of cereal crops, etc. The basidia develop from resting spores in the spring. In the Homobasidiomycetes — the mushrooms and toadstools — the spore-bearing cells occur at the tips of the threads which make up the fruiting body. The common mushroom *(Psalliota)* (Sally-oh-ta) is composed of masses of these threads which form numerous radiating gills under the cap. The spores develop on the surface of the gills and fall off to be scattered by the wind. Bracket fungi such as *Polyporus* produce spores on the linings of numerous pores on the underside. Puff-balls (e.g. *Lycoperdon*) have closed fruit-bodies and release their spores all at once when the covering splits.

Lichens

These organisms, which are usually the first to colonise bare rock faces, are symbiotic communities of a fungus (usually an ascomycete) and a green or blue-green alga. The fungal threads trap water and salts which the alga uses to make food. Many are brightly coloured (e.g. *Xanthoria*). Litmus indicator is obtained from a lichen.

see Plate 122

The World of Plants

Bryophyta — The Mosses and Liverworts

These plants, in general, frequent damp, shady places and always require the presence of water for their reproduction. Most of them are small, leafy plants but some of the liverworts are flat structures like large threads of algae.

Male and female sex-cells develop on the plant. After fertilisation of the female cell, a spore-bearing body *(capsule)* develops and scatters asexual spores. These grow into new plants.

Liverworts (=Hepaticae)

The plants, which may be leafy or flat, are attached to the soil by short, single-celled rhizoids which also absorb water and salts. The spore-capsule is normally short-lived and all the spores are scattered together. There are usually some rod-shaped cells *(elaters)* in the capsule. They help to scatter the spores.

The order *Jungermanniales* is the largest group and contains both flat and leafy forms. Examples include *Lophocolea* (leafy) and *Pellia* (flat).

Order *Marchantiales* are flat forms, usually having air-chambers in the tissues. The sex organs in *Marchantia* occur on stalked bodies, above the rest of the plant.

The order *Anthocerotales* contains flat liverworts which have long-lived spore-capsules. The spores ripen in turn from the top downwards and are released as the capsules split. In contrast to the capsules of other liverworts, these contain chlorophyll. Example: *Anthoceros*.

Mosses (=Musci)

The mosses are all leafy and are fixed by multi-cellular rhizoids. The leaves are very thin and are never notched. The spore-capsules are long-lived and normally contain chlorophyll. There are no elaters. When the spores germinate they form delicate branching threads (protonemata) from which the plants grow. This is why mosses normally grow in clumps — many small plants arise close together on the threads. There are no such threads in liverworts.

The order *Bryales* contains almost all the mosses — e.g. *Funaria, Hypnum, Mnium*. The spore-capsule is always stalked and has a lid. When ripe, the lid falls and exposes a series of water-sensitive teeth. In dry weather these curl up and the spores escape as the capsule sways in any breeze.

The bog moss, *Sphagnum*, is the only member of the order *Sphagnales* (Sfag-nail-ees). The tissues contain water-holding cells. The capsule has no chlorophyll and no water-sensitive teeth. It is not stalked, but the plant stem grows up when the capsule is ripe.

Order *Andreaeales* contains one genus — *Andreaea* — which forms dark cushions on rocks. The capsule has no chlorophyll, stalk, or water-sensitive teeth. It opens along four splits to release the spores.

see Plate 123

Plate 123

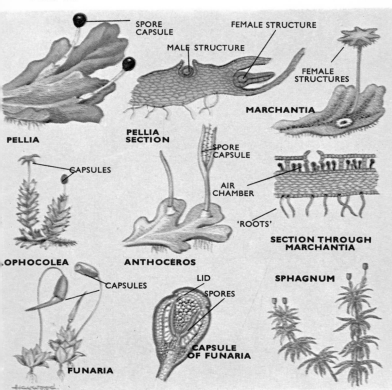

SPORE CAPSULE

MALE STRUCTURE

FEMALE STRUCTURE

FEMALE STRUCTURES

MARCHANTIA

PELLIA

PELLIA SECTION

CAPSULES

SPORE CAPSULE

AIR CHAMBER

'ROOTS'

SECTION THROUGH MARCHANTIA

OPHOCOLEA

ANTHOCEROS

CAPSULES

LID

SPORES

CAPSULE OF FUNARIA

SPHAGNUM

FUNARIA

BRYOPHYTA

Plate 124

CAPSULES

RHYNIA

PSILOTUM

LYCOPOD

CAPSULE ON LEAF

ISOETES

LEPIDO-DENDRON FOSSIL STEM

ROYAL FERN

ADDER'S TONGUE FERN

CAPSULES

FERN PROTHALLUS

SPORE CAPSULES

HORSETAIL

POLYPODY FERN WITH SPORE CAPSULES UNDER LEAF

SECTION OF MALE FERN LEAF WITH CAPSULES

SPORES

CAPSULES

PTERIDOPHYTA

The World of Plants

Pteridophyta (Terry-do-fight-a) —
The Ferns and their Relatives.

These are non-flowering land-plants showing a number of advances over the mosses. There are normally roots, stems and leaves, and, in contrast to the mosses, there is a special water-conducting system throughout the plant. In mosses the sex-organs develop on the green plant and spores are formed in a capsule which grows attached to the plant. The fern plant bears spores and is thus equivalent to the capsule of the mosses. Sex-organs arise on a small, usually short-lived body (*prothallus*), on or under the ground. This body develops from a spore and is equivalent to the moss-plant.

Order **Psilophytales** (Sill-o-fy-tail-ees) contains the oldest-known land-plants (e.g. *Rhynia*). Fossils show that they had no roots and that the leaves (if any) were scale-like. They lived (probably in swamps) about 300 million years ago.

The order **Psilotales** contains two living genera — *Psilotum* and *Tmesipteris* (Mess-ip-terris). They have no roots and their leaves are small. Spore capsules (*sporangia*) occur on some of the leaves. The body bearing the sex-organs is like an underground stem.

There are both living and fossil plants in the order **Lycopodiales.** The leaves are normally small and some of them have sporangia on them. These 'fertile' leaves are often grouped into 'cones' at the tips of the stems. *Lycopodium* and *Selaginella* resemble mosses but *Isoetes* is grass-like. *Lepidodendron* is a commonly found fossil form which had large woody stems.

The true ferns belong to the order **Filicales.** The leaves are large and usually divided into segments. Stems are usually underground (except tree-ferns) and rarely branch. Spore-capsules develop on the underside of the normal leaves but sometimes on special leaves or parts of leaves (e.g. *Osmunda* — the royal fern). The most primitive ferns (e.g. *Ophioglossum* — the adder's tongue) have large spore-capsules, but more advanced species such as *Polypodium* and *Pteridium* (Terr-id-ium) (bracken) bear clusters of tiny sporangia.

The order **Equisetales** (Ee-quiz-eat-ay-lees) contains the horsetails such as *Equisetum*. The simple leaves occur in whorls on the green stem. Those towards the tip may be modified to carry spore-capsules. Large woody species such as *Calamites* were common in Carboniferous times.

see Plate 124

The World of Plants

The Gymnospermae

These plants—the conifers and their relatives—are woody plants that reproduce by seeds. This is a big advance on the ferns. Whereas in the latter spores are shed before sex-organs are formed, in the seed-bearing plants the spores which give rise to female sex-organs are not shed. Male spores (pollen grains) *are* distributed and produce male-cells to join with the female-cells. The new embryo is well formed before it is shed—as a *seed*—from the parent. The spores develop in capsules *(sporangia)* attached to special leaves which are usually formed into cones.

The order **Pteridospermae** (Terry-do-spur-me) contains a number of extinct plants which resembled large ferns because of their large, divided leaves. *Neuropteris* is known from its fossil leaves.

The order **Cycadales** (Sigh-cad-ay-lees) contains several tropical palm-like plants (cycads) living today. The leaves are large and divided and arise from a thick stem. Male and female cones arise on separate plants.

There is only one living member of the order **Ginkgoales** (Gink-go-ay-lees). This is the *Ginkgo* or maidenhair tree, recognised by its fan-shaped leaves. There are no cones. The tree-form is very different from the structure of a cycad. *Ginkgo* is a native of China. Plants like *Ginkgo* were common in the Mesozoic era about 150 million years ago.

The **Coniferales** contains all the well-known cone-bearing trees such as *Pinus*, *Larix* (larch), *Juniperus* (juniper) and the monkey-puzzle tree *Araucaria.* The leaves are normally small and needle-shaped.

The yew *(Taxus)* belongs to the order **Taxales.** The seeds are borne singly and are surrounded by a fleshy growth called an aril.

The order **Gnetales** (Nee-tay-lees) contains three very different genera of plants, all of which show some advances towards the flowering plants. *Gnetum,* a tropical, climbing plant, has broad net-veined leaves. *Welwitschia* (Well-witch-ia) is a strange, desert-living plant of South Africa. It has only two leaves but these are large and grow continuously from a short, stocky stem. They are frequently split so that there appear to be several leaves. *Ephedra* is a shrubby plant of dry regions. Its stems and leaves are narrow.

see Plate 125

Plate 125

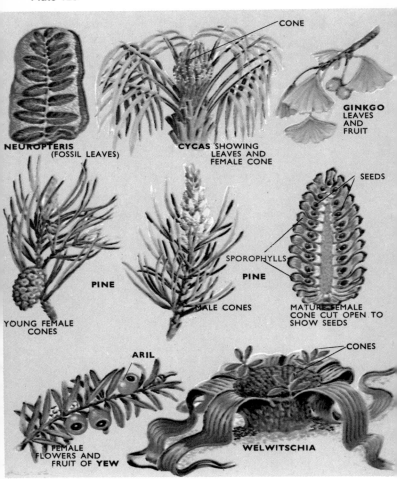

CONE

NEUROPTERIS
(FOSSIL LEAVES)

CYCAS SHOWING
LEAVES AND
FEMALE CONE

GINKGO
LEAVES
AND
FRUIT

SEEDS

PINE

PINE

SPOROPHYLLS

YOUNG FEMALE
CONES

MALE CONES

MATURE FEMALE
CONE CUT OPEN TO
SHOW SEEDS

ARIL

CONES

FEMALE
FLOWERS AND
FRUIT OF YEW

WELWITSCHIA

GYMNOSPERMAE

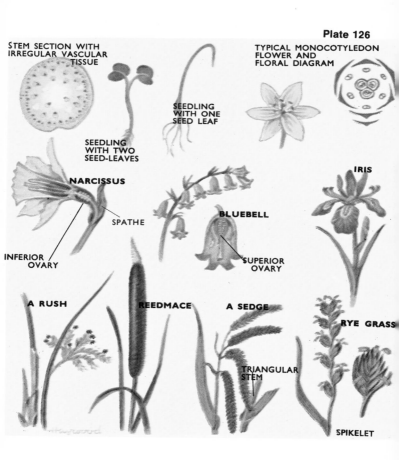

Plate 126

STEM SECTION WITH IRREGULAR VASCULAR TISSUE

TYPICAL MONOCOTYLEDON FLOWER AND FLORAL DIAGRAM

SEEDLING WITH ONE SEED LEAF

SEEDLING WITH TWO SEED-LEAVES

NARCISSUS

SPATHE

INFERIOR OVARY

BLUEBELL

SUPERIOR OVARY

IRIS

A RUSH

REEDMACE

A SEDGE

TRIANGULAR STEM

RYE GRASS

SPIKELET

ANGIOSPERMAE – MONOCOTYLEDONAE

The World of Plants

The Flowering Plants or Angiospermae

Like the conifers, the flowering plants reproduce by means of seeds, but there is an important difference between the two groups. The female structure *(ovule)* of the conifer lies exposed on the scale leaf of the cone, whereas that of the flowering plant is completely enclosed within the *carpel* or ovary which later forms the fruit.

In a cone, most of the leaves (scales) carry sex-organs, but in flowers, as a rule, only the central 'leaves' are fertile. The outer ones carry no reproductive structures and serve to protect the inner part, and in some cases to attract insect pollinators.

Angiosperms are divided into two major groups according to whether the seed contains one seed leaf (cotyledon) or two. The first group, *Monocotyledonae,* have narrow leaves with parallel veins. The conducting *(vascular)* tissues are in patches scattered throughout the stem. The floral parts are normally arranged in groups of three and may or may not be joined together to form a tube.

The most important family of monocotyledons (indeed probably of all plants) is the *Gramineae.* From it come all our cereals, sugar cane, many fibres and even bamboo, as well as animal fodder. The tiny flowers occur in *spikelets.* A spikelet is a very short branch enclosed by two bracts and supporting from one to several flowers, each with its own bracts, stamens and carpel (Plate 43). The flowers are pollinated by wind.

Other wind-pollinated monocotyledons are the rushes (family *Juncaceae*), sedges (Cyperaceae) and the reed-mace *(Typhaceae).* Most of these live in wet or marshy ground.

The family *Liliaceae* normally has two whorls of petaloid floral parts, six stamens and an ovary placed above the origin of the petals. Examples include the bluebell, tulip and the various lilies.

The *Amaryllidaceae* (Am-aril-iday-see), including *Narcissus* and snowdrops, are distinguished from the lilies only by the inferior ovary (i.e. below the origin of the petals). The trumpet of the narcissus is an outgrowth of the petals.

The family *Orchidaceae* contains some most striking plants. The flowers are usually so irregular that three-fold arrangement is difficult to detect. There are one or two stamens.

The duckweeds *(Lemna),* common on ponds and slowly moving streams, are also monocotyledons (family *Lemnaceae).* The flowers are minute and consist only of stamens or ovary.

Other monocotyledons include irises, crocuses, arum lilies, pondweeds and arrowhead.

see Plate 126

The World of Plants

Most families of flowering plants belong to the group called *Dicotyledonae,* that is to say their seeds contain two seed-leaves (cotyledons). Other features that distinguish this group from the *Monocotyledonae* are the broad, net-veined leaves, and the regular arrangement of the conducting tissues in the stem. The floral parts are normally arranged in fours or fives. Several schemes have been proposed for arranging the families into larger groups, according to similarities of flower structure. None is wholly satisfactory, however, and here only the more important families will be described.

Family *Salicaceae* (Say-lik-ay-see) contains the willows and poplars. The flowers occur in catkins, male and female ones on separate trees. There are no petals. Poplars are wind-pollinated and have hanging catkins with many stamens and branched stigmas. Willows produce nectar and are insect-pollinated. The catkins are normally upright.

Family *Betulaceae* contains the birches, hazel and alder. Male catkins are hanging and female ones upright. Both occur on one plant and are wind pollinated. Female catkins persist for some time. The fruit is a nut.

Beech and oak belong to the *Fagaceae* and are similar in many ways to the previous family. *Urticaceae* contains mainly herbaceous plants such as the stinging neetle. The tiny flowers have four (sometimes five) green 'petals' and either stamens or carpels.

The family *Caryophyllaceae* has flowers that are normally regular, with five free petals, and with structures of both sexes. Examples include chickweed and pinks.

Buttercups and anemones are included in the *Ranunculaceae.* Petals are often absent, in which case the sepals are brightly coloured. Some irregular flowers such as *Delphinium* also belong to this family.

The *Cruciferae,* including wallflowers, cabbage and cress, all have flowers with four free petals and six stamens (a whorl of four and one of two).

The *Papaveraceae* (poppies) are mainly herbaceous and usually contain a milky substance *(latex).* There are two sepals which fall as the flower opens.

Family *Violaceae* contains some trees and shrubs as well as the familiar violets and pansies. The flowers may be regular or irregular and the five petals are sometimes joined.

see Plate 127

Plate 127

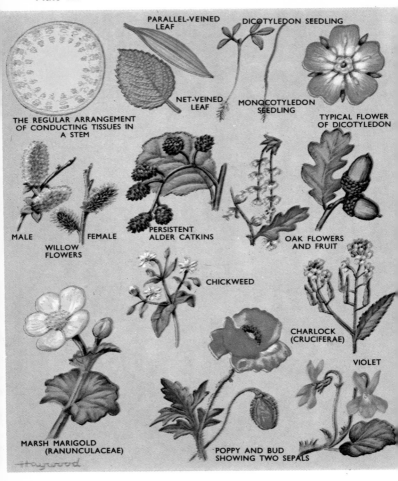

PARALLEL-VEINED LEAF

DICOTYLEDON SEEDLING

NET-VEINED LEAF

MONOCOTYLEDON SEEDLING

THE REGULAR ARRANGEMENT OF CONDUCTING TISSUES IN A STEM

TYPICAL FLOWER OF DICOTYLEDON

MALE

FEMALE

WILLOW FLOWERS

PERSISTENT ALDER CATKINS

OAK FLOWERS AND FRUIT

CHICKWEED

CHARLOCK (CRUCIFERAE)

VIOLET

MARSH MARIGOLD (RANUNCULACEAE)

POPPY AND BUD SHOWING TWO SEPALS

ANGIOSPERMAE – DICOTYLEDONAE

Plate 128

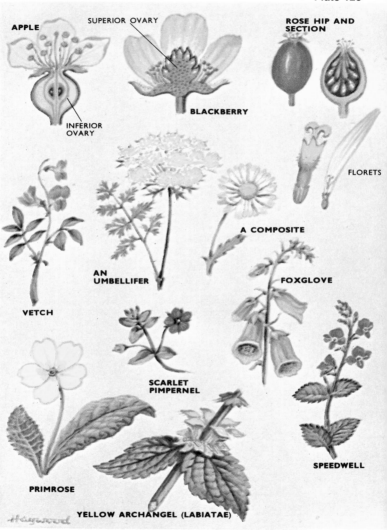

APPLE

SUPERIOR OVARY

INFERIOR OVARY

ROSE HIP AND SECTION

BLACKBERRY

FLORETS

VETCH

AN UMBELLIFER

A COMPOSITE

FOXGLOVE

SCARLET PIMPERNEL

SPEEDWELL

PRIMROSE

YELLOW ARCHANGEL (LABIATAE)

ANGIOSPERMAE – DICOTYLEDONAE

The World of Plants

Family *Rosaceae* contains herbs, shrubs and trees, most of which are perennial. The flowers are normally regular and the parts are arranged in groups of five. The receptacle on which the floral parts are arranged is often flattened at the outside (blackberry) or concave (rose). Other members include the apple, strawberry and plum.

Family *Leguminosae* all have irregular flowers with the parts arranged in fives except that there is a single carpel. The flowers are pollinated mainly by bees and the fruit is a characteristic pod *(legume)*. Peas, beans, gorse and vetch are typical members.

The *Umbelliferae* are mainly herbaceous (non-woody) plants with large leaves. The flowers are small and normally white or yellow. All parts other than the two carpels are free. The flowers are borne in *umbels*.

Family *Compositae* includes the daisies, dandelions and thistles. The flower heads are in fact tightly packed clusters of tiny tubular flowers called florets, each of which has its own sexual structures. The florets may have a strap-shaped *ligule* attached (e.g. dandelion and the outer florets of daisies). The calyx grows into a tuft of hairs when the fruit is ripe. This family is very wide-spread and successful.

Primulaceae are herbs with regular flowers. The sepals and petals are normally joined and form a tube. Examples include the primrose and the scarlet pimpernel.

Family *Scrophulariaceae* is a large one, usually with irregular flowers and only four stamens. Petals and sepals usually number five. Examples include snapdragons, foxgloves, and speedwells.

Family *Labiatae* is characterised by the square stem and opposite leaves. The flowers are irregular and the sepals persist—forming a protection for the fruit. The flowers are pollinated by various insects. The leaves often have scented oils. Examples include lavender, mint and deadnettles.

see Plate 128